CW00545714

THE TELLER

ESSAYS ON LITERATURE & CULTURE

& THE TALE

1990–2015

Gabriel Josipovici

CARCANET

First published in Great Britain in 2016 by

Carcanet Press Ltd
Alliance House, 30 Cross Street
Manchester M2 7AQ
www.carcanet.co.uk

A CIP catalogue record for this book is available from the British Library, ISBN 9781784102128.
Book design: Luke Allan.

The publisher acknowledges financial assistance from Arts Council England.

For Tamar

Contents

Preface

IT'S ONLY NOW that I have finished putting together this selection of essays and reviews written over the past quarter of a century that I see what a personal volume it is.

Three strands run through it: Jewish culture and experience; modernism and its discontents; and my own writing. Naturally they shade into one another. Thus the invitation to review a book on the Cairo Geniza allowed me to revisit my childhood in Egypt, while the review of a book on a family of Holocaust victims and survivors helped me understand how different is my own experience as a Jew with roots in the Middle East from that of the bulk of English and American Jews, who came from the Ashkenazi strongholds of North-Eastern Europe; meditation on the lives and writings of Kafka, Eliot, and Pasternak led straight to the heart of modernism, but questions of Judaism and anti-Semitism could not be avoided there either. Some of the later essays deal with problems I faced in writing various novels and short stories, and here I hope reprinting them will not be seen as mere self-indulgence; certainly in my own experience artists writing or talking about their work has been both intriguing and illuminating, even when I have not read or seen or heard that work or perhaps do not warm to it greatly.

I conclude with a response to an invitation to write about place, which allowed me to ponder what it means to me to live where I do, not far upstream from where Virginia Woolf drowned herself.

THE TELLER & THE TALE

Proust and I

MY DEAR DEPARTED FRIEND Gāmini Salgādo entitled his inaugural lecture as Professor of English at the University of Exeter 'Shakespeare and I', because, he said, that was his one chance of finding his name yoked to that of the writer he admired above all others. A similar impulse has led to my choice of title for this essay, but there are also deeper reasons (as, indeed, there were for Gāmini). Proust's *À la recherche du temps perdu*, like Dante's *Divina Commedia*, leads you in a spiral to the point where a door opens and you are invited – and find yourself able – to cross a threshold into a new life. You are able to do so because you have been trained for this purpose, much as a gymnast is trained, in the course of the three thousand pages that separate beginning and end. The book, like Dante's poem, is as much about us, the readers, as it is about Marcel. Proust was clear about this and often alluded to it in the course of the novel, and he was also clear, from the first, that the role of all art was to lead us forward to a place or a form of life we are all in search of but cannot by ourselves attain. When, for example, Swann first hears the Vinteuil sonata, it takes hold of him in a quite literal way: '*D'un rhythme lent elle le dirigeait ici d'abord, puis là, puis ailleur, vers un bonheur noble, inintelligible et précis.*' ['With a slow and rhythmical movement it led him first this way, then that, towards a state of happiness that was noble, unintelligible, and yet precise.'][1]

If this is the case then a response to the novel that is personal and biographical need not be merely anecdotal or self-preening but could, on the contrary, lead one into the very heart of Proust. For just as Marcel's story is seen (in the first instance by the relationship Proust establishes between Marcel and Swann) to be not merely the story of one person but of all human beings, so my personal response may turn out to be just one instance of a universal one. That, at any rate, is my hope for what follows.

I first read *À la recherche* at seventeen, in the year between school and university. In the mornings I was trying to write a novel and in the evenings I was reading my way through the great literature of the world, all borrowed from the wonderful Putney and Wandsworth public libraries. I read Dostoevsky and Tolstoy, Dickens and George Eliot, Yeats and Rilke – and then I read Proust. I felt at once that Proust was *true* in ways the others simply were not; they might be profound, tragic, funny, moving and many other things, but Proust's book had this peculiar quality of touching on my life at every turn, of actually being *about* me. Why did I feel this? What was it in the book that made me feel this?

At one level it was a plethora of tiny details, such as the pillow that appears in the second paragraph of the novel: '*J'appuyais tendrement mes joues contre les belles joues de l'oreiller qui, pleines et fraîches, sont comme les joues de nôtre enfance.*' ['I would lay my cheeks gently against the comfortable cheeks of my pillow, as plump and fresh as the cheeks of childhood.'] This is the kind of observation that tends to pass below the radar of most writers, but it catches in one short sentence the way a freshly ironed pillow-case, as one lays one's head to rest on it, brings flooding into one's body the sense of the protected nature of childhood, how in that blessed period we slept so well because we had no responsibilities, our lives taken care of by our loving parents. It doesn't tell us this but conveys it with that wonderful shorthand which is the privilege of great art – '*comme les joues de nôtre enfance*'. When I first read it I did not pause to think all this, and I did not see how it related to the theme of those opening pages and of the novel as a whole – it was just 'felt in the blood, and felt along the heart', as Wordsworth, who knew a thing or two himself about memory and the body, put it in *Tintern Abbey*.

Then there were the details of social behaviour, such as we get in the third paragraph of *Un amour de Swann*:

> Les Verdurin n'invitaient pas a dîner: on avait chez eux 'son couvert mis'. Pour la soirée, il n'y avait pas de programme. Le jeune

pianiste jouait, mais seulement si 'ça lui chantait', car on ne forçait personne et comme disait M. Verdurin, 'Tout pour les amis, vivent les camarades!' Si le pianiste voulait jouer la chevauchée de *La Walkyrie* ou le prélude de *Tristan*, Mme Verdurin protestait, non que cette musique lui déplût, mais au contraire parce qu'elle lui causait trop d'impression. 'Alors vous tenez à ce que j'aie ma migraine? Vous savez bien que c'est la même chose chaque fois qu'il joue ça. Je sais ce qui m'attend! Demain quand je voudrai me lever, bonsoir, plus personne!' S'il ne jouait pas, on causait, et l'un des amis, le plus souvent leur peintre favori d'alors, 'lâchait', comme disait M. Verdurin, 'une grosse faribole qui faisait s'esclaffer tout le monde', Mme Verdurin surtout, a qui – tant elle avait l'habitude de prendre au propre les expressions figurées des emotions qu'elle éprouvait – le docteur Cottard (un jeune débutant a cette époque) dut un jour remettre sa mâchoire qu'elle avait décrochée pour avoir trop ri.

[The Verdurins never invited you to dinner; you had your 'place laid' there. There was never any programme for the evening's entertainment. The young pianist would play, but only if 'the spirit moved him,' for no one was forced to do anything, and, as M. Verdurin used to say: 'We're all friends here. Liberty Hall, you know!' If the pianist suggested playing the Ride of the Valkyries or the Prelude to *Tristan*, Mme Verdurin would protest, not because the music was displeasing to her, but, on the contrary, because it made too violent an impression on her. 'Then you want me to have one of my headaches? You know quite well it's the same every time he plays that. I know what I'm in for. Tomorrow, when I want to get up – nothing doing!' If he was not going to play they talked, and one of the friends – usually the painter who was in favour there that year – would 'spin', as M. Verdurin put it, 'a damned funny yarn that made 'em all split with laughter,' and especially Mme Verdurin, who had such an inveterate habit of taking literally the figurative descriptions of her emotions that Dr Cottard (then a promising young practitioner) had once had to reset her jaw, which she had dislocated from laughing too much.]

At first sight this might be mistaken for Dickens, though it has a density perhaps alien to the Englishman's more expansive style. But it differs in a more fundamental way: in Dickens, all the time one is laughing one is pleasantly distanced from the object of laughter; in Proust, even in a grotesque passage like this, the uneasy feeling grows on one that the way Mme Verdurin behaves as she listens to music is only an exaggerated form of the way *we all* tend to behave. There is a deep mystery underlying this farcical scene: how do we express what we feel? What role do our bodies have in our attempts to convey to others – friends, acquaintances, lovers – how we feel about a particular thing? Put this way it is easy to see how this theme is central to the whole novel. But it is also something we all encounter every day. Is it intrinsically wrong, for example – hypocritical? condescending? – to grow solemn and nod without speaking when someone tells you they have lost a parent or that their marriage has imploded? We do this because we do not know *how* we feel about what we have just been told, so we reach out for what we know from our experience of the world we *should* be feeling, and then try out what we hope will be the expression appropriate for conveying this feeling. Scenes of this kind proliferate in Proust's novel; the paragraph about the Verdurins' musical evenings, climaxing in the hostess's dislocated jaw, is only one of the more extreme examples.

In this paragraph we are aware of the writer/observer, but we look past him, as it were, to Mme Verdurin and her salon. In other instances the laughter, the perception of truth and the awareness of the artist cannot be disentangled. Take this passage from the soirée at the Marquise de Saint-Euverte; Swann has just entered the hotel Saint-Euverte, thinking of Odette:

[p]our la première fois il remarqua, réveillée par l'arrivée inopinée

> d'un invité aussi tardif, la meute éparse, magnifique et désoeuvrée des grands valets de pied qui dormaient ça et la sur des banquettes et des coffres et qui, soulevant leur nobles profiles aigus de lévriers, se dressèrent et, rassemblés, formèrent le cercle autour de lui. L'un d'eux, d'aspect particulièrement féroce et assez semblable à l'exécuteur dans certains tableaux de la Renaisssance qui figurent des supplices, s'avança vers lui d'un air implacable pour lui prendre ses affaires. Mais la dureté de son regard d'acier était compensée par la douceur de ses gants de fil, si bien qu'en approchant de Swann il semblait témoigner de mépris pour sa personne et des égards pour son chapeau.
>
> [(h)e now noticed for the first time, roused by the unexpected arrival of so belated a guest, the scattered pack of tall, magnificent, idle footmen who were drowsing here and there upon benches and chests and who, pointing their noble greyhound profiles, now rose to their feet and gathered in a circle about him. One of them, of a particularly ferocious aspect, and not unlike the headsman in certain Renaissance pictures which represent executions, tortures and the like, advanced upon him with an implacable air to take his things. But the harshness of his steely glare was compensated by the softness of his cotton gloves, so that, as he approached Swann, he seemed to be exhibiting at once an utter contempt for his person and the most tender regard for his hat.]

Note, again, how the pleasure, the sense of recognition, here comes from the combination of observation, invention of metaphor, and precision of language. The first of the three sentences, which we joined half-way through, is a long, typically Proustian one, which seems to meander interminably but knows exactly what it is doing as it suddenly swoops in on its real subject with the startling image of the tired footmen as greyhounds. The second is much shorter and drives to its conclusion from the start, but it still has time to loop out and remind us of Swann's habit of comparing the world about him to his beloved Renaissance paintings, though the comparison of the footman to the headsman at an execution only reinforces the threat of its forward march, which is abruptly and comically undercut by the final phrase, '*pour lui prendre ses affaires*'. Just as we are trying to digest this we are thrust into a beautifully balanced passage in which two pairs of opposites are displayed, at the end, in a form of words which touches on the grotesque without quite tipping over into it: '*du mépris pour sa personne et des égards pour son chapeau*.' How I love these bravura passages and feel that, had I the skill, the imagination and the linguistic resources, they are the kinds of passages I myself would like to have written.

But there were deeper reasons why I felt, in that magical first reading of the novel, that Proust was speaking to me in a way Dostoevsky, Dickens and the rest simply were not, that he was bringing to the surface truths I already knew but had not been able to articulate. These were less easy to pin down because they suffused the text, but that did not mean that I did not feel them at the time.

There was the interconnection between love and need, which runs through the whole book from the initial scene of the mother's kiss to the disappearance of Albertine. Again, I sensed that what Proust was saying was 'true' in a way the other novelists and philosophers I had read were not, even though I could not at the time grasp – nor felt the need to – exactly in what this truth lay. Why, for example, does Marcel say, when his mother finally agrees to read to him that night: '*J'aurais dû être heureux: je ne l'étais pas* [...] *il me semblait que je venais d'une main impie et secrète de tracer dans son âme une première ride et d'y fair apparaître un premier cheveux blanc.*' ['I ought to have been happy; I was not [...] I felt that I had with an impious and secret finger traced a first wrinkle upon her soul and brought out a first white hair on her head.'] I didn't fully understand it at the time and yet, such is the way art works, I think I did: her giving in to him is the source of enormous relief for that one evening, makes the absolutely intolerable finally not just tolerable but pleasurable, but at the same time it heralds the end of his sense of his mother's absolute authority and therefore of her invulnerability. She can be swayed, she is human – but by that very fact she is suddenly vulnerable, subject to time like all of us and therefore will one day, eventually, die.

And then there is the extraordinary 'truth' with which *Combray* begins and ends:

> Certes quand approchait le matin, il y avait bien longtemps qu'était dissipée la brêve incertitude de mon réveil. Je savais dans quelle chambre je me trouvais effectivement, je l'avais reconstruite autour de moi dans l'obscurité, et – soit en s'orientant par la seule mémoire, soit en m'aidant, comme indication, d'une faible lueur aperçue, au pied de laquelle je plaçais les rideaux de la croisée – je l'avais reconstruite tout entière et meublée comme un architecte et un tapissier qui gardent leur ouverture primitive aux fenètres et aux portes, j'avais reposé les glaces et remis la commode à sa place habituelle. Mais à peine le jour – et non plus le reflet d'une dernière braise sur une tringle de cuivre que j'avais pris pour lui – traçait-il dans l'obscurité, et comme à la craie, sa première raie blanche et rectificative, que la fenêtre avec ses rideaux, quittait le cadre de la porte où je l'avais situé par erreur, tandis que pour lui faire place, le bureau que ma mémoire avait maladroitement installé là se sauvait à toute vitesse, poussant devant lui la cheminée et écartant le mur mitoyen du couloir; [...] et le demeure que j'avais rebâtie dans les ténèbres était allée rejoindre les demeures entrevues dans le tourbillon du réveil, mise en fuite par ce pâle signe qu'avait tracé au-dessus des rideaux le doigt levé du jour.
>
> [It is true that, when morning drew near, I would long have settled the brief uncertainty of my waking dream; I would know in what room I was actually lying, would have reconstructed it around me in the darkness, and – fixing my bearings by memory alone, or with the assistance of a feeble glimmer of light at the foot of which I placed the curtains and the window –

> would have reconstructed it complete and furnished, as an architect and an upholsterer might do, keeping the original plan of the doors and windows; would have replaced the mirrors and set the chest-of-drawers on its accustomed site. But scarcely had daylight itself – and no longer the gleam from a last, dying ember on a brass curtain-rod which I had mistaken for daylight – traced across the darkness, as with a stroke of chalk across a blackboard, its first white, correcting ray, than the window, with its curtains, would leave the frame of the doorway in which I had erroneously placed it, while, to make room for it, the writing-table, which my memory had clumsily installed where the window ought to be, would hurry off at full speed, thrusting before it the fireplace and sweeping aside the wall of the passage; [...] and the dwelling-place which I had built up for myself in the darkness would have gone to join all those other dwellings glimpsed in the whirlpool of awakening, put to flight by that pale sign traced above my window-curtains by the uplifted finger of dawn.]

We have all woken up in a strange bedroom and had to readjust rapidly our sense of where walls and cupboards and doors and windows were, but who before Proust had thought to talk about it? But of course this is more than the bringing to light of something well known and rarely discussed. It plays a positively Nabokovian role in the novel (Borges has written eloquently on how reading Kafka leads one to see the 'Kafkaesque' in earlier writers, and though Proust is a greater novelist than Nabokov, the particular artistic strategy I am exploring at this moment is more central to Nabokov's cruel imagination than it is to Proust's), forcing us, as happens so often in this book, to discover that firmly held beliefs are actually erroneous, and by so doing giving a solidity and 'reality' to the new beliefs which no Flaubertian realist could ever achieve. In *Dreaming by the Book*, a fascinating exploration of how writers, via their works, teach us to use our imaginations, Elaine Scarry argues that Proust gets us to imagine the solid surface of his bedroom precisely by concentrating on the immateriality of the images the magic lantern projects lightly over the walls: 'the perpetual mimesis of the solidity of the room', she says,

> is brought about by the 'impalpable iridescence' of Golo fleeting across its surfaces [...] Taken in isolation, the walls, the curtains, the doorknob are for the reader (as opposed to Marcel inside the book) certainly as thick and impalpable as the bright coloured images issuing from the magic lantern. Yet by instructing us to move the one across the surface of the other, the transparency of one somehow works to verify the density of the other.

This may be true, but Scarry misses what is to me the central reason for our sense of the solidity of the room: the fact that for so long it is so flexible. Precisely because the walls and cupboards and windows of the room are moved by the power of habit and imagination this way and that, when sleep is finally banished and the erstwhile sleeper fully awake, we assent to the reality of this room and forget that it too is, after all, just as much the product of Proust's imagination and writerly skills as all the other rooms that have been paraded before us: two minuses make a plus.

But all this is really a prologue to my central theme. The real reason why I felt that *À la recherche* was 'true' (was in some sort of way 'my truth', while other novels, great though they might be, were like distant mountains I could admire but which in the end could be of no help to me in my life) lay in Proust's relation, in the book, to the art and act of writing books. I had felt the frisson, the angel passing over my face, in the previous year, when, at sixteen, I had read *The Waste Land* and encountered the lines:

> On Margate sands
> I can connect
> Nothing with nothing.
> The broken fingernails of dirty hands.

I had no idea what that was about, but I knew it was vital to me. Now of course I see that it moved me because there, in the middle of what was undoubtedly a great poem, was a raw cry of despair at the impossibility of holding the world together for long enough to make any kind of art. And here in Proust, in the midst of this gripping and charming narrative of bucolic childhood, was a passage in which the hero, seized with the desire to speak of the beauty of the day, is reduced to banging his umbrella on the ground in frustration and crying out: 'Zut, zut, zut, zut.' A little later, daydreaming about Mme de Guermantes, he writes:

> Et ces rêves m'avertissaient que puisque je voulais un jour être un écrivain, il était temps de savoir ce que je comptais écrire. Mais dès que je me le demandais, tâchant de trouver un sujet où je pusse faire tenir une signification philosophique infinie, mon esprit s'arrêtait de fonctionner, je ne voyais plus que le vide en face de mon attention, je sentais que je n'avais pas de génie ou peut-être une maladie cérébrale l'empêchait de naître.
>
> [And these dreams reminded me that, since I wished some day to become a writer, it was high time to decide what sort of books I was going to write. But as soon as I asked myself the question, and tried to discover some subject to which I could impart a philosophical significance of infinite value, my mind would stop like a clock, my consciousness would be faced with a blank, I would feel either that I was wholly devoid of talent or that perhaps some malady of the brain was hindering its development.]

I too had, at seventeen, been reduced to the equivalent of 'zut, zut, zut, zut' again and again. I too was feeling, even as I read this book, the sense of impotence every time I contemplated the notion of writing 'A Novel'.

A little later I came across Kafka's *Diaries*, and found there the same paradox that was so troubling me at the time: the violent need to write, to express something, and the impossibility of doing so – not having the words for it, not having the form for it, not even knowing what it was that I was so desperate to 'express'. If Proust and Kafka and Eliot had felt this, I thought, and gone on to write what they had, then perhaps there was hope for me; perhaps I was not doomed to a lifetime of frustration, a physical feeling so intense that I felt at times I was about to blow up.

But of course reading *À la recherche* did even more for me. It gave me the powerful sense that *it didn't matter* if one could not see one's way forward, *it didn't matter* if one was silly and slow and confused, *it didn't matter* if one had got hold of the wrong end of the stick – what mattered was *to keep going*. I began to see that the doubts I had were in a sense the temptations of the Devil, the attempt to make me give up at the very start by presenting things in absolute terms (I can do it / no, I can't do it); and that what Proust (like Dante before him, I later discovered) was offering was a way of fighting that by saying: All right, I am confused, then let me start with my confusion, let me incorporate my confusion into the book or story I am writing, and see if that helps. If I can't start, then let me write about not being able to start. Perhaps, after all, confusion and failure are not things one has to overcome before one can start, but deep human experiences which deserve themselves to be explored in art. Perhaps, indeed, the stick has no right end and therefore no wrong end.

I had, in effect, begun to understand Proust's tactics in *À la recherche*. For Marcel differs from Bloch or M. de Norpois or Mme Verdurin not because he is more intelligent than they are but because, unlike them, he is uncertain of what he feels and thinks; he differs from Swann not because he suffers more from the agonies of jealousy and betrayal, but because he will not let go of his anguish and confusion by taking refuge in a convenient cliché, such as 'she was not my type'. Instead, he goes on worrying at his responses – to love and desire, to the acting of la Berma, to his disappointment with Balbec or Venice on a first visit – and incorporates his misunderstandings into the narrative. What this does, again, is to make the book feel 'true', because understanding, here, as in life, is always seen as provisional and capable of being reversed at any moment.

It also leads to the spiralling movement of the novel. As is well known, behind the three or four abortive starts of the book proper lie the many rejected openings, and behind those the years of uncertainty. All of this is not airbrushed out of the picture but acknowledged and overcome by being incorporated into a larger rhythm, which gathers momentum as the book develops, moving in ever wider spirals, but always returning to its origins, until the end, which both closes and finally opens the book to us, its readers, in precisely the same movement as Dante's.

It also leads to a kind of spiralling within the layers of the self and the ages of one's life. Whenever I read in the middle of the episode of the goodnight kiss, suddenly, abruptly, '*Il y a bien des années de cela*' ('this was many years ago'), I want to burst into tears. Of course in one way that has been prepared for by the opening word of the whole novel, '*Longtemps*', which implies a *maintenant*, a now. But this sense of looking back from a present in which the book is both being written and – one of the miracles of literature – read (with none of the nostalgia of English versions, such as L. P. Hartley's 'The past is a foreign country') is, for some reason, deeply moving. Let me quote the whole passage. Marcel's father and mother have come upon him on the staircase outside his bedroom and his father, with that gesture which reminds him of the Abraham of Benozzo Gozzoli telling Sarah to go and be with Isaac, has just uttered the amazing words of reprieve, '*couche pour cette nuit auprès de lui*' ('stay with him tonight'). '*Il y a bien des années de cela*,' he goes on,

> la muraille de l'escalier, où je vis monter le reflet de sa bougie n'existe plus depuis longtemps. En moi aussi bien des choses ont été détruites que je croyais devoir durer toujours et de nouvelles se sont édifiées donnant naissance à des peines et à des joies nouvelles que je n'aurais pu prévoir alors, de même que les anciennes me sont devenues difficiles à comprendre. Il y a bien longtemps

aussi que mon père a cessé de pouvoir dire à maman: 'Va avec le petit.' La possibilité de telles heures ne renaîtra jamais pour moi. Mais depui peu de temps, je recommence à très bien percevoir si je prête l'oreille, les sanglots que j'eus la force de contenir devant mon père et qui n'éclatèrent que quand je me retrouvai seule avec maman. En réalité ils n'ont jamais cessé; et c'est seulement parce que la vie se tait maintenant davantage autour de moi que je les entends de nouveau, comme ces cloches de couvents que couvrent si bien les bruits de la ville pendant le jour qu'on les croirait arêtées mais qui se remettent à sonner dans le silence du soir.

[Many years have passed since that night. The wall of the staircase up which I had watched the light of his candle gradually climb was long ago demolished. And in myself, too, many things have perished which I imagined would last for ever, and new ones have arisen, giving birth to new sorrows and new joys which in those days I could not have foreseen, just as now the old are hard to understand. It is a long time too, since my father has been able to say to Mamma: 'Go along with the child.' Never again will such moments be possible for me. But of late I have been increasingly able to catch, if I listen attentively, the sound of the sobs which I had the strength to control in my father's absence, and which broke out only when I found myself alone with Mamma. In reality their echo has never ceased; and it is only because life is now growing more and more quiet round about me that I hear them anew, like those convent bells which are so effectively drowned during the day by the noises of the street that one would suppose them to have stopped, until they ring out again through the silent evening air.]

Somehow, going backwards and forwards into the self and its history is one with having the courage to start wherever you are and go forward, however stupid and inadequate you feel yourself to be, because the impulse to utter and to make is one which must be given its heed if we are not to deny what is deepest and most basic to us.

This leads me to my final point. It has to do with a misunderstanding of Proust that was in vogue some years ago and is perhaps less so now. Back in the seventies Claude Simon came to the University of Sussex and gave an eloquent lecture. His thesis was that with Proust one could start anywhere and move on from there to the entire novel, and he demonstrated this by starting with the episode of the great fish being brought to the table in the restaurant in Balbec. It was a beautiful and illuminating performance. It was also given in the heyday of structuralism and when both Simon and Robbe-Grillet were rather more in thrall to the theories of Jean Ricardou than was good for either of them. When I challenged Simon at question time and asked why, if indeed with Proust we had an example not of *the writer* at work but of *writing* at work, as he was suggesting, using a contrast popular at the time, he should have had such difficulty starting, should have spent ten years struggling to find his subject and his way into his subject, he brushed my question aside. But I think it is a pertinent one. Proust, thank God, is not Ricardou. He is not even Robbe-Grillet. They may all come out of him, as Hockney and Bacon came out of Picasso, but there are deep differences. Proust's work is so moving because his message that we must start anywhere and have the courage to go on has to do not just with writing but with living. It is because the two are inseparable that I find him, like Dante, in the end, so profoundly satisfying a writer. But then I would. I owe him everything.

1 References are to the 1987, four-volume Pléiade edition of *À la recherche du temps perdu*, with C. K. Scott Moncrieff's translations from the six-volume edition revised by Terence Kilmartin and then by D. J. Enright (London: Chatto & Windus, 1992).

Tristram Shandy: Not Waving But Drowning[1]

YOU'VE COME HERE to listen to a lecture. You are looking forward to a pleasant evening – instructive, you hope, but also funny. But what if, when you arrive, there is no lecturer? What if, instead of facing a podium and a lectern, you sit down and find yourselves looking at a large mirror which takes up the entire end wall of the room and which reflects back to you nothing but yourselves, sitting and waiting? And what if nothing happens in the course of the evening but the sitting and the waiting and the looking at yourselves sitting and waiting?

That, in effect, is what happens in *Waiting for Godot*. The two tramps are a surrogate for the audience. Just as the audience has come in the expectation of something happening, of being taken out of themselves (is that not why we go to the theatre?), so the two protagonists have come in the hope that today Godot will come. And as the audience waits, so they wait; as they wait in vain, so too the audience. This is extremely disconcerting. We don't know what to make of it. We don't know how to respond. In our bafflement we may get angry at the playwright for not fulfilling his part of the tacit bargain (I pay for my seat and you entertain me), or we may laugh and declare the play the funniest thing we have seen and the evening well spent. But we will know deep inside ourselves that both responses are inadequate to the experience.

And this of course is what happens when we pick up *Tristram Shandy* and settle down with it for a good read. It is, after all, a classic, and we have much enjoyed *Middlemarch* and *Little Dorrit*. Why should we not enjoy this? But the story's inability to move forward consistently frustrates our palpable need to settle into a good story, and we even have the horrible suspicion that what story there is, as in *Waiting for Godot*, merely dramatises and reflects back at us our own frustrations.

Admirers of the book of course defend it by pointing to its humour, to this frustration as a means of generating laughter. If they are of a more moralising bent they may suggest that this is a way of teaching us about ourselves, and I will, at the end of this lecture (yes, relax, it is a lecture) go down that route myself. But what I wish to concentrate on this evening, just because it tends to be passed over in discussion of the novel, is the element of anxiety that inhabits and, I would say, drives the novel, no less than it does Beckett's dramatic masterpiece. And I want to suggest that it is this that makes the book great and quite different from the many imitations it has spawned.

What is the source of this anxiety, in both Sterne and Beckett (for it is the same source in both cases)?

Let me approach the question by going on with my analogy of the lecture. Just as you came in the expectation of an instructive and enjoyable evening, alerted to the lecture by our host, so I too have come, summoned by Patrick, with a clear brief and the expectation of an audience of Sterne enthusiasts. But what if I had had no brief, nor even any invitation, yet found myself drawn to giving a lecture? Not a lecture on Sterne, of course, because I have not been invited anywhere, but a lecture *tout court*. Here I am, fancying myself as a lecturer, an avid reader of other people's lectures, of course, certain of my ability to impress an audience, but no one has asked me to lecture. What do I do? Do I stand in my room and look in the mirror, try out different postures, and then start? But start what? And start how? And start why?

This, I want to suggest, is the situation in which Sterne finds himself. And he is not alone. Before him, and known to him, are a number of authors who seem to have struggled with the same set of problems, a number of works which seem to explore the same predicament: Rabelais, Cervantes, Burton, the Swift of *A Tale of a*

Tub. From all of these Sterne will draw the strength and the confidence to do what he feels drawn to do, and all of these will figure prominently in his own book. After him will come, apart from Beckett, Kafka, Proust, Mann, Kundera, Bernhard, and many others who have in turn drawn strength from Sterne and the Renaissance tradition of which he was the last great representative.

That tradition is often referred to as the tradition of learned wit. I would prefer to call it the tradition of learned anxiety. In each case we are faced with a situation in which the author feels the desperate need to speak but feels at the same time that he lacks the authority to speak, and that without that authority his work lacks all legitimacy. You remember Kafka's Land Surveyor in *The Castle*. He insists that he has been called, but the inhabitants of the Castle and the village deny that. You can stay here and be a land surveyor if you wish, they say, but no one has asked you to come. K, however, feels that he cannot remain and be a land surveyor unless he has been called. Stalemate ensues.

What does it mean, to be called? You all, I am sure, remember the story of the Burning Bush. It is to be found in chapter 3 of the Book of Exodus. Moses is tending his father-in-law's sheep out in the desert, when he comes upon a bush which seems to be burning but is not consumed by the flames. Astonished, he approaches, and as he does so God calls to him out of the bush: 'Moses! Moses!'

> And he answered, Here I am. And the Lord said, Do not come closer. Remove your sandals from your feet, for the place on which you stand is holy ground. And the Lord said, I am the God of your fathers, the God of Abraham, the God of Isaac, and the God of Jacob. And Moses hid his face, for he was afraid to look at God. And the Lord continued, I have marked well the plight of my people in Egypt and I have heeded their outcry… Come, therefore, I will send you to Pharaoh, and you shall free my people the Israelites, from Egypt. (Exod. 3: 4–10)

God speaks to Moses and orders him to go to Egypt and free his people, and there is no question but that he must obey. This is what being called implies. Alas, no such encounter precedes K's visit to the Castle, and it is the absence of such an encounter which constitutes the subject of Kafka's novel.

Consider now the opening of Homer's *Iliad*: 'Sing, Goddess, the wrath of Achilles'. The Goddess invoked is the Muse, and what follows, the whole mighty epic of the *Iliad*, is nothing other than the bard's transmission of her song. That song is neither true nor false, for such terms do not apply: it is simply the account of the way things are, and the singing of that account by the bard helps reinforce the memory of it in the community that listens. Judaism and Christianity retain a version of this in their communal repetition of their founding stories in the annual festivals of Passover and Easter, and (in abbreviated form) in the daily or weekly services attended by the faithful. But such communal assent and renewal no longer holds where our artefacts are concerned.

It still did in the West in the High Middle Ages. For example, the sculptors of the churches and the great cathedrals that were the focus of the community received their instructions as to *what* to portray from the clergy who commissioned them; and *how* they portrayed the hands of Jesus, say, or the beard of Moses they learned as apprentices in the workshop where they had worked since their youth. This did not make all medieval sculpture identical, as we well know, but it did free them from having to make personal choices of content or form in any self-conscious way, and gave to their work a freshness, an innocence, which all who love medieval art treasure, and which modern artists such as Proust and Eliot, Picasso and Maxwell Davies, relish in the art of the Middle Ages.

English literature is particularly rich in examples, and I merely pick out one tiny poem to bring home to you how working within a strictly defined tradition, drawing on conventional doctrines and images, makes for a freer rather than a more subservient art, and certainly for a confident and moving art:

Now goth sonne under wod:
Me reweth, Marye, thy faire rode. [*rood*, cross]
Now goth sonne under Tre:
Me reweth, Marie, thy sone and thee. [*me reweth,* I feel pity for]

The poet sees the sun going down behind the trees, as it does every evening, and meditates on the crucifixion, the 'setting', as it were, of the Son of God. He expresses his sense of pity for both Mary and her child, but that pity is tempered for him and the listener/reader by the knowledge that just as the sun will rise again the following morning, so the Son of God will rise, and, by so doing, save the world and us. The poem effortlessly brings together the natural world, with its cyclical pattern of recurrence, and the unique Christian story. In twenty-three simple words it manages to lament, praise and re-affirm.

It was probably written in the thirteenth century, but such poems (though few as good) went on being recited and then written down till the fifteenth. By the end of that century, though, the world which had given rise to it, as to the churches and cathedrals, was disappearing. By 1600 the consensus on which such art rests had gone for good, the victim of a massive crisis of authority which touched on all areas of society. At a political level the crisis had to do with who rules the land and by what authority. This is explored by Shakespeare in his great cycle of history plays which begins chronologically with the murder of a bad king, Richard II, yet a king who is accepted as God's regent on earth. The question for Richard's successors is, if it is legitimate to depose a king because he is bad who is now to decide who is bad and who is good? Any powerful faction can accuse the incumbent king of being bad and proceed to depose him (or, of course, her). This is mirrored in (and deeply intertwined with) the religious crisis of the time. If the Pope is corrupt, as Luther made out, and his authority to be rejected by all right-thinking persons, what happens when other right-thinking persons do not see eye to eye with Luther?

In the realm of art, what happens when the authority of the traditions in which artists had been working for centuries is suddenly called into question? The answer many theorists as well as artists came up with, is that individual genius replaces the dead hand of tradition. This is the story of the Renaissance that was most actively promulgated by the Renaissance itself, and that still seemed persuasive to the nineteenth and early twentieth centuries. It is the one still popularly held today. But why should the logic that applies to kingship and biblical interpretation not apply to art? In other words, why should not he who seems to himself to be a genius seem merely a madman to others? That is what Cervantes set out to explore. Don Quixote thinks that, like Moses, he has been called, but we know that he is self-deluded. He may be a charming and well-intentioned madman, but as soon as he tries to impose his vision on the world around him it leads to havoc.

Albrecht Dürer, as we know, was one of Luther's staunchest supporters. But in 1514, three years before Luther nailed his theses to the church door in Wittenberg, the gesture which is usually regarded as marking the start of the Reformation, he produced a number of remarkable engravings, amongst which were two which he obviously saw as a pair because in every instance but one he gave them away together. The first was entitled *St Jerome in his Study* and the second, rather more mysteriously, *Melencolia I*. I don't think it's fanciful to see them as Dürer's response to the crisis of authority I have been exploring. The *St Jerome* depicts the saint who gave the Christian West its Latin Bible as a man at ease within the tradition, quietly translating the Bible, with his dog at his feet. A skull and an hourglass remind him of his mortality, but he accepts that as a natural part of being human, a small but necessary part in the great chain of tradition. *Melencolia I* depicts what happens when that sense of tradition has vanished. A large woman sits in the open, next to a ruined house, with her head on her hand, a compass in the other, but she is not working. Her eyes are wide open but she is looking not out at the world but into herself. From her belt hang a bunch of keys and an open purse. Round her, in disarray, lie various measuring instruments and tools, behind her an hourglass and a magic square. Sitting above her is a *putto*, visibly scribbling. An eerie moonlight blankets the scene and, on the left, above a sheet of water, a bat spreads its wings on which the mysterious title is displayed. The two figures convey an overwhelming impression of tension and anxiety in the midst of both chaos and stasis.

This, we feel, is what happens when the authority of tradition no longer has a hold on us. Far from being liberating, the new freedom leads to melancholy and the inability to act. The condition of melancholy was so prevalent in the Renaissance that all the arts explored it, Dowland and Monteverdi in music, Shakespeare and others in poetry, Dürer and Cranach in art. Robert Burton wrote an 'anatomy' of the condition that ran to thousands of pages. Sterne, anticipating Baudelaire, called it Spleen. Freud rightly intuited that it is a condition brought on by a powerful sense of loss for which the psyche lacks the mechanism to mourn adequately because it is unclear exactly what it is that has been lost.

We can see it at work in a play which was to become pivotal for the Romantics but which already exercised an inordinate fascination for Sterne: *Hamlet*. And *Hamlet*, of course, from first to last, is concerned with this question of legitimacy. How does it open? With a ghost stalking the battlements of Elsinore. Hamlet is called, the ghost reveals itself as his father, the former King of Denmark, who commands Hamlet to avenge his murder by the brother who has now married his widow and rules in his place. But – and it is a very big but – is the ghost to be believed? Protestant hostility toward the doctrine of Purgatory means that this figure who arrives on stage to urge a killing would have presented audiences, as he presents Hamlet, with a startling set of choices: he might represent a (Catholic) soul returned from the dead, or a demonic apparition inviting the prince to commit a mortal sin; he might even be the result of a brainsick, melancholic fantasy. How to determine which it is?

The ghost, in a remarkable phrase that haunts Sterne's novel, is said to be 'unhouseled, disappointed, unanealed', that is, deprived of his last rites: not having received the Eucharist, vocal confession, or extreme unction. Yet his command to Hamlet, 'Remember me!' is of the kind that expects to be obeyed. How is Hamlet to respond to these contradictory demands on him? Not knowing what to think or how to act, he decides first to prevaricate and then to improvise in the hope that illumination will follow.

Towards the end of the play, still unclear as to what to do, he finds himself in the graveyard where his erstwhile love, Ophelia, another victim of the ghost's demands, is to be buried, and he overhears two gravediggers talking about their profession. As with the garden scene in *Richard II*, we seem to be in what one might describe as the medieval and allegorical antechamber to the play. Here what is at issue is *memento mori*, the Christian contemplation of death, usually depicted as the contemplation of the human skull. In the fifteenth century it would have driven home to every Christian the lines from Job used in the burial service, that 'dust we are and unto dust we shall return' – but that, as Christ's children, we can take comfort from the thought that if we repent our sins and partake of the sacraments of the Church, we may be confident that we will cheat death and attain eternal life. This is how we are to take it in Dürer's engraving of St Jerome in his study. By the year 1600, roughly when *Hamlet* was written and performed, all it does is bring us face to face with our end, our unimaginable end. Like the hourglass which hangs over the head of Melencolia, it is there merely to remind us that we cannot stop time, that it is to this we are all heading. In the face of this knowledge the only response seems to be either laughter or sentimentality:

> Alas, poor Yorick! I knew him, Horatio, a fellow of infinite jest, of most excellent fancy. He hath borne me on his back a thousand times. And now how abhorred in my imagination it is! My gorge rises at it. Here hung those lips that I have kissed I know not how

> oft. Where be your gibes now? Your gambols, your songs, your flashes of merriment that were wont to set the table on a roar? Not one now to mock your own grinning? Quite chapfall'n? Now get you to my lady's chamber, and tell her, let her paint an inch thick, to this favour she must come.

Heaven is as doubtful as Purgatory. All we are left with is the shining hardness of the grinning skull. Yet we have our desires, our memories of childhood joys and of those whom we loved in those days – how to reconcile that with the brute fact of the skull?

Marlowe and Shakespeare represent the first wave of excitement in the Elizabethan theatre when playwrights were discovering that audiences were willing to pay to be moved and entertained. Marlowe, like Verdi in the nineteenth century, was only too willing to oblige, and created on stage characters for whom imagination, if powerful enough, overcame reality. Shakespeare, like Mozart, seems to have been more interested in exploring the nature and implications of such imagination. That too was the area to which Rabelais, Cervantes and Sterne were instinctively drawn. But for those driven to writing prose fiction and not plays there was a further problem. We all remember the painting of Chaucer reading aloud to the court of Richard II, and Dante, it is known, read parts of his *Commedia* to the ducal court of Cangrande della Scala when he was an exile in Verona. The advent of print had given Rabelais and Cervantes a far wider audience than Dante or Chaucer ever enjoyed, but this came at a price: they no longer knew their audience nor their audience them. They wrote in the privacy of their rooms and what they wrote might be read in far-away cities. In their rooms they had no Muse to guide them, no Church to commission them and instruct them what they were to write, only their own imaginations. But, as we have seen, the products of that imagination were, to them, deeply suspect. What to do, then? How to write? What to write?

There is an interesting moment in *Tristram Shandy* when Tristram contrasts himself with Pope:

Pope and his portrait are fools to me [....] but I have no

Zeal or Anger – or
Anger or Zeal

He is thinking here, the invaluable Melvyn New tells us in his notes, of the portraits of Pope receiving inspiration from the Muses that could be found in the Collected Works edited by Warburton, and probably of La Mettrie's comment on them in his popular book of 1747, *L'homme machine*. 'Let us view the picture of the famous Mr Pope,' writes La Mettrie. 'The efforts and nerves of his genius are strongly represented in his physiognomy, it seems to be in a sort of convulsion [...] because the source of the nerves is [...] in labour, and the whole body [...] feels the pangs of a painful delivery.'[2] Today our image of the Romantic artist, driven by inspiration, is more likely to be derived from the portraits and busts of Beethoven than of Pope. Yet Pope, who had died in 1744, some fifteen years before the first volumes of *Tristram Shandy* hit the bookstalls, was in many ways closer to Beethoven than he was to Swift and Sterne. He was the first English writer to live by his pen, and he marketed himself assiduously as the new Homer, the inspired Bard. All this was anathema to Sterne, for all the reasons I've outlined above. Sterne, like Rabelais and Cervantes, wanted his reader to remember that the book he held in his hands was not the product of inspiration but of accident and whim. 'I wish you saw me half starting out of my chair, with what confidence, as I grasp the elbow of it I look up – catching the idea, even sometimes before it half-way reaches me,' he writes in the paragraph immediately preceding his little riff on Pope.

Not that he would not *like* to be able to write like Homer or Dante – but unfortunately that is not how things are:

Oh ye POWERS (for powers ye are, and great ones too) – which enable a mortal man to tell a story worth hearing – that kindly

> shew him, where he is to begin it, – and where he is to end it, – what he is to put into it, – and what he is to leave out, – how much of it he is to cast into shade, – and whereabouts he is to throw his light! – Ye, who preside over this vast empire of biographical freebooters, and see how many scrapes and plunges your subjects hourly fall into, – will you do one thing?
>
> I beg and beseech you [...] that where ever in any part of your dominions it so falls out, that three several roads meet in one point as they have done just here, – that at least you set up a guide-post in the center of them, in mere charity to direct an uncertain devil, which of the three he is to take.

The Muses, however, remain silent, and the uncertain devil must do the best he can with nothing but his own wits to help him.

But to help him do what? Once upon a time the word of the Bard meant something. Kings took their poets into battle with them because it was felt that their castigations of the enemy would help destroy them. In the culture that produced the cathedrals, the poems of Dante, and lyrics like 'Now goth sone under wode', a curse pronounced with all the appropriate procedures upon someone or something was felt to have a lethal force. Now, like the curse of Ernulphus, which Walter forces poor Dr Slop to read aloud, it is an occasion (for the reader) for mirth rather than awe and terror:

> By the authority of God Almighty, the Father, Son and Holy Ghost, and of the undefiled Virgin Mary, mother and patroness of our saviour, and of all the celestial virtues, angels, archangels [...] and of all the holy patriarchs [...] and of the holy innocents, who in the sight of the Holy Lamb, are found worthy to sing the new song [...] and of all the saints together with the holy and elect of god – May he [Obadiah] be damned [for tying these knots] – We excommunicate, and anathematise him, from the thresholds of the holy church of God Almighty, etc.

We laugh, and rightly so, at the disparity between the size and solemnity of the curse (it is in Latin, the language of authority), the time it takes to deliver it (when so much is happening upstairs), and the absurd object at which it is directed (Obadiah, who has tied the knots of Dr Slop's medical bag so tight that when Slop's obstetrical tools are needed they are not to be got at); but, once again, there is a serious, not to say a desperate point behind that laughter. All the way through the book Sterne/Tristram, like a good Anglican, takes swipes at (as he sees it) Catholic superstition; but this set of practices, which to the eighteenth-century Englishman looks so utterly absurd, is the remnant of what was once, as we have seen, simply a product of a thriving religious culture, and, importantly for this book, one in which words *mattered*.[3]

Today they no longer seem to matter. Most novelists ignore the change. They may be isolated, they may lack legitimacy, but they have learnt how to tell a story that will hold their readers, and that is enough for them. Sterne can do this too, naturally, and he shows the reader how in the course of the little lesson Uncle Toby, of all people, gives to Trim in the art of realistic story-telling. The episode occurs in volume eight, and its occasion is Trim's desire to tell the story of the King of Bohemia and his seven castles. 'There was a certain king of Bohemia,' begins Trim, 'but in whose reign, except his own, I am not able to inform your honour.'

> I do not desire it of thee, Trim, by any means, cried my uncle Toby.
>
> – It was a little before the time, an' please your honour, when giants were beginning to leave off breeding; but in what year of the Lord that was –
>
> – I would not give a half-penny to know, said my uncle Toby.
>
> – Only, a' please your honour, it makes a story look the better in the face –
>
> – 'Tis thy own, Trim, so ornament it after thy own fashion

Trim, like many a beginner, does not know what to put in and what to leave out. He is obsessed with setting the scene in a historically precise time, thinking that this will give more credence to his story, but his efforts to do so in fact undermine the credibility of the narrative. Toby has to remind him that after all it is not history he is writing, the story is his, so he should tell it how he likes.

He starts again. 'In the year of our Lord one thousand seven hundred and twelve, there was, a' please your honour –.' But again Toby interrupts him:

> To tell thee truly, Trim [. . .], any other date would have pleased me much better, not only on account of the sad stain upon our history that year [. . .] – but likewise on the score, Trim, of thy own story; because if there are – and which, from what thou has dropt, I partly suspect to be the fact – if there are giants in it –
>
> There is but one, an' please your honour –
>
> – 'Tis as bad as twenty, replied my uncle Toby – thou shoulds't have carried him back some seven or eight hundred years out of harm's way, both of criticks and other people [...]

First of all Toby comes up against a problem all writers of fiction face: what you are writing about may simply not be of interest, or, worse, may be positively disliked by your readers, so that no matter how well you write they will be reluctant to read you. 1712 was not a good year for the English army, and Toby, as a good soldier, would hesitate to pick up a book set in that year. But Toby also criticises Trim's method. If you are going to have giants in your story, he tries to get Trim to understand, you need to set it in a time when giants still walked the earth, or at least when your readers might believe they did. But it's only one giant, pleads Trim in mitigation. One giant is as bad as twenty, Toby says severely, trying to inculcate the basic principles of narrative realism.

All this is splendid, and we would no doubt find it replicated in creative writing courses up and down the country in 2013. The rest of the novel, though, tells us what Sterne himself thinks of it: that it is not so much nonsense as profoundly misguided. For what we need is not lessons in how to produce the *effect* of reality, what we need is a questioning of the whole basis on which narratives that rely on this for their authority are founded.

Chapter 8 of volume two is a classic example:

> It is about an hour and a half's tolerable good reading since my uncle *Toby* rung the bell, when *Obadiah* was order'd to saddle a horse, and go for Dr *Slop,* the man-midwife, so that no one can say, with reason, that I have not allowed Obadiah time enough, poetically speaking, and considering the emergency, both to go and come; – though morally and truly speaking, the man has scarce had time to get on his boots

Many different things are going on here at the same time. Sterne, as he so often does, deliberately confuses reading time and narrative time so as to jolt us into realising that there are in fact three time-scales: there is the time the narrative itself uses (one day in the case of *Ulysses*, a lifetime in the case of Proust's *À la recherche*); there is the time the reader takes to read the book; and there is the time the writer takes to write it. Realist novelists deliberately occlude the latter two so as to give the impression that the novel we are reading is not a construct but is somehow natural, like a tree. Sterne, in the interests of truth, wants to stress the opposite. So, in this instance, only a few minutes have elapsed in narrative time between Toby's ringing for Obadiah and ordering him to fetch Dr Slop and the appearance of the latter, but Sterne begins by pretending that, since he has placed so much reading matter in the form of digressions between the two moments, that is time enough for the Doctor to have got the message, packed his bag, and come. He then admits that 'morally and truly speaking', in other words within the time-frame inside the narrative, 'the man has scarce had time to get on his boots'.

However, Tristram continues,

> if the hypercritick [...] is resolved after all to take a pendulum, and measure the true distance betwixt the ringing of the bell and the rap at the door, – and, after finding it to be no more than two minutes thirteen seconds and three fifths, – should take upon him to insult over me for such a breach in the unity, or rather probability of time

If he is so resolved, Tristram has an answer for him, which consists in a rapid summary of Locke's argument about the duration of ideas. However,

> If my hypercritick is intractable, – alledging that two minutes and thirteen seconds are no more than two minutes and thirteen seconds, – when I have said all I can about them; – and that this plea, though it might save me dramatically, will damn me biographically, rendering my book, from this very moment, a profess'd ROMANCE, which, before, was a book apocryphal: – If I am thus pressed – I then put an end to the whole objection and controversy about it all at once, – by acquainting him, that Obadiah had not got above threescore yards from the stable-yard before he met with Dr Slop; – and indeed he gave a dirty proof that he had met with him, – and was within an ace of giving a tragical one too.

If you want me to furnish you with an explanation that accords with the reality effect, Sterne is saying, then I can easily invent one: Obadiah did not have to ride all the way to the doctor's house and the two of them ride all the way back, for Dr.Slop was in fact himself already on his way to the Shandy household, was so close, in fact, that the two collided only minutes after Obadiah had set out.

The whole farcical episode is only another assertion by Sterne that he will have nothing to do with what critics expect (or, we might say, with what creative writing courses try to teach), that he will go about things in his own way and will not be beholden to any man. As Borges says, reality needs to move steadily forward in time, but why should a piece of fiction? If, Sterne argues, he wishes to insert a Preface in the middle of his book, why shouldn't he? If he wishes to write a chapter on whiskers, why shouldn't he? If he wishes to introduce one of his own sermons, into the narrative, why shouldn't he? It is, after all, as Toby said to Obadiah, his story, and he should be allowed to tell it in his own way.

What Sterne cannot bear is having to toe the realist line, tediously going from A to B, tediously describing a new character each time he or she is introduced, and so on and so forth – you can fill in more examples from your reading of realist novels – merely so as to satisfy critics who are besotted with the idea that a novel must continuously uphold the reality effect. Sterne is unwilling to play this game. All it would do, he feels, would be to make a drudge of him, something he has no intention of becoming. Rather, he writes to assert his freedom, as Trim asserts his by the twirl of his stick.

And he will assert his freedom, paradoxically, by insisting on his helplessness in the face of accident and chance.

Both Rabelais and Cervantes, in their prefaces, dramatise themselves in the act of writing, sucking their pens, clutching their heads, having a drink to revive their flagging spirits, and so on. This, as I have been explaining at perhaps tedious length, is done partly in order to alert the reader to the fact that the book they are about to read is not a work like that of Homer or the Bible – underwritten, as it were, by the Muse or by God – but merely a piece of improvisation by a very human scribbler. Rabelais's giants and cunning tricksters may be alter egos, but it was left to Cervantes to draw an explicit link between himself and his hero:

> Idle reader, without my swearing to it, you can believe that I would like this book, the child of my understanding, to be the

> most beautiful, the most brilliant and the most discreet that anyone can imagine. But I have not been able to contravene the natural order; in it like begets like. And so what could my barren and poorly cultivated wits beget but the history of a child who is dry, withered, capricious, and filled with inconstant thoughts, never imagined by anyone else.

Sterne's stroke of genius was to make his hero not only a writer like himself, but also to afflict him and his family with all the misfortunes to which, he sensed, the modern writer is inevitably subject (though most choose to hide this, even from themselves).

It is obvious from the start that the novel is dogged with issues of paternity and impotence. Who is Tristram's father? What is the significance of the mistake which has landed Walter's coach with a coat of arms that figures a bend sinister, the sign of bastardy? Why does Tristram suffer a threefold blow almost before he is born – botched conception, wrong name, broken nose? Why does he then have to endure possible castration when the sash window falls upon him as Susannah holds him up to the window in the absence of a chamber pot? Why does the book end with an impotent bull and itself admits to being nothing but a Cock and Bull story?

The answer to all these questions is of course that Tristram's story is the story of the book – it is both the story the book *recounts* and the story the book *enacts*. It is extremely doubtful, for example, if in real life the distraction of the parents in the act of copulation leads to a weak and distracted child being born, but Sterne plays with the mechanistic thought of the time to suggest that this is precisely what happened – while of course at the same time asking us to recognise that this is all nonsense. Mrs Shandy's question, Tristram avers, 'scattered and dispersed the animal spirits, whose business it was to have escorted and gone hand-in-hand with the HOMUNCULUS, and conducted him safe to the place destined for his reception.' A paragraph later the homunculus is quite a little gentleman:

> Now, dear Sir, what if any accident had befallen him in his way alone? – or that, thro' the terror of it, natural to so young a traveller, my little gentleman had got to his journey's end miserably spent; – his muscular strength and virility worn down to a thread; his own animal spirits ruffled beyond description, – and that in this sad disorder'd state of nerves, he had laid down a prey to sudden starts, or a series of melancholy dreams and fancies for nine long, long months together. – I tremble to think what a foundation had been laid for a thousand weaknesses both of body and mind, which no skill of the physician or the philosopher could ever afterwards have set so thoroughly to rights.

What in Cervantes was merely melancholy resignation is transformed by Sterne into high farce. But this should not distract us from grasping that while what he is saying is absurd as far as *procreation* is concerned, it is only too true where *the creation of a work of art* is concerned. Unlike the image Warburton/Pope want to present of the creative process, Sterne wants to remind us of the myriad slips that may occur between the conception and the production of a novel – or even a chapter, a sentence, a word.

This kind of thing happens again and again in the course of the book:

> – This unfortunate drawbridge of yours, quoth my father –
> – God bless your honour, cried Trim, 'tis a bridge for master's nose. In bringing him into the world with his vile instruments, he has crushed his nose, *Susannah* says, as flat as a pancake to his face, and he is making a false bridge with a piece of cotton and a thin piece of whalebone out of *Susannah*'s stays, to raise it up.
> – Lead me, brother Toby, cried my father, to my room this instant.

Toby hears the word 'bridge' and immediately thinks of fortifications; Sterne, however, wants the reader to think about his book, which, like Tristram's nose, has been patched up with the equivalent of the piece of cotton and the piece of whalebone out of Susannah's stays. Dickens and George Eliot both know that this is how books are made, but they prefer to hide it from their public – and even from themselves.

But now we come to the key question: If this is the case, then what is Sterne saying when he tells of Trim flourishing his cane and uttering his stirring words in praise of freedom? That he is writing a book that is as free as the twirl of the stick, a book that will forever raise two fingers to the bigoted critic and his desire for realism? True enough. But not the whole truth. Toby and Trim have marched up to the Widow Wadman's front door. Toby is about to propose to her and so change his life forever. 'Nothing,' Trim says, 'can be so sad as confinement for life – or so sweet, an'please your honour, as liberty.' 'Nothing, Trim,' responds Toby. 'Whil'st a man is free – cried the Corporal, giving a flourish with his stick thus – '

The discussion is not about liberty in the abstract but about marriage and its discontents. And Tristram's comment on the image of the twirling stick which Sterne/Tristram reproduces on the page for us, makes this explicit: 'A thousand of my father's subtle syllogisms could not have said more for celibacy.'

The question is this: Will Toby be happier married or celibate? We know what he chooses, and the book implies that he was bound to choose this, since the wound in his groin debarred him from what he explicitly affirms to be the main function of marriage, the production of children. But the further question arises: Was the wound itself not, in a sense, an essential part of Toby and not the result of a mere accident? Is Toby not in a sense 'really himself' in his celibacy and perpetual childhood, with his fortifications to keep him amused and his pipe and Lillabulero? Or is his dearest wish to change this condition so that he may at last grow up and be like other men?

And the question then arises, what of Sterne? Is he playing with his reader or can he really not get his book written? Is his inability to get his book written a cause for celebration or lament? Is the book a paean to freedom or a cry of despair?

The philosopher Robert Pippin has a fascinating paragraph in his book *Modernism as a Philosophical Problem*. Here is what he says:

> In Weber's essay, 'Science as a Vocation', he offers an interpretation of Tolstoy's late novels in order to emphasise a point he is making in his own way about modernity as, by and large, exclusively, loss (the disenchantment of the world, the loss of all forms of authority other than bureaucratic or charismatic). Tolstoy had noted that in pre-modern times, or times oriented around the centrality of nature and not historical time, the prospect of death was much easier to bear. The cycle of life and death had (or was experienced as having) a regular and predictable pattern. After some stretch of time, if one were fortunate enough to have lived into middle age, one could console oneself with the thought that one had basically seen all that life had to offer. The cycle of birth, growth, work, love, reproduction and death had run its course. What more there was to see would likely be only a repetition. Even the great events on the world stage, wars, famine and so forth, were themselves the return of the eternal troubles of the human heart, were themselves repetitions. With the advent of a historical consciousness, though, and so some belief in the uniqueness of historical events, especially the unrepeatability of historical moments, it was impossible to avoid the crushing sense that death was completely meaningless, occupied no place in any natural cycle; was an event without possible consolation [...] One's death became a mere ending at some arbitrary point; there would always be something, probably an infinity of distinct and unprecedented events, to 'miss'.[4]

This anxiety over death is something I have already touched on as providing the undertow in *Hamlet*, and it is of course prevalent in *Tristram Shandy*, not only in the figure of Yorick – who, with Toby, acts as a kind of surrogate father for the impotent Tristram – but also in the whole of volume seven, Sterne's jokey but angst-ridden account of a journey undertaken to escape death – whether by visiting healthier climes than those of Yorkshire or in good medieval fashion by outwitting the figure of Death himself is another ambiguity Sterne refuses to unpack.[5] As Weber argues, in Pippin's summary, the sense that there is so much still to do and that one will never be able to do it in one's lifetime is what makes modern life so frustrating, so angst-ridden. It is this that the nineteenth-century novel explored, in particular *Crime and Punishment* and *Madame Bovary*. For Rabelais and Cervantes, long before, it was an issue that was directly connected with their sense both that writing was what they wanted to do and that it was essentially a waste of time, and therefore something keeping them from doing that which might justify their lives.

Now just this link between the need to write, the absurdity of writing, and the sense that by so doing one is frittering away ones life is something that pervades Kafka's writing from the start. There is nothing closer to the ambiguous complexity of Trim's gesture than the early letter in which Kafka remarks to Brod: 'When people ask us about the life we intend to live, we form the habit, in spring, of answering with an expansive wave of the hand, which goes limp after a while, as if to say that it was ridiculously unnecessary to conjure up sure things.'[6] Late in his life he ponders in his diary the link between such gestures and his writing: 'Childish games (though I was well aware that they were so) marked the beginning of my intellectual decline. I deliberately cultivated a facial tic, for instance, or would walk across the Graben with arms crossed behind my head. A repulsively childish but successful game. (My writing began in the same way […])'[7]

A late story brings out the link Weber touched on between the sense of a life not fully lived and a death not properly accepted. It is called 'The Hunter Gracchus'. A boat arrives in the little harbour of the Italian town of Riva. In it is a bier on which a man is lying.

The Burgomaster, who in the night received a message which said: 'Tomorrow the dead Hunter Gracchus is coming: receive him in the name of the city', comes down to the harbour and kneels by the bier: 'Are you dead?' he asks the man. Yes, replies the man. 'Many years ago,' he explains, 'I fell from a precipice in the Black Forest – that is in Germany – when I was hunting a chamois. Since then I have been dead.' 'But you are alive too,' says the Burgomaster.

> 'In a certain sense,' said the Hunter. 'In a certain sense I am alive too. My death ship lost its way; a wrong turn of the wheel, a moment's absence of mind on the pilot's part, the distraction of my lovely native country, I cannot tell what it was; I only know this, that I remained on earth and that ever since my ship has sailed earthly waters. So I, who asked for nothing better than to live among my mountains, travel after my death through all the lands of the earth.'

'The Hunter Gracchus' is Kafka's clearest expression of a feeling he often referred to in his journals, the feeling that he has never really been born and therefore can never really die, that he has no past and no future but only a hopeless present.

Of course Sterne is no Kafka. Kafka was triply isolated, as he often pointed out in his letters and journals: a German-speaking Jew in a Prague that was starting to feel the stirrings of Czech nationalism; a Jew no longer at home in the religion of his forefathers yet unable to believe in the new religion of financial success and upward mobility espoused by his father. Sterne was a deeply rooted Yorkshireman, a clergyman of the Church of England, whose grandfather had been Archbishop of York, and he was deeply loved and respected in his community. And yet, strangely enough, he seems to have been infected (from one point of view), or had his eyes opened (from another) by Rabelais, by Cervantes, by Shakespeare, by Swift, and when, late in his life, he began to write, he produced a work which harks back to those earlier writers but also forwards to Kafka and

Beckett and other modern masters. That is why his contemporaries can still be enjoyed today as great eighteenth-century writers, but he, we feel, is very much our contemporary,

'The history of a soldier's wound beguiles the pain of it,' writes Tristram of his uncle Toby's need to talk about how he got his wound at the siege of Namur. 'Beguiles' is, as always with Sterne, precisely the right word. One of its meanings is 'to divert attention in some pleasant way from'. So Uncle Toby enjoys recounting the story of how he got his wound, and the enjoyment is genuine; but he also tells the story to divert his attention from the pain, which seems to stretch beyond the physical and take on an almost metaphysical dimension: it is the pain of not being able to engender, as well as the pain of solitude. The two things, the pleasure and the pain, co-exist, and who is to say which is the main one? The late Stevie Smith, in her best-known poem, stressed one side of the equation:

Not Waving But Drowning

Nobody heard him, the dead man,
But still he lay moaning:
I was much further out than you thought
And not waving but drowning.

Poor chap, he always loved larking
And now he's dead
It must have been too cold for him, his heart gave way,
They said.

Oh, no no no, it was too cold always
(Still the dead one lay moaning)
I was much too far out all my life
And not waving but drowning.

But I cannot let Stevie Smith have the last word. I think that it is precisely because *Tristram Shandy* is built on such dark foundations that it is so wholesome, so much more nourishing than those modern works that claim kinship with it – Robert Nye's *Falstaff*, the novels of Salman Rushdie, and many others. Sterne's story of Tristram's accidents and misfortunes, the accidents and misfortunes which dog his own book, remind us that we are not independent beings, free to mould our own destinies, as a long tradition of Western philosophy since Descartes, and of fiction since Defoe, has suggested. On the contrary, we are, from first to last, dependent on others and grow into ourselves through our reciprocal relations to others. Moreover, chance and accident, to which we can only respond by patching and mending, are not misfortunes that befall us but the very things that make us human. Sterne helps us to recognise our own dependence on chance and on other people, makes us understand that though we may dream of purity and independence, we are creatures embodied and in this world. It is a lesson we are grateful to learn.

1 Delivered as the annual *Tristram Shandy* lecture at Shandy Hall, May 2011.

2 Laurence Sterne, *The Life and Opinions of Tristram Shandy, Gentleman*, with a preface by Christopher Ricks and an introduction and notes by Melvyn New, edited by Joan New and Melvyn New (Harmondsworth: Penguin Books, 1997), p. 649.

3 I have explored Tristram's scepticism about the relics he encounters on his journey through France, and how this is paralleled by his sense of the absurdity of the modern tourist's desire to see objects of purely cultural value, such as the Tomb of the Lovers in Lyon, in 'Escape Literature: Tristram Shandy's Journey Through France', in Gabriel Josipovici, *The Singer on the Shore* (Manchester: Carcanet, 2006), pp. 104–118.

4 Robert B. Pippin, *Modernism as a Philosophical Problem: On the Dissatisfactions of European High Culture* (Oxford: Blackwell, 1999), p. 155.

5 See my essay referred to in note 3.

6 28 August 1904.

7 24 January 1922.

Empty Rooms[1]

THE FIRST ROOM of the Hammershøi exhibition at the Royal Academy is already breathtaking. Three tiny paintings of farm buildings in an indeterminate landscape, which remind one of Morandi in their muted tones, blurred edges and almost abstract balancing of shapes. Then a larger painting entitled *The White Door*, which shows, through an open door, set in a greenish yellow wall, a white closed door beyond, warm as a pail of fresh milk. The only other feature is a stove in the corner of the first room, a dark shape set against grey walls. The brown floor drinks in a bit of colour from the white door beyond but grows almost black around the stove. The absence of any other objects or of any sign of human life forces upon us words like 'silence' to convey its atmosphere, but though the predominant tones are dark the rhythm established between closed and open doors, white door and dark stove conveys a sense of calm exhilaration rather than doom or despondency.

Hammershøi's contemporaries sensed this. 'The picture bearing the fine name, The White Door,' wrote Emil Heilbut in 1905, 'is a work of perfect beauty. The open white door is really alive, its wood shimmers! The other door, which leads backwards from the room, is also open. They seem to be talking to each other, these two open doors. Very slow-ly, very slow-ly, Jens Peter Jacobsen would say.'[2] Rilke, who had first come across Hammershøi's work in an exhibition in Düsseldorf in 1904, travelled to the Danish capital to meet the artist, about whom he planned to write an essay which, sadly, never materialised. 'Hammershøi is not one of those about whom one must speak quickly,' he wrote to Alfred Bramsen, the painter's champion in Copenhagen. 'His work is long and slow, and at whichever moment one apprehends it, it will offer plentiful reasons to speak of what is important and essential in art.'

Hammershøi's life was as uneventful as his art. Born in 1864 into an upper-middle-class merchant family, he quickly showed artistic talent, which was encouraged by his mother. At fifteen he began attending art school. In 1891 he married Ida Ilsted, the sister of a former fellow student, and travelled with her to Holland, Belgium, Germany, Italy and London. Between 1898 and 1909 they lived in a flat in Strandgade 30, in the centre of the city, where many of his greatest and most characteristic work was done, and, when they were forced to leave because the building was being sold, moved to a flat across the road where Hammershøi died of cancer of the throat in 1916, aged 51.

Uneventful perhaps, certainly not bohemian, but not exactly conformist either. 'I have a pupil who paints most oddly. I do not understand him, but believe he is going to be important,' said one of his first teachers. At twenty-one, in 1885, he entered an Academy competition with a portrait of his sister Anna. To us today it looks innocent enough, but its lack of sharp contours and any clear background scandalised the jury. In the following years, though he had already become something of a celebrity among his contemporaries in Copenhagen, the Academy rejected two more of his submissions, and he never again submitted work to it. In the 1890s he travelled to Paris with his new bride. His mother was anxious lest he fall prey to the new painterly fashions. She need not have worried. The one painting he brought back was a painstaking copy of a fragment from a marble relief of the Three Graces from Thasos, dated 470 BC, in the Louvre. Yet it is not quite a copy. By blurring the features and outlines ever so slightly he brought out the beautiful rhythm that seems to animate the three women, and makes of this, to me, almost as powerful an image of the dance that inheres in the universe as Matisse's much more celebrated painting. Here was a man who knew almost from the start what it was he wanted to do, and had the means to do it.

His rare comments on his art suggest someone who has thought long and hard about his craft and is totally confident about his aims and ambitions, though unwilling to probe too deeply into his motivations. 'Why do I use just a few, muted colours? [...] It seems perfectly natural to me, but I can't say why [...] I'm utterly convinced that a painting has the best effect in terms of its colour the fewer colours there are.' And: 'What makes me choose a motif are [...] the lines, what I like to call the architectural content of an image. And then there's the light, of course. Obviously, that's also very important, but I think it's the lines that have the greatest significance for me.'

Though Hammershøi painted a number of characteristically empty and timeless landscapes and buildings and streets in Denmark and in London (the way he renders the railings of the British Museum courtyard fill one with joy), it is the interiors which form the bulk of his work and of the RA exhibition. When he and Ida moved into the flat in Strandgade 30 they emptied it out and had it repainted. Photos included in the catalogue give an impression of what it must have been like, and how strikingly different, in its lack of clutter, it was to most bourgeois habitations of the time. But what they establish is that even though bare by standards of the day it was a great deal fuller, more 'inhabited' than it appears in the paintings. Clearly Hammershøi, when devising his paintings, treated his flat as a sort of stage set. He emphasises the elegant panelling of the rooms and, sometimes, a few items of furniture such as a square piano, a table with a vase or a Dutch ceramic bowl on it, a chair or two. Sometimes there is a flower in the vase, sometimes not. Occasionally there is only the room, with the light streaming in through the windows – like Vermeer, Hammershøi is conscious of air as more than a transparent medium; it has substance, like water, and the room is bathed in it.

There is something uncanny about these empty rooms, reminding one a little of de Chirico and even more of Magritte. But the similarity surfaces only to vanish again, for there is nothing wilful about this emptiness, no point to be made. It is the same with another name that comes to mind: Hopper. The catalogue would seem to want to push us in the direction of Hopper, but the abrasive greens and reds of the American exude an urban angst which is quite alien to the Dane.

Sometimes a single woman inhabits these rooms. Clearly Hammershøi had seen Vermeer, and he has his figures sometimes sewing or reading or stirring a cup of coffee in a desultory way. These are not his most successful pictures. Vermeer was fascinated by the way a woman in the exercise of a simple manual task such as pouring milk or sewing, or even just reading a letter, becomes at once all surface and all depth. The viewer, looking at this silent activity which is neither inner nor outer, comes to understand what it means to be embodied. Hammershøi's vision is quite other. He prefers his women to have their backs to us. In one, *Interior, Strandgade 30* the woman sits at a table to the left of the picture, the bulk of which is taken up with a window, through which the light comes and patterns the floor behind her, and a door. The woman is half but only half turned towards the window and the light. We cannot tell if she is looking outwards or inwards. Unlike Friedrich's *Rückenfiguren*, those figures with their backs to us such as the dramatic *Wanderer above the Sea of Fog,* she is not our means of access to a vision beyond. She is, in fact, no more than another element in the room. To call her 'Ida Hammershøi' as the catalogue constantly does is to give us a false sense of access to her mystery. In another work, also dated 1909, *Interior with Stove*, the woman, holding a plate against her left hip, stands a little to the side of an open door, through which one can see further rooms and, at the end, a window filled with sunlight. In the corner, with a framed picture next to it, a stove glints. This image of a woman, seen from behind, carrying a plate against her left hip while facing to the right, clearly meant much to the artist, for we find her again, in a picture dated 1904, this time three quarter length, enclosed in the cube of the room (the door is invisible, to the right, we surmise).

What is the source of the hold these paintings have over us?

Islamic artists believed that mathematics, when embodied in pattern, revealed the secret rhythms underlying the universe. It does not matter if the pattern is cut off at any one point on the surface, because we have been given more than enough to allow us to intuit these rhythms. In the same way Hammershøi's pictures establish a rhythm, and the cutting off of a panel or a bookcase by the edge of the picture only confirms that the rhythm inheres in all things, and can become accessible to us if we sit quietly enough, listen intently enough. That rhythm was already there in the Louvre's *Three Graces*; in the later work it is embodied in the purely abstract play of shape against shape, light against dark, hip and plate against shoulder and cheek. But it is more than that, and when we grasp what that 'more' is we grasp why Hammershøi, like so many modern painters, having fully internalised the reasons for the drive towards abstraction, nevertheless wished to remain within the realm of figuration. And not just figuration, but the depiction of the ordinary. No Matissian dance for him. If the woman is taking part in a cosmic dance (and she is) then she does not know it, and it is important that she does not. At the same time these pictures convey a powerful sense of the radical contingency of each moment: it is this moment, now, and no other. But also, the radical contingency of our Western, urban civilisation: it is a late-nineteenth-century room or street in Copenhagen or London, here, now – and it could so well have been other. There is a political direction in which this could go, of course, but it is not the direction Hammershøi chooses: having understood that our world has not been given but made, in a dizzying series of chances and choices, he has no desire to change it; he is content to stay poised at the perfect midpoint between where we are and where we cannot be. There is no need to overcome this condition. It just is, transient, transitory. That is enough. No wonder Rilke wanted to write about him.

This exhibition is timely. Not just because Hammershøi is practically unknown in this country (he was forgotten by the whole world from the time of his death till the seventies), but because it is perhaps only now that we are ready for him. The grip of teleology in the matter of Modernism that has for so long held critics, artists and the public in thrall, is beginning to relax. There has been a growing recognition that there are many ways of being modern: there is the way of Malevich and there is the way of Bonnard, the way of Duchamp and the way of Balthus, the way of Pollock and the way of Bacon. As one walks round this masterly exhibition one has the feeling that it is Hammershøi who has been waiting, quietly, for us to catch up with him. We will talk of it for many years to come.

1 A review of the exhibition *Vilhelm Hammershøi: The Poetry of Silence*, Royal Academy of Arts (Sackler Wing), London, 28 June–7 September 2008.

2 *Hammershøi*, edited by Felix Kramer, Naoki Sato, and Anne-Birgitte Fonsmark (London: Royal Academy of Arts, 2008).

A Napoleon of Thought: Paul Valéry and his Notebooks[1]

Paul Valéry seems to have crept into the pantheon of European Modernists by the back door. There are few in the English-speaking world who have read him, fewer still who have understood or enjoyed what they have read, but perhaps for that very reason his status has never really been in doubt: if everyone says he is a great poet and thinker, then that's what he must be. And it's not very different in France, where his reputation has never really dipped, as has that of Claudel. In a strange way, he seems to be above criticism, gazing down with cool disdain at the world below.

The publication after Valéry's death of the notes he jotted down every morning for fifty years between 3.30 and 7 a.m., only served to reinforce this image. For what we have here is not an intimate journal, like that of Kafka, but an unwieldy mass of notes, sketches, diagrams and stray thoughts on every conceivable subject, from maths to prosody, from the transcript of conversations with Mallarmé and Gide to tiny prose poems, from delicate little watercolours to attempts to translate the law of the conservation of energy into a general principle governing the dynamism of mental activity. No surprise, then, that the publication first of a facsimile of the vast manuscript (260 notebooks) in twenty-nine volumes shortly after his death, then of a selection in two fat Pléiade volumes, and finally the ongoing publication of a complete transcript of the two initial decades of the *Cahiers* (1894–1914), should only have reinforced the view of Valéry as godlike, out of reach, someone one would never read but who it was comforting to know had existed.

Richard Sieburth, in what must surely be one of the finest reviews ever written for the *TLS* (22 September 1989), made an impassioned plea, however, for the continuing relevance, indeed the central place of Valéry, and of the notebooks in particular, in our culture: 'Logbooks of a mind restlessly seeking to recalculate its position every day', he wrote, 'these early *Cahiers* chart what Valéry refers to as "rhumb line", that is, the course of a ship sailing always oblique to the meridian in the direction of one and the same point of the compass – the adventure of thought as a sustained "écart par rapport à une constante esssentielle"'.

Valéry began the *Cahiers* in 1894, two years after the great crisis of his youth when, having published some precocious poems in his teens, he suddenly ceased to write poetry and withdrew from literary life for over twenty years. Even after his triumphant re-entry into the world of letters with the publication of *La Jeune Parque* in 1917, which culminated in his election to the Académie Française in 1925, he continued his daily dawn jottings – they were his 'travail de Pénélope', he said, the moment when he could feel that he was closest to his true self. At the same time he on several occasions considered preparing the *Cahiers* for publication, feeling even late in his life that they were his most important contribution to literature. As early as 1908 he began extracting what he thought was the most valuable material and hired a secretary to type it out. From then until the end of his life, as he tried one system of classification after another, Valéry employed a series of secretaries more or less permanently to transcribe his notes in duplicate and arrange the typescript under various headings for eventual annotation and revision. In a bizarre Ionesco-like drama, the sheer physical bulk of the *Cahiers* began to occupy more and more room in the Valéry apartment, threatening to oust the human occupants. Death, however, intervened.

Now, under the guidance of three leading English Valéry scholars, the *Cahiers* are at last being published in English translation – not the *Cahiers* Sieburth waxed so eloquent about, but the two-volume Pléiade edition published in 1973–74 by Judith Robinson-Valéry.[1] And one can see why. Sieburth was reviewing the first two volumes of what would eventually be a twelve-volume edition, but even that would only transcribe four of the twenty-nine volumes of the 1948 CNRS facsimile edition. As the editors Paul Gifford and Brian Stimpson say in their introduction to *Reading Paul Valéry* (1998), this in effect means that 'the finest of Valéry's mature thought is excluded.' However, there are real problems with the Pléiade edition, problems which take us to the heart of Valéry's own ambivalence about his *Cahiers*, and, indeed, of his life-work as a whole.

The two-volume Pléiade prints about one-tenth of the 260 *Cahiers*, thematically organised according to the system of 31 headings and 215 subheadings that Valéry sketched out between 1935 and 1945. 'Exceptionally well edited and annotated,' says Sieburth, 'this edition nonetheless imposed a factiously synchronic order on a manuscript that had for half a century remained in flux. Neatly enshrined in two Pléiade volumes, Valéry's *Cahiers* ran the risk of becoming a canonical monument – whereas their real interest lay in their textual history as an ongoing ruin.' Judith Robinson-Valéry herself acknowledged in her Pléiade introduction that the divisions were rather arbitrary, that 'Ce serait fausser complètement sa pensée que de croire que le chapitre *Langage*, par exemple, représente la somme de ses reflections à ce sujet.' It was, however, she felt, better than any of the alternatives. The English editors, while by and large keeping to Robinson-Valéry's plan, have, for inexplicable reasons, themselves made a few further changes. They have, for example, moved the thoughts of Valéry on writing, and on his own writing in particular, 'Ego Scriptor', from what would seem to be its natural place after 'Ego' at the start of volume I (where it is in the Pléiade), to the very end of the second volume (their edition will eventually comprise five volumes instead of the French's two). No doubt they have their reasons, and one could go on arguing about order for ever, since the whole enterprise rests on such arbitrary divisions. They have also annotated the text more fully, and while some of these annotations are helpful, others seem bizarre, such as trying to explain Valéry's aesthetics in five lines; or quite misleading, such as telling us that Valéry was the first to adopt for literary purposes the biological term 'tropism', only given currency 'much later' by Nathalie Sarraute in her novel of that name, to which the date of the English translation (1957) is attached, whereas the book came out in French in 1939.

Much more worrying, though, is that the Pléiade edition, as Sieburth points out, completely distorts the way we read these notes. Hived off in separate compartments, entitled 'Poetry', 'Literature', 'Psychology', etc., what should have been seen as stray thoughts, dawn jottings, take on the shine of aphorisms, and not only does this go against the very idea of a daily notebook, they are also often simply not up to it. 'I can't help it, everything interests me', is all right as a private jotting but comes over as insufferably pompous when isolated and published. 'The task of poetry is to produce a handful of perfect examples of a nation's language in action' is not exactly profound, and neither is 'Architecture is an ode to space itself', though, again, as jottings they would be perfectly acceptable. The travel notes are hardly better: 'Magnificent countryside near Sidi Bou Saïd. The town is a kind of gem [...] I love this Arabic architecture and decoration.' And of the course the few notes which do give a glimpse of the human being behind the comments such as 'This morning I got up as though to flee from myself – Had a very strong coffee. And I still haven't calmed down. I am, I feel like a violin string vibrating at its highest pitch' – are positively damaged and mocked when divorced from the continuum of life and placed in a section marked 'Ego'.

What complicates matters is that Valéry himself, in his lifetime, not only gave a good deal of thought to how he might publish these notes, but actually mined his notebooks for quotable passages, which he reproduced in various collections, such as *Tel Quel* and *Mélange*. We must assume that he was proud of them. Yet, though Valéry's supporters make huge claims for him, it is difficult to see how the notebooks bear these out. *Reading Paul Valéry*, a companion volume to the notebooks by one of its editors, Paul

Gifford, is a veritable compendium of such claims: 'Writing here signifies the ethic of a research vocation espoused with radical integrity and recalled with terse insistence,' writes Paul Gifford. 'Valéry is now seen as one of the major thinkers of the century', enthuses Régine Pietra, though nothing in her essay goes the least way towards backing up the claim. 'The startlingly original, high-voltage prose poetry of a consummate artist' is how the poet Stephen Romer describes the contents of the section 'Poèmes et PPA (petits poèmes abstraits)', and since he is himself the translator of that section in the English edition it is possible to test his claims. 'The jetties were flying past like arrows', reads an entry for 1894, and while this would be quite passable in a diary (though Kafka's early entry in his diary of 1910, 'The onlookers go rigid when the train goes past', is infinitely superior, catching as it does the speed of the train and the reaction of those on the platform in a few deft words – Kafka, one feels, is utterly in thrall to the event, Valéry jotting down a pleasing *aperçu*), it hardly bears out Romer's extravagant claims. A little later we have: 'The sun melts, liquefies, and pours onto the domes and tiles, in a magnificent marshland of copious roofs / in a copious marshland of magnificent roofs', which is simply ridiculous. An entry entitled 'Star' reads: 'In the uniform matt dark blue sky, black-bodied, – pierces something infinitely soft, vibrant and elevated – accompanied by radiance, distance, purity, penetration, finesse, isolation – presence.' It's not as clumsy in the French ('Au ciel uni mat bleu sombre, a corps noir, – quelque chose infiniment douce, vive et élevée perce [...]') but hardly merits the term 'prose poem'. Better is an entry on rocks, which Valéry thought well enough of to reproduce, with variations, in *Autres Rhumbs, Tel Quel*:

> Some black, some silver, others flesh-pink. Some shining and cube-shaped with mossy, flattened edges. Others with clean, sharp breakages, or with very thick, ragged slates, others large and rounded. To each its nature, and in accordance with that, its face,

which is also its history.

The form depends on the substance and on events, on links and forces.

I walk among this chaos, to the sound of the sea.

Good, but not exactly in the Coleridge or Hopkins class.

When it comes to comments on artists and on the history of art and literature, Valéry was extremely limited: he was against the Romantics and for Racine and Mallarmé, but he never moves outside the canon of French literature, and, when he deals with the visual arts, never outside a narrow tradition that goes from the Renaissance to Degas. His early passion for Leonardo's notebooks should, one would have thought, make him a particularly astute critic of the painter, but again one is disappointed: 'The smile of the *Mona Lisa* is empty of thought. Her smile signifies: "I'm not thinking of anything – Leonardo is thinking for me."' Valéry despised Proust (though one wonders if he ever read him) but Proust, writing about the same subject at roughly the same time (1906–07), pierces us with the sense of something fundamentally important being said. In his preface to his translation of Ruskin's *Bible of Amiens*, Proust contrasts his experience of the statue of the Virgin on the south porch of Amiens Cathedral with the 'Mona Lisa' in the Louvre. The 'Mona Lisa', though obviously painted by a specific person in a specific place, is now uprooted, he says, rather like a wonderful woman without a country ('quelque chose comme une admirable "sans-patrie"'). By contrast her sister, the Virgin of Amiens, is a local girl, made of local stone, with the sun of that region shining on her and its winds beating for ever on her face. In order to see her we need to take the train, enter an unknown city, walk. These two factors, her rootedness in a specific countryside and the effort we must make to get to see her, cannot be removed from our response to her. And Proust ends this contrast with one of those simple but devastating remarks which so often lift his criticism into the realm of greatness: 'In my room,' he says, 'a photograph of the Mona Lisa retains only the beauty of a masterpiece. Near her a photograph of the Vierge Dorée takes on the melancholy sadness of a souvenir.' Proust is here raising questions about the new genre of portable oil painting, about just where we stand in relation to the Middle Ages and the Renaissance, about museums, about the power of photographs, and about the very nature of aesthetics and of its place in our lives. By contrast Valéry makes a dubious point about Leonardo without making us either look or think again.

Proust was probably the only major French writer of the early twentieth century to have read deeply if not widely in nineteenth-century English literature. He responded to Ruskin because Ruskin's passion for the Middle Ages confirmed his own, and because this gave both of them a standard with which to confront their own times. Eliot found in Laforgue and Donne hints as to how to escape from the stifling atmosphere of late-nineteenth-century poetry. By contrast, Valéry clung to a narrow view of literary history, seeing in himself the culmination of a line that ran from Poe through Mallarmé, and that had as its single weapon a dislike of the excesses of Romanticism. This was not a very good basis on which to launch a career either as a poet or as a cultural critic.

Yet such was the impact of Mallarmé on the young Valéry (Sieburth suggests that the entirety of the early *Cahiers* was an attempt to come to terms with the overwhelming personality of the Master) that it forced Valéry into a lifetime of thought about the possibilities and the nature of art. If we do not take him at his own evaluation but try to understand why he needed to create a certain myth about himself, we will find that here and there, scattered throughout the *Cahiers*, lie some fascinating insights not only into his own work and temperament, but into the peculiar problems of modernism and its remarkable triumphs.

The crisis of 1892, the 'nuit de Gènes' as Valéry called it, was sparked by his sudden understanding, during a sojourn in that city, of the implications of living in a world without God. 'Nuit effroyable [...] Je me sens AUTRE ce matin. Mais se sentir AUTRE

– cela ne peut durer.' ('Dreadful night [...] I feel myself OTHER this morning. But to feel oneself OTHER – that won't last.') Like Mallarmé thirty years before him, like Hofmannsthal's Lord Chandos and Thomas Mann's Adrien Leverkühn, it suddenly dawns on him that he cannot, in all conscience, go on with the charade of 'being an artist' – society does not need him and there can be no such thing as a vocation, since there is no one to call him. The only response appears to be to retreat into silence. 'Je ne suis pas un Poète,' he wrote to Gide, dramatising himself as a latter-day Bartleby, 'mais le Monsieur qui s'ennuie.' ('I am not a poet, but a bored gentleman.')

Boredom, however, takes many forms. Valéry may, at twenty-one, have given up writing poetry, but he had not given up either writing or thinking. Soon, after an intense reading of Leonardo's journals and an immersion in mathematics, physics, and the history of science, he began to develop a notion of what the silent poet – the poet who had been too clear-headed to be enticed by the false myths of his time, including the myth of the uniqueness of the 'creative artist', but who nevertheless believed in the human mind and spirit – could do. Each of us, he suggests, is put on earth with massive potential, but few of us realise even a tenth of that potential. Someone like Leonardo developed nine-tenths or more, refusing to be limited by any one type of activity precisely because he recognised that all natural and human activities have the same source and the same underlying shape:

> Leonardo [...] He is the angel of morphology. Cartilages of the larynx, flowers, rocks, draped cloth, are treated by him with the same gaze – a view always complemented by a determination to understand – to be fanciful and abstract, so much so that his drawings are plans and must have left him feeling he had grasped something, You might say that through drawing he perceived the forces of formation.

Introduction à la méthode de Léonard de Vinci (1894), as the title suggests, brought together Leonardo and Descartes. Armed with Descartes' method of starting from scratch and thinking everything out afresh for himself and Leonardo's morphological vision, Valéry felt he could now do anything. Other, perhaps more surprising models, were Napoleon and Cecil Rhodes. In his self-imposed poetic silence, Valéry meditated on the sources of human power and imagined himself a new Leonardo, a Napoleon of the mind. Other models are the chess player, the fencer, the athlete and the dressage expert, for all of these have learnt how to use their potential to the utmost, not for any practical purpose but for the sheer pleasure of the exercise. That is 'The Way to Uebermensch' as Valéry noted in a curious mixture of English and German, Pietism and Nietzscheanism.

My feelings, thought Valéry, are the least interesting part of me. They are what I share with everyone. Right through his life he constantly tested himself against Gide, the great moralist, the great explorer of the emotions, the great exposer of the self. All this, Valéry felt, was both tedious and banal. The only way to live fully was to be constantly exploring one's limits, not spouting ready-made feelings; to be doing, if one was a man of the intellect, the intellectual equivalent of dancing and dressage. In Monsieur Teste he created an alter ego, and in time was able to slip fragments from his notebooks straight into the Teste cycle: 'Je suis rapide ou rien' ('I am all speed or I am nothing'), asserts M. Teste, and he describes himself as a man 'toujours debout sur le cap Pensée, à écarquiller les yeux sur les limites ou des choses, ou de la vue' ('always upright on Cape Thought, straining my eyes to attain either the limits of things or of sight').

Valéry always prided himself on his inaccessibility. Unlike Gide, his works, he said, required to be read more than once to be understood. That was because he was concerned to train the reader as he had trained himself. It is natural then that those who have made the effort have felt both grateful and protective towards Valéry. In their eyes he can do no wrong. But it remains to be asked whether he was not intoxicated by a peculiarly post-Romantic dream of conquest and totality. For the truth of the matter is that thought and literature are *not* like dancing and dressage. We may admire the intensity of Leonardo's gaze, but it is only intense because it is directed *at* something. To work for that intensity as an end in itself is like trying hard to be humble.

The image of Valéry as the lonely thinker 'toujours debout sur le cap Pensée' (after Caspar David Friedrich), as the master gymnast of thought (after Schiller and Kleist) is a myth he fostered himself – not out of cynicism, but because he desperately wanted to believe it – and it is one which has for over a century been faithfully trotted out by his admirers. There is no evidence in the *Notebooks* of such thinking and writing, only of the fantasy. And perhaps it was the gradual realisation of the falsity of seeing himself as the Napoleon of thought that led to his gradual return, from 1913 on, to the writing of poetry.

But it would be a poetry very different from that of his predecessors and contemporaries (apart, of course, from the glorious exception of Mallarmé). It would be a poetry of retardation, as Bach's Suite in D Major remained for Valéry all his life the supreme example of a music of retardation ('delay laden with emotion'), a music that is all process and no goal (in stark contrast to the symphonies of Beethoven); a poetry that moved constantly between sound and meaning, that abolished the difference between foreground and background, so that the 'meaning' and the 'action' would rest as much in the so-called formal procedures as in the so-called subject; a poetry that would come alive with the first word and die with the last, leaving a powerful aftertaste in the mouth, the memory of a voice in the head. Hence:

La mer, la mer, toujours recommencée!
O recompense après une pensée
Qu'un long regard sur le calme des dieux!

('Le cimetière marin')

Hence:

> Et toi, maison brûlante, Espace, cher Espace
> Tranquille, où l'arbre fume et perd quelques oiseaux.
>
> ('Été')

As Geoffrey Hartman pointed out many years ago in what is still one of the best essays ever written on Valéry the poet, one's first impression in the second example is that the poet is describing a tree, the mist around it, and birds flying away. But further reflection leads to the conclusion that what is really at issue here 'is a yielding of the materiality of matter to the brightness of burning space'. Valéry is only interested in the tree, the mist, the birds, because they set up in him a sense of something general and universal, of how matter yields to space. Valéry, in other words, is interested in man as a being in the world, in the physicality of sight, the nature of loss, the brevity of life. Art for him is a way of seeing man as if from the outside, as a product of contingency, and of seeing the world like that as well. 'L'étonnement, ce n'est pas que les choses soient; c'est quelles soient *telles*, et non telles autres' ('what is surprising is not that things are; it's that they are *such* and not other'), he writes in the 'Note et digression' he appended to his Leonardo essay in 1919. This is profoundly opposed to the pragmatic and positivist English tradition, which takes the world and ourselves for granted and sees the task of art as the simple (or not so simple) exploration of the vagaries of life and the problems of morality. It is this, we could say, that makes it difficult for the English to respond to the manifestations of European modernism, which is too often accused of 'abstraction' and 'deliberate obfuscation', whether it be the poetry of Rilke and Paul Celan, the philosophy of Heidegger and Derrida, or the novels of Alain Robbe-Grillet and Thomas Bernhard. For the English reader and critic, not to be interested in nature for its own sake, not to be interested in the moral dimension of murder and adultery, is not merely a literary but a human failing, a sign of a fatal abstraction, an unwillingness to engage with life as it is. For Valéry or Robbe-Grillet, to be interested in a tree or a bird – or a murder or a jealous husband – for its own sake, is to be concerned merely with the anecdotal and ephemeral. What interests them is what bird-leaving-tree tells us about our condition, it is the nature of murder and of jealousy.

There is no need to take sides. What is important here is to understand that what one can call the modernist vision leaves the artist who espouses it with the perpetual sense not just of failure but of betrayal, for language covers over the *strangeness* of our being in the world. The most successful modernists have been those who have faced the problem squarely and have integrated it into their work, like Proust and Beckett; or who have discovered subjects which would yield what they wanted, like Kafka, Eliot and Wallace Stevens. Valéry, in thrall to the notion of his powerful mind, was strangely helpless before his poetic gift, though by 1913 he had relented enough to accept that he would be a writer of poems as well as a gymnast of the intellect. As a result, we can see with hindsight, he produced a few perfect short poems, which are among the minor masterpieces of twentieth-century poetry – 'La Dormeuse', 'Les Pas' – and some longer poems full of brilliant lines and passages – 'Le Cimetière Marin', 'La Jeune Parque'. Because Valéry never discovered (as Eliot, Kafka and Brecht did) an aesthetic outside the post-Romantic one, which would help him move beyond Poe and Mallarmé, his poetry constantly resorts to the exclamation marks, the *oh*s and *ah*s, so typical of nineteenth-century French poetry, and never escapes from the highly limited vocabulary of the period, for which he tries to compensate by an unfortunate tendency to echo the line of Racine, for example:

> Lumière!... Ou toi, la mort! Mais le plus prompt me prenne!...
> Mon cœur bat! Mon cœur bat! Mon sein brûle et m'entraîne!
> Ah! qu'il s'enfle, se gonfle et se tende, ce dur
> Très doux témoin captif de mes réseaux d'azur...
>
> ('La Jeune Parque')

Reading Valéry one longs for the realism and wit of Donne and Laforgue that Eliot learned to adapt, for the street cries of Paris that Proust used to such good effect, for an element of demotic speech – but it is nowhere to be found.

Yet much that Valéry says about poetry and the novel is of abiding interest, and still as relevant to poetry and the novel today as it was in the early years of the last century. When he asks: 'What is the point of an art whose practice does not transform me?'; when he says: 'I have too much respect for my hours, or quarters of an hour of natural work of the mind to use them in constructing false lives or exploiting what I remember of feelings, women, etc.', he is talking about more than himself. He is scratching an itch that lies behind all the greatest writing of the twentieth century. What worries him about novels is that they do nothing for him, either as a reader or as a (potential) writer:

> I can write down: 'The countess caught the 8 o'clock train.' Or 'The marchioness caught the nine o'clock train.' Yet what I can vary indefinitely in this way, *so malleably* – any fool can do in my stead [...] My concern however – is with the things that cannot be substituted – that are crucial to me.

He worries away at this, returning to it again and again:

> Novels. If I say: the marquise closed the door, or else, Elise was thirty years old – No one will be able to contradict me. It's neither true nor false, since Elise does not exist any more than the marquise or the door. They are postulates. Novelists consequently try to shore up their postulates by the consequences they have. *Real* consequences from gratuitous postulates. – And sometimes to create reality by the accumulation of postulates, i.e., by sheer activity. An addition of arbitrary propositions equals a non-arbitrary effect.

But it is not only the arbitrary nature of plot that disturbs him; it is also the falsity of novelistic description: 'The realist novel always introduces the description of the things surrounding the characters [...] which have never been visible or noticed by the characters themselves [...] A character has never seen the colour of the bed-spread.' 'A long poem by Hugo is a collection of brilliant solutions to infantile problems,' he remarks, and his comments on Stendhal, Flaubert, Zola, and Gide suggest he would say the same about them. In a very Nietzschean vein he notes that 'the real drama takes place here on the writing table; and the fictional drama is just one of the players in it.' At times we could be reading Adorno or Benjamin: 'Literature – discredited – no longer instructive, no longer a counsel, a precept, known by heart, ornamenting the memory for life – but a pastime in the passage of time – and then the writings can no longer endure in the memory – cannot sustain reflection on their subject.'

And yet, when he is thinking of his own work he gives us a sense of the possibilities that still inhere in art, if it is properly undertaken. Here, for example, no doubt meditating on *La Jeune Parque*, he could be talking about Beckett or Pinget:

> How many poems, long poems, very long poems, have begun with a fragment of a line that shaped itself quite by itself not in the mind but in the secret mouth-ear of the author! Then who is the author? The fragment takes over, obsesses like an inescapable need, like the germ of something. It has something better than a meaning: an urge to be continued [...] You have to find what comes after it, or else what gives rise to it, its justification

And one of the many notes about the dawn cannot help but remind one of what lies at the heart – the secret heart – of the works not only of Rilke but of Proust and Marguerite Duras, the sense of a mode of writing which would convey the silence that comes before all writing:

> Black dawn – Lamp – Vigil – I feel like the only existing or thinking being at the centre of a world in which sleeping men play out the role of nothingness. This instant, a triumph of suspense and potential. This emptiness and silence experienced as a positive acquisition – richness – a waiting spell – a good black soil for a stray idea to germinate and come to full flower. – Extent to which I feel I *am* the sole monologue set up against the universal muteness.

The meeting with Mallarmé was not the only reason for Valéry's crisis of 1892. Equally important was a mysterious encounter with a Catalan lady in Montpellier with whom the eighteen-year-old Valéry fell in love, a passion which lasted several years, though he was too shy to approach or write to her. The retreat into literary silence was thus also a retreat into the fortress of the self, where he would make sure that he would henceforth be protected from the pain that the outside world, with all its unpredictability, could cause him. The effort seemed to have succeeded, but, as with Georges Perec's Bartlebooth, who decides at the age of twenty-five to devote himself to a wholly useless and totally passionate inner life, the world has a habit of getting its own back on those who try to deny it. In 1923 Valéry fell in love with Catherine Pozzi, the estranged wife of the boulevard playwright Édouard Bourdet. Their affair was doomed from the start: Catherine's passion for mystical spirituality was not something Valéry found easy to tolerate, and he was appalled by her impulsive desire that he should immediately divorce his wife. But even as late as 1928 he was still thinking of her, and though he fell in love, unhappily, several times more in his life, the 'crisis of 1921', as he referred to it, was a second turning-point. For the first time he realised that, however hard he tried, he could not close himself off from the world and its pain. The most moving extracts from the *Notebooks* concern this period in his life: 'You gave me everything, but have taken back more than everything, for the very thing you gave me bore the promise of infinitely better

things, and I counted them inwardly and thought they were mine,
But taking back your gift you withdrew much more.'

In an essay on Flaubert, Nathalie Sarraute (who herself penned one of the few really critical pieces on Valéry) wrote:

> Il n'est pas possible qu'une oeuvre vivante, toute entière fondée, comme toute oeuvre d'art authentique, sur la sensation pure, plongeant ses racines et tirant sa sève de l'inconscient, se situe toute entière, avec ses significations profondes et ses résonances, dans la conscience claire de son auteur. Cela n'est ni possible ni souhaitable.[2]

> [It is not possible for a living work, entirely based, as all authentic works of art must be, on pure sensation, digging its roots into and drawing its sap from the unconscious, to be situated in its entirety, with all its resonances and profound significations, in the clear consciousness of its author. That is neither possible nor desirable.]

Valéry's admirers do him a disservice to stress his extreme lucidity as a virtue. What the *Notebooks* show is that this man, who spent so much of his life thinking about himself, knew himself but scantly; that, far from being the Napoleon of thought, he was as confused about his talents, his aims and his desires, as most of us are. That is perhaps what saved him.

1 A review of Paul Valéry, *Cahiers / Notebooks*, edited by Brian Stimpson, Paul Gifford and Robert Pickering, two volumes (New York: Peter Lang, 2011).

2 Nathalie Sarraute, 'Flaubert le précurseur', in *Preuves* no. 168, ed. François Bondy (Paris: Congres pour la liberté de la culture, 1965).

Reading Kafka Today[1]

ON 26 MARCH 1911 Kafka noted in his diary: 'Theosophical lectures by Dr Rudolf Steiner, Berlin'. After commenting on Steiner's rhetorical strategy of giving full weight to the views of his opponents, so that 'the listener now considers any refutation to be completely impossible and is more than satisfied with a cursory description of the possibility of a defence,' he goes on:

> Continual looking at the palm of the extended hand. – Omission of the period. In general, the spoken sentence starts off from the speaker with its initial capital letter, curves in its course, as far as it can, out to the audience, and returns with the period to the speaker. But if the period is omitted then the sentence, no longer held in check, falls upon the listener immediately with full force.

Only Kafka could experience language with such intensity and express his response in such a strange and striking way. Two days later he comes back to Steiner in his diary, either to another or to the same lecture, which he proceeds to paraphrase in dead-pan fashion, interspersing this with comments about his neighbour:

> Dr Steiner is very much taken up with his absent disciples. At the lecture the dead press so about him. Hunger for knowledge? But do they really need it? Apparently, though [...] He stood very close to Christ [...] Löwy Simon, soap dealer on Quai Moncey, Paris, got the best business advice from him [...] The wife of the Hofrat therefore has in her notebook, 'How does One Achieve Knowledge of the Higher Worlds? At S. Löwy's in Paris.' [*How Does One Achieve Knowledge of the Higher Worlds?* was the tantalising title of one of Steiner's books.]

Yet Kafka is sufficiently impressed to make an appointment to see Steiner in his hotel. 'In his room I try to show my humility, which I cannot feel, by seeking out a ridiculous place for my hat, I lay it down on a small wooden stand for lacing boots.' Steiner is gracious, however, and tries to put the young man at his ease by asking if he has been interested in theosophy long. Kafka pushes on with his prepared speech: A large part of his being seems to be striving towards theosophy, while at the same time he greatly fears it. 'I have, to be sure, experienced states (not many) which in my opinion correspond very closely to the clairvoyant states described by you, Herr Doktor.' However, in those states he did not write at his best, and since 'my happiness, my abilities, and every possibility of being useful in any way have always been in the literary field', he is terribly torn.

We never hear how Steiner responds to what Kafka has told him. Instead, this:

> He listened very attentively without apparently looking at me at all, entirely devoted to my words. He nodded from time to time, which he seems to consider an aid to strict concentration. At first a quiet head cold disturbed him, his nose ran, he kept working his handkerchief deep into his nose, one finger in each nostril.

And with that Steiner disappears from the diaries.

June Leavitt, who begins her book *The Mystical Life of Franz Kafka*[1] with this episode, describes Kafka here as 'ridiculing' Steiner's claims and 'satirizing' his psychic powers and self-appointed mission of enlightening humanity, describing the last paragraph as facetious. However, she argues, 'Kafka's yearning for transcendental mind continued despite his disappointing meeting with Steiner.' Throughout his life, she maintains, Kafka was torn between his desire to write and his experience of out-of-body states, which he longed for yet dreaded.

This brings out well how even the most learned and well-meaning, if they are not very careful, will start with a slight misreading and end in the further reaches of lunatic assertion. For Kafka's description of Steiner's lecture and of their meeting follows the same pattern as everything else he jots down in the diary: he notes everything he sees and that happens to him with puzzled and scrupulous detachment. *Pace* Leavitt, he is not satirising Steiner or the Frau Hofrat (or himself for the comedy with the hat), but merely noting it all, as though trying to pierce a mystery which is immediately comprehensible to everyone but himself.

Leavitt is surely right to remind us of the enormous popularity of theosophy and related notions in the European fin-de-siècle. Not only Steiner but Mme Blavatsky too seemed, for many thinking people in the West who had lost faith in organised religion, to provide the answer to their spiritual yearnings. Yeats, Maeterlinck, Kandinsky, and Mondrian were all adepts and excited proselytisers at one time or another in their careers, and Eliot introduced a 'famous clairvoyant' into *The Waste Land*. It's not at all surprising that Kafka should have been interested in and knowledgeable about theosophy, and Leavitt is right to suggest that his apparent fascination with Jewish mysticism, which scholars have made much of in recent decades, probably came to him via Christian (and debased) sources.

Eliot's take on 'Mme Sosostris' was, of course, at the opposite pole from Yeats's or Kandinsky's. Where does Kafka stand? He was, we know, a notorious faddist, solemnly subjecting himself to nature therapy, raw food diets and gymnastics, Mazdaznanism, Fletcherism and the rest. But what of his writing, which is surely the important thing? Leavitt trawls his *oeuvre* to find examples of mystical experiences and out-of-body states, but her insensitivity to context and nuance grows more pronounced with every page.

She examines in detail the long, abandoned story, 'Description of a Struggle', written around 1904. The narrator here seems able merely to wish something for it to happen: 'So I happily spread out my arms in order to fully enjoy the moon. And by making swimming movements with my weary arms it was easy for me to advance without pain or difficulty [...] My head lay in the cool air.' This indeed seems to be an example of levitation, and Leavitt quotes from Steiner and Blavatsky in order to explain that we are in the presence of an 'ether-body', which is the true body, not the physical body we carry around with us. Now this may be theosophical doctrine, but one wonders if the main reason why Kafka abandoned the work was not that it was all too easy to do this sort of thing in fiction: if you can make the body fly merely by wishing it, you can do anything – but by the same token you have done nothing. Kafka is looking for a form of art that will be true to all our desires – including the desire to escape the body – but will also be ready to examine these desires. That is why when he does finally agree to let his close friend and confidant, the writer Max Brod, find a publisher for his early work he ignores the long and complex but ultimately unsatisfactory 'Description of a Struggle' and selects instead tiny fragments that seem to him more 'true', such as 'The Wish to be a Red Indian':

> If one were only an Indian, instantly alert, and on a racing horse, leaning against the wind, kept on quivering jerkily over the quivering ground, until one shed one's spurs, for there needed no spurs, threw away the reins, for there needed no reins, and hardly saw that the land before one was smoothly shorn heath when the horse's neck and head would be already gone.

Later Leavitt examines one of Kafka's last stories, 'The Bucket Rider', written when he had finally escaped Prague and gone to Berlin with Dora Diamant, to endure there a terrible winter of freezing conditions and dreadful food scarcity. 'To grasp the inverted perspective of "The Bucket rider",' says Leavitt, 'it is necessary to penetrate the narrative façade, which Kafka critics have not done.' These are the kinds of sentences that set alarm bells ringing: they usually herald a total misreading, and this is indeed what we get here. 'Coal all spent, the bucket empty; the shovel useless; the stove breathing out cold, the room freezing; I must have coal; I cannot freeze to death; behind me is the pitiless stove, before me the pitiless sky.' This is a terrifying evocation of human destitution and desperation. The narrator goes on: 'So I ride off on the bucket. Seated on the bucket, my hands on the handle, the simplest kind of bridle, I propel myself with difficulty down the stairs; but once downstairs, my bucket ascends [...] And at last I float an extraordinary height above the vaulted cellar of the dealer.'

But, alerted by the idea of flying, Leavitt is away: 'Mystical logic allows expansion of perspective beyond the conceptual framework of time and space. I claim that the narrator has already frozen to death; he is a disembodied spirit. The narrative concerns a soul in crisis.' The story ends: 'And with that I ascend into the regions of the ice Mountains and am lost forever.' Leavitt fastens on the expression *Nimmerwiedersehen*, literally 'never to be seen again', and concludes: 'This bucket rider has relinquished his craving for materiality to migrate to a higher world.' With that the pain of the story's realism is dissolved into a cosy mysticism which may bring comfort to some but does a gross disservice to a great and painfully honest writer.

The book grows ever more dotty and ill-written: 'The canine narrator of "Investigations of a Dog" refers to the Word, a cipher for Jesus, in a text rippled [*sic*] with early 20th-century occult expectations about universal enlightenment.' 'Some of the hermeneutical void surrounding his work can be filled if we read his corpus [*sic*] as a series of mystical reports, written by a clairvoyant, or at least by a person who could masterfully represent the clairvoyant state.' The pity is that Leavitt has a good though modest point: that Kafka's interest in theosophy and other forms of fin-de-siècle religiosity aligns him with a great many of the major artists of the period, and that a dismissal of this as due to personal fads, or an exclusive emphasis on Jewish mysticism distorts the picture. But as so often in Kafka studies an initial insight is ruined by insensitivity to the way language works in the texts and to the overall evidence of the diaries, the letters and the rest of the fiction.

This is strikingly evident in David Suchoff's *Kafka's Jewish Languages*.[2] Suchoff has much less than Leavitt to work with: a long diary entry of 24 December 1911, on the literatures of minority languages already mined by Deleuze and Guattari; an address on the nature of Yiddish given in February 1912 to introduce an evening of Yiddish readings by his actor friend Yitzhak Löwy; diary entries on his reading into the history of Hebrew literature; and his late decision to learn Hebrew along with his one letter in Hebrew to his old teacher on her return to Palestine. Suchoff examines these with a manic zeal and reports on his findings in a contorted language that veers from the clumsy to the incomprehensible: 'In Pines [Meyer Pines' *Histoire de la littérature Judéo-Allemande*], Kafka read an interpretation that placed German in the Jewish hot seat in the New York form of this question.' Further on:

> The 'dog-like muzzle' imposed here [in Kafka's description on 14 October 1911 of a performance of a play by the Yiddish Theatre at the Café Savoy], like the one mocked in *The Trial*, is the censorship that would condemn every species of national identity to perform a stereotype of itself. To wear the 'muzzle' is thus not to squelch [*sic*] the animal – whether coded as Jewish, African, or Irish, or any other national type – but to transform the canine voice into a murderous singularity of form.

When he comes to examining actual works, Suchoff is as sure of himself as Leavitt and as misled by his obsession. Commenting on the terrible conclusion to 'The Judgement', the story that came to Kafka in the night of 22–23 September 1912, and which he always felt marked the moment when he found his true voice, he writes:

> 'I sentence you to death by drowning!' [the terrible curse of the father that leads to Georg Bendemann's precipitous suicide]

> names [*sic*] the conclusion of the story as a movement toward life, reflecting Kafka's recovery of the meaning of Yiddish from the dour Jewish fathers of his generation. Georg's final position between bridge and river thus defines Kafka's trajectory toward the fluidity of the multilinguistic imagination that animates his later prose.

My favourite, however, is his disquisition on Leni's webbed hand in *The Trial*. Readers have always felt a frisson of disgust when this detail is revealed, but not Suchoff: 'In linguistic terms,' he informs us, 'German and Jewish speakers are all held in Leni's hand. Joined by the "Verbindungshäutchen" or "connective tissue", invisible to each of its speakers, as Kafka said of the "Verbindungen" between "Jargon" and German, Leni in this way points to the delicate connection between seemingly discrete and opposite realms.'

Suchoff does have interesting things to say about the fact that all languages are 'impure', and especially about the way both Goethe and Jacob Grimm, Germany's greatest classic writer and the first historian of its language, recognised and explored this. And he is interesting too on the debates that took place around the establishment of Hebrew as the language of the Jews of Palestine (Kafka's Hebrew teacher, Puah Ben-Tovim, was the daughter of Zalman Ben-Tovim, a distinguished Hebraist who was also the neighbour in Jerusalem of Eliezer Ben-Yehuda, the father of modern Hebrew). The pity is that he felt he had to tie all this to poor Kafka, who perhaps should by now be allowed to rest in peace, or at least not have to suffer the indignity of having his lucid but mysterious works mangled by all and sundry.

That is not going to happen so long as academics have to prove that they are more than just good teachers. Two books of essays both co-edited by Stanley Corngold, who seems to have established himself as the doyen of American Kafkaists, bear this out. Ruth Gross's Preface to *Kafka for the Twenty-First Century*[3] sets the tone. The idea, she explains, was 'to assemble a number of distinguished Kafka researchers from North America and Europe to examine together the ways in which this extraordinary writer, who so decisively shaped our conception of the twentieth century, might suggest fruitful strategies for coping with the twenty-first.' But who ever imagined that writers should give us 'fruitful strategies for coping', even if we knew what that meant? They have quite enough on their plate trying to say what they feel they have it in them to say. She goes on: 'How do we compose a complete and coherent account of a personality with so many often contradictory aspects?' Again, this sounds good, but what on earth would a 'complete and coherent account' of anything be? Should we even aim for that? Maybe we would do better simply trying to understand why, after all this time, Kafka still affects us as he does?

Some of the essays are just as unenlightening as the preface would suggest, in particular the ones on 'Kafka and Israeli Literature' and on 'Kafka and Italy', which explore the writers in those countries whose work exhibit 'familiar Kafkaesque themes, such as metamorphosis, existential absurdity, bureaucratic nightmares, marginality, power, and identity.' One had hoped Kafka studies had progressed beyond such banalities, but apparently not. Some, though, start off by opening up interesting areas of research, only to follow the Leavitt-Suchoff route of crazy obsessiveness. Thus Roland Reuss asks us to go behind the printed texts to the manuscripts, where we will find that the editors, however sensitive, have all had to make decisions which cut out alternatives left open by the manuscripts. This dilemma is not unique to Kafka editors, *pace* Reuss, but has been interestingly explored in recent decades by those working on the manuscripts of Proust and Joyce – it is of course particularly the case with works, such as the later volumes of *À la recherche* and many of Kafka's stories, where the work was not published in the author's lifetime. Thus the story Brod called 'Prometheus' is found in the Octavo Notebooks, but entirely crossed out. The Fischer editors, who claimed that they would not include anything that had been crossed out, clearly felt that crossing out an entire story did not count and silently included it. But there is a further problem. The concluding paragraph in Brod reads in English: 'Legend attempts to explain the inexplicable; because it arises from a ground of truth, it must end again in the inexplicable.' But the Fischer editor noted an insertion sign in the manuscript at the start of the story, and so placed it there, thus dealing a blow to Hans Blumenberg, who had based his entire interpretation of the story, in his great *Work on Myth*, on its coming at the end. However, notes Reuss, and he gives us photographs of the manuscript to prove his point, there are not one but two insertion signs in the story, at different places – where should the sentence really go?

This is a fascinating reminder that what we deal with in reading this material is something written, and often written in the heat of inspiration. It is less a *text* than a *process*. This is important, but Reuss does his cause no good when he goes on to examine another passage, this time from the manuscript of 'The Hunter Gracchus' which reads: '*ich tot tot tot. Weiss nicht warum ich hier bin*.' (I, dead dead dead. Know not why I am here.') The first five words, he points out (and again shows us the evidence) are on one line, the last five on another. This suggests, he says, that we must take *ich tot tot tot Weiss* as a unit, and read the last word as a noun, white, and not a verb, to know – which gives us the Mallarméan line 'I (the written word, black on the white page) dead dead dead white'. We are back in Leavitt-Suchoff territory.

Elsewhere John Zilcosky has a fascinating essay on Kafka and trains, alerting us to the fact that in the early twentieth century there was as much anxiety about what train travel might do to you as there is today about jet travel: 'After the legal debate heated up in the 1890s about whether train-induced neuroses were physio- or psychogenic, researchers still insisted on the pathogenic importance of material vibrations, the train's shaking seemed to transfer directly to the body. Many doctors cited passengers who even continued to tremble in their sleep.' Other symptoms of travel sickness were failing vision and eye fatigue, caused by the unnatural speed of trains. Gregor Samsa, we learn early on in *The Metamorphosis*, is a commercial traveller. Could it not be that what he feels he has become, an insect, whose vision is getting worse by the day, is the result of the unnatural life he has to lead? Indeed, he himself wonders if perhaps what has happened to him is simply that he has contracted a 'standing ailment of commercial travellers'. At the end of the story, Zilcosky suggests, we move from inhuman trains and what they can do to you to the much more 'human' tram, which takes Samsa's parents and sister out into the country, 'ins Freie'. Though whether that ending is 'positive', as everyone in these books seems to think, or bleak in the extreme, as Blanchot – who is strangely absent from modern academic discourse on Kafka – suggests, persuasively in my opinion, is an open question.

One of the virtues of Zilcosky's essay is that it doesn't imagine that trains will explain everything in Kafka. The same modesty inheres in Ritchie Robertson's essay on the new awareness of and writing about bureaucracy at the turn of the century and how Kafka taps into that, and in Doreen Densky's essay on Kafka and the insurance business. But the best moments in *Kafka for the Twenty-First Century* are those which return us to the detail of Kafka's own writing, often of fragmentary and little-regarded bits and pieces, which immediately reminds us why we read Kafka in the first place. Mark Harman, for example, noting that in much of Kafka's writing there is a tension between his amazing linguistic ability and his doubts about the adequacy of language, quotes the very first piece of writing by Kafka that has come down to us, an entry in a girl's keepsake album:

> How many words there are in this book! They are meant for remembrance! As though words could remember! For words are poor mountaineers and poor miners. They cannot bring down the treasure from the mountains' peaks, or up from the mountains' depths.

Kafka was seventeen when he wrote that, in 1900. It reminds us that from the start he had extraordinary gifts allied to an extraordinary clarity of mind that would not allow him to deploy those gifts unquestioningly.

In another interesting essay Uta Degner takes a close look at a tiny piece, 'Absent-Minded Window-Gazing' ('Zerstreutes Hinausschaun'), which, like the little Indian narrative I quoted earlier, Kafka included in his first volume, *Betrachtung* (1913). She shows how carefully and with what a fine ear Kafka used language:

> The title already has a certain phonetic effect: the two sounds 'shhh' and 's,' in a form of inverted, or mirrored reduplication: 'ZerSHHtreuteS HinauS-SHHaun' [...] A sign that Kafka used this principle of 'harmonic opposition' intentionally is the elision of the 'e' of 'Hinauschauen', which shortens the word to three syllables, establishing the equal balance of syllables and the impression of sound-contiguity between the title words.

This, as she points out, mirrors the story, which tells of a 'you', who goes to the window and looks out as the sun is setting after a grey day and sees it lighting up the face of a little girl 'who strolls along looking about her', but is 'eclipsed' by the shadow of a man overtaking her. 'And then the man has passed and the little girl's face is quite bright,' the piece ends. The man, Degner suggests, 'embodies a linear reader, who passes through the text quickly; the girl follows a more sedate model of reading' – 'absent-minded' in fact, but letting her mind, as we should let ours, hover over the story, noting mirrorings and correspondences, and not rushing to any conclusions.

It is clear that much of the power felt by readers from the start in Kafka's works, as in Eliot's, has as much to do with their authors' incomparable ear as with any theme, such as 'despair' or 'alienation' – though it is an ear always working in the interests of the whole. Both Kafka and Eliot were fastidious in what they published.

Kafka's diaries are full of laments at how 'dead' and 'inert' he finds what he has just written; very occasionally, though, he grants that some of it 'lives'. We need to understand what constitutes the life, for him, of these mysterious works.

The volume of essays by Corngold and Wagner, *Franz Kafka: The Ghosts in the Machine*,[4] is largely dominated by an attempt to come to terms with a recent addition to the Kafka corpus, his *Office Writings*. This is not surprising, since Corngold and Wagner are the editors of that volume too. And it's not quite like Faber publishing Eliot's *Collected Blurbs* (though I wouldn't mind reading that). Kafka, they remind us, was not a simple cog in a large administrative machine, but a lawyer with the Prague Workmen's Accident Insurance Institute dealing with the whole of Bohemia. And as they make clear, workers' accident insurance was something fairly new and the result of a great shift in thinking about individuals and their responsibility for their lives. For in an accident, and especially an accident that occurs in the workplace, we are at the intersection of the individual (who has, say, had his thumb cut off) and the statistical average. Kafka, they plausibly suggest, mines this duality in his literary works. Unfortunately the curse of the Kafka critic soon takes over. Talking of the little parable 'The Building of the Great Wall of China' they write in their introduction: 'Invaders and invaded share the risk of mutual destruction. At the same time the paradox of the breachable wall almost certainly [words which, where Kafka is concerned, should always set alarm bells ringing] alludes to Kafka's affirming a system of comprehensive accident insurance for both on-site and off-site industrial injuries that nonetheless allows for negotiable gaps.' Soon we are mired deep in academic waffle, with Corngold much the worse offender. Let one example suffice. It concerns the ending of 'The Judgement':

> In the case of Bendemann, the condemnation and self-sacrifice of the normal life of the family man in the name of the intensive life of the bachelor brings about the liberation of literature as the

> act of dissolution of the 'unsalvageable ego' into the twofold immortality of the data-flow of the average man and the scriptive traffic of literature.

Benno Wagner can be equally seduced by academic jargon and his own cleverness, but the volume as a whole is redeemed by ten wonderful pages in which he compares two descriptions of street accidents: the opening of Musil's *The Man Without Qualities* and a passage from Kafka's account of his early trip to Paris with Brod.

On 'a beautiful August day in 1913', in the heart of Vienna, a heavy truck has knocked down a pedestrian. Thus begins Musil's enormous, unfinished novel. 'The event unfolds as the collision between technology and life,' suggests Wagner.

> The crowd of onlookers, while agreeing that the truck driver was not at fault, is incapable of taking individual action: all they can do is kill time until the rescue service arrives. This substitution of human instinct by technological process recurs in the conversation between two of the spectators, a gentleman and a lady. While the lady is overcome by a wave of nausea 'which she credited to compassion', the gentleman offers relief in the form of a technical explanation relating the accident to the long braking distance of heavy vehicles. Accidents, he explains, are a necessary evil, citing statistics from America, according to which 190,000 persons were killed and 450,000 wounded annually in traffic accidents.

Ten years before Musil began his novel, Kafka described in his travel diary for September 11, 1911 an accident he had witnessed at a busy crossroads in Paris:

> Automobiles are easier to steer on asphalt surfaces, but also harder to bring to a stop. Especially when/if the gentleman at the wheel, taking advantage of the wide streets, the beautiful day, his light motor-car and his skill as a driver [...] at the same

> time weaves his car in and out at crossings in the manner of pedestrians on the pavements. This is why such a motor-car, on the point of turning off into a side-street and while yet on the large square, runs into a tricycle; it comes gracefully to a halt, however, does little damage to the tricycle, has only stepped on its toe, as it were.

'Musil and Kafka channel the narrative momentum of the accident in different ways,' Wagner notes. 'Musil uses the genre of the novel to generate a – however decentred and fluid – allegory of the psychological dynamics of prewar Central Europe. His account aims at a representational relation between fiction and reality. Kafka's diary takes us outside this distinction. His account moves in the epistemic space of the probable event, a type of event that, by a continuous scale of probabilities, erodes the distinction between fiction and reality.' There follows a fine analysis of the passage, in which Wagner shows how Kafka moves from the general ('automobiles') to the more specific ('harder to bring to a stop', 'on asphalt'), as *this particular event* is narrated, though it's difficult to say when precisely we move from one to the other, the transition perhaps resting on the ambiguity of the German *wenn*, which could be either temporal (when, whenever) or conditional (if). By the third sentence we are with the specific accident, though even that is hedged in by the generalising 'This is why such an automobile [...] runs into a tricycle.' 'We are now,' says Wagner, 'close to the centre of Kafka's writing, which arises from the permanent oscillation between the real space of the factual event and the virtual space of the probable event.' And he proceeds to explore this by following Kafka's account of what then happens: first the mute replaying of the incident as 'the automobile owner with raised palms simulates the approaching automobile [...]'; then the gathering of a crowd of spectators, all of whom have views about what has just taken place; and finally the arrival of the policeman, who proceeds to write down in his notebook what has happened. Unfortunately,

Kafka goes on, 'something has gone wrong with the policeman's notes, and, for a while, in his effort to get it right, he sees nothing further. He had, that is, begun to write on the sheet of paper at a point where for some reason or other he should not have begun [...] He has to keep turning the paper around over and over again to persuade himself of his having incorrectly begun the statements.' The hope of the spectators that the authoritative figure of the policeman would finally bring order and clarity is quickly seen to be vain. The passage ends with the policeman still scrutinising what he has written and trying to bring some order into *that*.

This is not one of the great stories but an early passage in a travel diary, and yet so many of the elements we associate with Kafka are already in place. By treating it with the attentiveness it deserves Wagner makes us recognise how all Kafka's writing is of a piece, from first to last. I feel Wagner could have developed his analysis even further by showing how the desire of the reader (if not of the spectators who soon become participants in the event) for clarity – for a transcendental authority or its representative to tell us exactly what is what – looks, with the arrival of the policeman, as if it is about to be fulfilled, but then the vertical is, as it were, subsumed once more into the horizontal, as the pronouncement of judgement is turned into the endlessness of (merely human) writing. But he has done what we require of all good criticism: not provided answers but set us on our way to appreciation.

Shachar Pinsker's *Literary Passports*[5] hardly mentions Kafka – Kafka wrote in German, not Hebrew or Yiddish, the field Pinsker has chosen to write about – yet he succeeds in throwing genuine new light on him. Pinsker is concerned to rescue writers of Hebrew and Yiddish poetry and fiction in the early years of the twentieth century, who were in large part Russian, from the Israeli narrative in which they have usually been placed. Rather than being forerunners of a vibrant Israeli literature, he argues, we must see them as being rooted in European modernism, sharing many of the same interests and obsessions as their non-Jewish contemporaries all over

Europe. And, of course, of their Jewish contemporaries such as Kafka, who happened to write in German.

Pinsker divides his book into three large sections, of which the first – in which, with the aid of old photographs, he explores the cities and cafés where these writers congregated, from Odessa to Whitechapel in London – is the most original. By focusing on café culture in the old Europe he makes us understand how European modernism grew out of a combined sense of rootlessness and comradeship. We had known this with Picasso and his circle in prewar Paris, and with the Viennese intellectuals, but by casting his net so wide Pinsker makes us grasp how the cafés were in a sense the soil out of which so much that was radical flourished and grew. His second and third sections, on sexuality and the problematics of tradition, are a little more predictable, but still profoundly illuminating. And illuminating for Kafka as well, who, no less than Brenner, Agnon, and David Fogel, spent much of his early years in literary cafés, was wracked with contradictory and confusing sexual urges, and struggled all his life to define his personal relation to tradition. But, paradoxically, this is so illuminating for those interested in Kafka because it brings out starkly his uniqueness, the way in which, tackling common themes and issues, he spoke in a voice that was, always, utterly, his own. Thus Pinsker quotes a fascinating passage from an early novella, *Mi-saviv le-nekuda* ('Around the Point'), written by Brenner while he was living in Whitechapel in 1904 and never translated. Here the hero, Ya'acov Abramson, undergoes a crisis on a bridge as he is about to commit suicide. It's a powerful passage and Pinsker performs a little miracle of exegesis in bringing out its biblical and cabalistic echoes – but it is still fairly conventional in the way it explores the inner life of the protagonist. We are in a world made familiar by another solitary figure on a bridge, the protagonist of Munch's *The Scream*. The end of Kafka's 'The Judgement' also figures a bridge and the hero's suicide, but its brevity, speed, quietness and disconcerting oddness (Bendemann's prowess as a diver is evoked as he plunges into the waters below), as well as its extraordinary last sentence, puts it in a class apart.

'Impatience led to our expulsion from paradise', wrote Kafka in one of his aphorisms, 'and impatience stops us returning.' The sin of the Kafka critic is impatience, the need to locate the mystery and then solve it, as it were, the need to move, like the man in that early story, across the text from beginning to end, not stay with it, savour it, allow it slowly to come into focus. To do this we have first of all to recognise that the best way in to Kafka is not via an idea – Kafka and mysticism, Judaism, the insurance business or the condition of modernity – but via his unique way of approaching his material. If we return to the episode with which we began, Kafka's visit to Steiner, our awareness of his tone, which is neither 'ironic', as Leavitt suggests, nor purely descriptive, will be enhanced by our sense of other passages in his writings where a figure of authority comes under intense scrutiny in an effort to understand where the wellspring of his power lies. The Letter to his Father is the classic example, but it is to be found everywhere in Kafka. In 1916, during a stay in Badenheim, for example, he describes to Brod in great detail the surprise visit of the holy rabbi of Belz with his solemn entourage:

> He inspects everything, but especially the buildings; the most obscure trivialities interest him. He asks questions, points out all sorts of things. His whole demeanour is marked by admiration and curiosity. All in all, what comes from him are the inconsequential comments and questions of itinerant royalty, perhaps somewhat more childish and more joyous. At any rate they reduce all thinking on the part of his escort to the same level. Langer tries to find or thinks he finds deeper meaning in all this: I think that the deeper meaning is that there is none, and in my opinion this is quite enough. It is absolutely a case of divine right, without the absurdity that an inadequate basis would give to it.

There is nothing in the outward appearance or in the actions of the holy rabbi of Belz which would indicate holiness. On the contrary. Yet that is precisely what is so terrifying and authoritative about him. His very childishness is proof of the gap that lies between him and us. He is imbued with a totally mysterious power and authority, whose source we can never hope to understand. All we can say for certain is that we don't have it.

1 A review of the following five books:

June O. Leavitt, *The Mystical Life of Franz Kafka: Theosophy, Cabala, and the Modern Spiritual Revival* (Oxford: Oxford University Press, 2011).

David Suchoff: *Kafka's Jewish Languages: The Hidden Openness of Tradition* (Philadelphia: University of Pennsylvania Press, 2012).

Kafka for the Twenty-First Century, edited by Stanley Corngold and Ruth V. Gross (Rochester, New York: Camden House, 2011).

Stanley Corngold and Benno Wagner, *Franz Kafka: The Ghosts in the Machine* (Evanston, Illinois: Northwestern University Press, 2011).

Shachar M. Pinsker, *Literary Passports: The Making of Modernist Hebrew Fiction in Europe* (Stanford, California: Stanford University Press, 2010).

The Stories of the Germans[1]

Why do we need another edition of Grimms' *Tales* when there are already several complete editions in English and any number of picture book selections for children, with new ones appearing every Christmas? Instead of answering this question directly let us take another example of a 'world classic', the Bible. Though there are countless editions of the Bible around, and a large number of commentaries, OUP's World's Classics edition, published in 1996 filled a yawning gap. Edited by an Old Testament scholar with a real feeling for literature, Robert Carroll, and a literary critic with a strong interest in the Bible and its afterlife in literature, Stephen Prickett, this contained a very long and extremely interesting introduction and copious notes. It did not try to summarise the many biblical commentaries, which tend to be theological and historical, but rather to raise questions about the Bible as a book and a great literary document, which of course it is, as well as being a religious and cultural one. In a similar way Joyce Crick, a fine scholar of German literature who has always been adept at addressing a larger audience than simply her fellow *Germanisten,* has set out here to rescue Grimms' *Tales* both from children and from folklorists, and to help us see it as a major literary work. Like Carroll and Prickett, she has done a magnificent job, and both she and OUP are to be congratulated.

Carroll and Prickett had no problem selecting their master text: it had to be the 1611 King James Bible, which has been a 'world classic' from the moment it was published. Where the Grimms are concerned the choice is a little more difficult. To understand why, one needs to understand the publishing history of the *Tales*.

The brothers Jacob and Wilhelm Grimm were born within a year of each other (in 1785 and 1786) and, as law students in Marburg, were drawn to the study of the past of the Germanic people, as were many idealistic youths in the troubled period of the early nineteenth century, when Napoleon's armies were conquering Europe, arousing nationalist opposition in the areas they occupied while also spreading the creed of liberty in states still in the grip of petty princelings and feudal rule. Roped in by the young Romantic writers Ludwig Achim von Arnim and Clemens Brentano, who were compiling their anthology of German folk-songs, *Des Knaben Wunderhorn*, to compile a parallel anthology of the earliest German prose narratives, by 1810 the two brothers had prepared a manuscript consisting of thirty tales and dispatched it to Brentano. In 1812, volume one of their *Kinder- und Hausmärchen* (Children's and Household Tales) appeared, followed by a second volume in 1815. This was so successful that they thoroughly revised and enlarged it for a second edition in 1819. A 'little edition' appeared in 1825, consisting of most of what have become the best-known tales, and this was quickly translated into other European languages, and followed by further revised and enlarged editions in 1837, 1840, 1843, 1850 and 1857. These versions were mainly the work of Wilhelm, the more literary of the two, while Jacob pursued his philological and mythographical interests, becoming a leading figure in the founding of *Germanistik* as a formal field of study. They died within four years of each other, Wilhelm in 1859, Jacob in 1863.

The question is, what edition does one choose as one's master text? As Heinz Rölleke, the leading scholar in the field (constantly acknowledged by Joyce Crick in her introduction and notes), has pointed out, no two editions are identical, for even when no major changes were made between editions Wilhelm was constantly rewriting and 'improving'. Rölleke has chosen the 1837 edition as the master text for his edition of the *Tales* for the German equivalent of the Pléiade, the Deutsche Klassiker Verlag. Most complete English editions choose to work from the last edition, of 1857, and this is what Joyce Crick has done. That makes sense, for it yields not only the last word of the Grimms on the subject, but provides us with a translation of a mid-nineteenth-century children's classic. I cannot help feeling, however, that an opportunity has been missed and that a selection from the first edition, of 1812/15 would have given us not just a classic of German tales for children but one of the great books of world literature.

To understand why this should be so we need to look in a little more detail at the differences between the 1810 manuscript and subsequent editions. Crick is well aware of these differences, discussing the issue in her introduction, pinpointing details in her notes to the tales, and printing selections from earlier versions in Appendix A, while in Appendix B she prints a selection of tales that were in the first edition but were subsequently removed. Yet I don't feel she has fully grasped what is at issue here.

Though the brothers had been set to work by von Arnim and Brentano, they quickly realised that they were unhappy with the attitude of the two Romantic writers to their sources, which, they felt, was cavalier in the extreme. For their part, instead of using the ancient German poems and stories as launching pads for their own Romantic effusions, they wanted to present to the world what the ancient Germans had said in as unadulterated a form as possible. This is how they put it in the opening of their introduction to the first edition of 1812, repeated in 1819:

> It is good, we find, when an entire harvest has been beaten down by storm or some other heaven-sent disaster, that beneath lowly hedges and wayside bushes some small corner has still managed to preserve a shelter, and single heads of corn have remained standing. Then, if the sun shines kindly again, they go on growing solitary and unnoticed: the sickle does not cut them down early for storage in great barns, but in late summer, when they have ripened and grown full, the hands of the poor come in search of them, and, laid head to head, carefully bound and more highly prized than are entire sheaves elsewhere, they are borne home, providing nourishment all through the winter and also, it may

> be, the only seed corn for the future. That is how it seemed to us when we saw how, of so much that once flourished in times past, nothing has survived – even the memory of it has been almost entirely lost – except, among the common folk, their songs, a few books, legends, and these innocent household tales... We were perhaps only just in time to record these tales, for those who should be their keepers are becoming ever fewer.

However, as nineteenth-century collectors from Scott in Scotland to Lonnröt in Finland quickly discovered, this is easier said than done. Even today, with the help of aural and even visual recordings, it is not so easy to decide what is part of the authentic tradition, what is embellishment by the modern singer or narrator, and exactly how to transcribe what one is hearing. The Grimms, we must remember, were working long before folklore studies were established, though by the time of the last edition, and thanks in large part to them, the situation was very different.

Here, then, to demonstrate the problem, is the opening of the very first story in the collection, 'The Frog King, or Iron Henry'. In the 1810 manuscript it is called 'The King's Daughter and the Enchanted Prince'. As Crick points out, the drafts in the manuscript were 'written down with little attention to style, often with abbreviated forms, insertions, and minimal punctuation', which she has normalised:

> The king's youngest daughter went out into the forest and sat down by a cool well. Then she took a golden ball and was playing with it when it suddenly rolled down into the well. She watched it falling into the depths and stood at the well and was very sad. All at once a frog reached his head out of the water and said: 'Why are you wailing so much?' 'Oh! You nasty frog,' she answered, 'my golden ball has fallen into the well.' Then the frog said: 'If you will take me home with you and I can sit next to you, I'll fetch your golden ball for you.' And when she had promised

> this, he dived down and soon came back up with the ball in his mouth, and threw it onto land.

And here is the 1812 version; because it is longer I will only give the very opening:

> There was once a king's daughter who went out into the forest and sat down by a cool well. She had a golden ball which was her favourite toy; she would throw it up high and catch it again in the air, and enjoyed herself as she did [this to my ear, does not quite capture the self-absorbed quality of 'und hatte ihre Lust daran.']. One day the ball had risen very high; she had already stretched out her hand and curled her fingers ready to catch it when it bounced past onto the ground quite close to her and rolled straight into the water [*rollte und rollte und geradezu in das Wasser hinein*].

Finally, the 1857 version:

> In the old days, when wishing still helped, there lived a king whose daughters were all beautiful, but the youngest was so beautiful that the sun itself, which after all has seen so many things, marvelled whenever it shone upon her face. Not far from the king's palace there lay a big, dark forest, and in the forest, beneath an ancient linden tree, there was a well. Now if it was a very hot day the king's daughter would go out into the forest and sit at the edge of the cold well; and if she was bored she would take a golden ball, throw it up high and catch it again; and that was her favourite toy.

The first version clearly is very raw. It plunges straight in, a little too breathlessly perhaps. The second version provides the classic fairy-tale opening, 'There was once'. And, since in this story, unlike the majority, the fact of being the youngest child is irrelevant – the tension develops between the girl and her father (who holds that once she has given her promise to the frog she can't take it back) and not between siblings – it removes that bit of information, needlessly provided by the first version. But after that it's difficult to decide if its greater expansiveness weakens or strengthens it. What is important is that the girl is playing with a ball which falls into the pond and is only given back to her by the frog in exchange for a promise to let him sit next to her. Perhaps we need to be told that it was 'her favourite toy' but not that 'she enjoyed herself' as she threw it up into the air – for isn't that conveyed by the statement that when it fell into the water 'she was very sad'? Why add that 'she had already stretched out her hand and curled her fingers ready to catch it' when it evaded her and fell into the water? It's not necessary, though perhaps it helps fill out our sense of her in that decisive moment. In other words, do we want the story as taken down verbatim (but is it?) from one speaker, or the story developed a little in the quiet of the study in order to make it more readable and interesting?

The 1857 version carries this trend further. Now we can definitely hear the voice of the kindly and wise old narrator, telling us that 'In the old days, when wishing still helped…'; that 'the youngest was so beautiful that the sun itself, which after all has seen so many things [!], marvelled whenever it shone upon her face'; that the forest was big and dark, that the pond lay 'beneath an ancient linden tree'; that the day was very hot; that 'if she was bored' she played with her ball.

These changes are not radical; it could be argued that they merely fill out the story, make it easier for us to visualise. Yet cumulatively they do affect our response. What they bring out is that, despite the Grimms' Romantic claim (echoed of course by nearly all the great early collectors of folktales and songs) that they were preserving the precious seed of the Folk that was in grave danger of disappearing, we can never get at *a* version that is absolutely 'authentic', that every version will bear the imprint of the last speaker or compiler, no matter how 'neutral' and scientific' he may try to be. As Italo Calvino points out in the introduction to his collection of 'fiabe italiane', the task of the compiler is to be as sensitive to the essential nature of his material as possible and to try and 'render' it as well as possible, using all the resources at his command. My own feeling is that the Grimms achieved this in their first, 1812/15 edition, but moved further and further away from it in the subsequent editions.

Crucially, in the wake of the success of the first edition and of the many letters it elicited, they began to think of their work not as a collection of the earliest Germanic narratives but as a book designed specifically for children. Thus propriety, or what was acceptable to children, became a key issue. Some tales, such as the magnificent brief 'Wie Kinder Schlachtens miteinander gespielt haben' (printed by Crick in an appendix under the title 'Playing Butchers'), two versions of which were offered in 1812, were omitted from the second edition after parents had complained that they were too violent for their children (English readers have long been surprised though at the violence and sadism that was left in or even increased in subsequent editions, but it seems that so long as punishment was deserved the Grimms did not mind including it). Then there are changes made for propriety's sake. In the 1812 version of 'Rapunzel', for example, the girl, shut up in the inaccessible tower by the sorceress, but letting her long hair down to allow the prince to climb up to her when she is alone, gives the game away by saying to the sorceress: 'Tell me, Godmother, why my clothes are getting so tight on me, they don't fit me any longer?' This becomes, in the later versions: 'Tell me, Dame Godmother, how is it that you are much heavier to draw up than the young king's son, who only takes a moment to reach me?' In 'Snow White' the 1812 version gives us a wicked and jealous *mother*, but she is changed by 1819 into the clearly more acceptable wicked *stepmother*. In that mysterious tale, 'Allerlei-Rauh' ('Coat-o'-Skins') a father falls in love with his daughter after the death of his wife, and becomes obsessed by the desire to marry her. She escapes and wanders, disguised, in a forest where she is found by 'the King, her betrothed' in the 1812 edition, and by 'the king to whom that forest belonged' in the 1819 edition, in an effort to distinguish her rescuer from her pursuer.

But it was not just a question of propriety. As they thought of their collection more and more as tales for children rather than as ancient Germanic household tales, the Grimms inevitably altered them in the light of a particular and culture-bound notion of 'the child' – one which developed, especially in Germany and England, in the course of the nineteenth century, and which we, today, rightly find deeply suspect. But the changes were also dictated by more mysterious needs, of which the Grimms were certainly not conscious. Joyce Crick, in one of her excellent notes (to 'The Goose-Girl') remarks that the tales 'are invitations to interpretation, but never yield a single meaning'. This is true even of the most elaborated tales in the 1857 edition, which, as she points out, have lost much of their oral origin and become quite literary. Why then did the Grimms, who began by contrasting their method with the cavalier attitude to their sources of Romantic writers like von Arnim and Brentano, end up elaborating their own tales almost as much as their more literary contemporaries? Why, thinking that they were merely 'making sense' of what had come down to them in crude and fragmentary form, did they in fact alter them almost beyond recognition?

What we are witnessing in the transformation of a stark and 'unexplained' tale into something that makes moral, psychological, and narrative sense is very similar to what we find at other moments in other cultures. Eric Havelock tried to explain it in ancient Greece in his *Preface to Plato*. We see it in Jewish tradition in the transformation of biblical narratives into midrash. God calls Abraham – why? The Bible does not say. But Jewish tradition finds it hard to live with the apparently arbitrary ('How odd of God to choose the Jews'), and so elaborates a series of stories about the childhood of Abraham, about his belief in the one God, his hatred of idol-worship, and his persecution for that reason by the builder of the Tower of Babel, King Nimrod. *That*, then, is why God called Abraham and told him to leave his house and home and go where he, God, would tell him. We are at the point of transition, in all these cases, between two different attitudes to the world and to storytelling. Walter Benjamin struggles to express this in his essay on 'The Storyteller', contrasting the storyteller with the novelist:

> The storyteller takes what he tells from experience – his own or that reported by others. And he in turn makes it the experience of those who are listening to his tale. The novelist has isolated himself. The birthplace of the novel is the solitary individual, who is no longer able to express himself by giving examples of his most important concerns, is himself uncounseled, and cannot counsel others.

The novelist deals with information, the storyteller with wisdom. This wisdom is artisanal, it belongs to shared work, in the fields, in the house. Moreover, 'storytelling, in its sensory aspect, is by no means a job for the voice alone. Rather, in genuine storytelling the hand plays a part which supports what is expressed in a hundred ways with its gestures trained by work.'

Benjamin is not simply looking at the differences between stories and novels, he grasps that to make sense of both sets of phenomena you need to have some understanding of what it is that *drives* storytelling on the one hand and novel-writing on the other. More light is shed on this in a remarkable entry by Kierkegaard in his journal for 1837 (he was twenty-three). It is worth quoting in full:

> There are two recommended ways of telling children stories, but there are also a multitude of false paths in between.
>
> The first is the way unconsciously adopted by the nanny, and whoever can be included in that category. Here a whole fantasy world dawns for the child and the nannies are themselves deeply convinced that the stories are true, [...] which, however fantas-

> tic the content, can't help bestowing a beneficial calm on the child. Only when the child gets a hint of the fact that the person doesn't believe her own stories are there ill-effects – not from the content but because of the narrator's insincerity – from the lack of confidence and suspicion that gradually envelops the child.
>
> The second way is possible only for someone who with full transparency reproduces the life of childhood, knows what it demands, what is good for it, and from his higher standpoint offers the children a spiritual sustenance that is good for them – who knows how to be a child, whereas the nannies themselves basically *are* children [...]

This is an extraordinary passage. It suggests that what happened to the Grimms' *Tales* in the course of their fifty years of tinkering with them was that they were transformed from tales told by speakers who, in one way or another, were deeply convinced that they were true (whatever meaning one assigns to the term *true*) into tales told by writers (Wilhelm Grimm, in effect) who did not believe in them and therefore substituted scene-setting, morality and psychology for truth. It also gives us a hint as to why a novelist like Dickens had the effect he had on his readers (and still does): he was one who knew 'how to be a child'. However, it was perhaps Kleist alone among nineteenth-century writers who understood what was really at issue here. His great novella, *Michael Kohlhaas* takes many of the elements that go to make up the Grimm tales and stands them on their head, bidding an anguished goodbye as it does so both to community values and to wishful thinking. But Kleist had no successors and, by and large, nineteenth-century novelists and storytellers took the path of midrash and romance – still the staple diet of readers of twentieth-century fiction – with neither writer nor reader quite believing in what they are doing, but under a strange compulsion to pretend that they do.

The strange thing about the changes the brothers made to the *Tales* in the course of the different editions is that at some level they seem to have understood the nature of the material they were dealing with better than anyone else. As Joyce Crick is at pains to point out, even though they kept adding new tales (and occasionally removing old ones) they had a very clear sense of the overall shape they wanted their collection to have. All the editions begin with that mysterious and powerful tale, 'The Frog Prince', and all end with the tiny tale, 'The Golden Key', whose theme is identical to 'The Fox and the Geese', with which the first, 1812 volume ended: A poor lad goes out into the snow to find wood and comes across a golden key. 'Now he thought that where there was a key there must be a lock to match, so he dug in the earth and found a little iron casket.' He eventually manages to fit the key in the lock. 'Then he turned it once – and now we must wait until he has unlocked it completely and lifted the lid, and then we shall find out what marvellous things were in the casket.' Here, surely, is a parable about parables, as Kafka would put it later, an injunction to be patient, to read and savour and not rush to interpret. For, as Kafka said elsewhere, 'perhaps there is only one cardinal sin: impatience. Because of impatience they were expelled, because of impatience they do not return.'

Joyce Crick has given us the best guidance possible to the world of the storyteller as exemplified by the Grimm *Tales*. For one thing, she provides a generous selection of other writings by the Grimms – prefaces, circulars and the like – to help us understand what it was they were trying to do. Secondly, as I have said, she is alert to the overall shape of the collection, recognising that the brothers put it together with the care of a Yeats or a Wallace Stevens in bringing a new volume of poems before the public. Thirdly, instead of focussing exclusively on the tales of magic and transformation, as do most recent commentators, she gives us a large enough selection of tales to make us grasp the sheer variety of the collection, which is a crucial part of its meaning and significance.

There are at least four distinct genres represented, with many hybrid tales, and the Grimms alert us to this with the first four tales of their collection. The first is the 'fairy-tale' of the frog prince who in the end returns to his rightful shape as a beautiful young man; the second, 'Cat and Mouse as Partners', is an animal fable, though 'fable' is the wrong term for what are often imaginative if anthropomorphic representations of the animal world; the third, 'Our Lady's Child', is a religious piece – the *Tales* are deeply imbued with the pietistic spirit so prevalent in German popular culture of the time, a spirit which is at times deeply repugnant to us in its mixture of morality, cruelty and smugness, but which is indubitably there; the fourth, 'The Boy Who Set Out to Learn Fear' introduces us to a key figure in these German tales: the *Dümmling* or simpleton: 'There was once a father who had two sons. The elder was clever and sensible and knew the right thing to do in all circumstances, but the younger boy was stupid and couldn't understand anything or learn anything.' Here we can see laid out for us the different directions taken by the tale and the novel. For the hero of the novel is by and large the astute and cunning youth, who knows the ways of the world and uses them to his own advantage, and yet who is ready to learn in the course of the narrative. By contrast the hero of the *Märchen* is the simpleton, who doesn't understand the world and learns nothing, but who triumphs because in his innocence he is at one with nature and with the animal kingdom (he literally speaks the language of beasts and birds and is always kind to them, for which they usually reward him). The title of the story doesn't accurately reflect its contents, for the boy doesn't want to learn *fear* but rather 'what it means to make the flesh creep'. The ending is as wonderfully (and sexually) ambiguous as anything in the *Tales*, for when his new bride's resourceful chambermaid pours a bucketful of little fishes over him as he is asleep he wakes up and cries: 'Oh, my flesh is creeping! My flesh is creeping, wife dear! Yes, now I do know what flesh-creeping is.'

For too long these haunting tales have been yanked out of context and subjected to mythological and psychological exegesis. Joyce Crick has done us an enormous service by returning them to their context in the Germanic lands of early modern Europe (Bruegel and Rabelais, it has always seemed to me, are a better key to interpretation than Freud, Marx or Mircea Eliade). Though she does not include some of my favourite stories (the wonderfully Surrealist 'Herr Korbes', and 'Läuschen und Flöhchen' for example); though she can do nothing about conveying the huge linguistic range of the collection; and though I feel she has missed an opportunity by not using the first edition as her base text, this is nevertheless a volume to treasure and one that should renew interest in a masterpiece of world literature.

1 A review of Jacob and Wilhelm Grimm, *Selected Tales* (Oxford World's Classics), translated with an introduction and notes by Joyce Crick (Oxford: Oxford University Press, 2005).

The Legends of the Jews [1]

In the Garden of Eden there are many strange creatures, none stranger than the Man of the Mountain. His form is that of a human being, but he is fastened to the ground by means of an umbilical cord, upon which his life depends. If the cord snaps, he dies. No creature may venture to approach within the radius of his cord, for he seizes and destroys whatever comes within his reach. To kill him, one must not go near him, but instead sever the umbilical cord from a distance by means of a dart. When Abraham was born, his mother abandoned him in a cave, and he began to wail. God heard him and sent Gabriel down to give him milk to drink, and the angel made it flow from the little finger of the baby's right hand, and he sucked at it until he was ten days old, when he got up and walked out of the cave. When King David was exploring the foundations of the temple in Jerusalem, he came upon a plug. He tried to pull it up, but the plug said: 'You cannot do it.' 'Why not?' said David. 'Because I rest upon the abyss,' replied the plug. Nevertheless David lifted it, and the waters of the abyss rose and threatened to flood the earth. Fortunately, Ahitophel was standing close by, and he had the Name of God transcribed upon the plug and had it thrown into the abyss. At once the waters began to subside.

You can't remember reading about these things in the Bible? That's not surprising, for they are not to be found in any Bible, only in stories that grew up in time around the Holy Book. At the turn of the last century, a remarkable scholar from Lithuania, originally a student of mathematics, but also a published poet in German – a language he had only learned five years previously, after wandering through Russia, Germany and France before ending up in America – decided to gather these tales and legends into one volume for the delectation of his fellow Jews and to further the scholarly understanding of his people. The project was not completed until almost forty years later, in 1937, and by that time it had swelled from one volume to seven.

Louis Ginzberg's plan was to produce a two-tiered book. He would retell these stories, culled from a huge variety of sources, Jewish and Christian, in large part accessible only to scholars on the shelves of university libraries; he would organise his material so as to make it run parallel to the Bible, from the Creation to Ezra and the return of the exiles from captivity; and in a series of learned footnotes, many of them miniature essays, he would give his sources, discuss philological and other issues, and refer to the work of other scholars.

The finished work, which quickly became a classic, thus consisted of four volumes of retellings, two volumes of notes, and a volume of indexes. It has been out of print for sixty years, and now Johns Hopkins University Press has reissued the entire set in paperback with a lucid preface by James L. Kugel, one of the foremost scholars of the Bible and its later traditions.

As Kugel points out in his foreword, the very title, *The Legends of the Jews*, as well as the work's conception, place Ginzberg's enterprise firmly in its time. For this was the heyday of collections of legends – of the Greeks, the Romans, the Celts, the Germans, the Russians, the Chinese: a tradition which had its roots in Romanticism and whose first great exemplar was the collection of German folktales by the Brothers Grimm. By 1900 it was taken for granted that every self-respecting people had to have three things: a national homeland, a national language, and a national literature. The Jews were, of course, lobbying hard to establish their own homeland; modern Hebrew was already being spoken in Palestine after two millennia of silence broken only by the chanting of the liturgy. Surely it was time to show the world that they too had a national literature? The title, though, conceals the fact that these Jewish legends differ from those of other peoples in that they are all directly related to one source, the Bible. Nevertheless, there is some justification for Ginzberg's choice of title, for if Jews could not conceive of story-telling divorced from meditation on the Bible, that did not stop these stories from acquiring their own identity, one very different from that of the Bible.

The nature of this doubleness – of the Bible and yet not of it – has been the subject of much scholarly study in recent years. Michael Fishbane, in his magisterial *Biblical Interpretation in Ancient Israel* (1985) and in numerous essays, has sought to show that interpretation of the Bible is part of the fabric of the Bible from its earliest strands, and that later retellers managed the delicate feat of both interpreting the Bible and developing their own very different world-views. In an essay called 'Five Stages of Jewish Myth and Mythmaking', he argues that there was another tradition than the demythologising one of Maimonides, one which 'begins with the myths of Scripture and develops new ones of much daring and drama throughout antiquity and the Middle Ages. There are no breaks here, only layers of hermeneutical transformation.' Howard Schwarz, who has done more than anyone since Ginzberg to make available to the general public the wealth of Jewish folk and fairy tales, echoes this in his book *Reimagining the Bible: The Storytelling of the Rabbis*. 'The aggadic tradition', he writes,

> is a continuing process of the reintegration of the past into the present. Each time this takes place, the tradition is transformed and must be reimagined. And it is this very process that keeps the tradition vital and perpetuates it. For despite the inevitability of this metamorphosis, the essential aspect of the tradition remains eternal and unchanging.

Fishbane and Schwarz are all too conscious of the fact that these stories did not develop spontaneously 'in the folk memory', but were the result of two unrelated but essential features of the Bible: its sacred status and its laconic style. Because it is sacred, everything in it must not only be true but significant; because it is so laconic there is an urgent need to fill in the details. What, for example, happens to Cain after he is cursed by God and sent out into the wilderness? The Bible says he founded cities, but where and how it does not say, and it does not tell us how he died. The rabbis turned to the enigmatic passage about Lamech, his two wives, and his confession to having murdered a man (Genesis 4: 23–4). When Lamech says: 'I have slain a man for wounding me', he is referring, they suggest, to Cain, who wounded him by being the ancestor responsible for the curse that hangs over his descendants. When Lamech was very old, his eyes grew dim, and he was led about by his son, Tubal-Cain. They were walking in a field when the young man saw what he thought was a wild beast, which he shot and killed. In fact, it was Cain, whose horn and way of life had almost transformed him into a beast. The story thus explains the enigmatic lines about Lamech, and suggests that the killer is slain for his crime.

Kugel, in his foreword, gives another example of this process at work. The Book of Genesis tells us that when Joseph was sold as a slave by his brothers and taken down to Egypt, his master's wife attempted to seduce him. The Bible simply says: 'Joseph was fair of form and appearance. And it came to pass after these things, that his master's wife cast her eyes upon Joseph and said, "Lie with me".' (Genesis 39: 6–7). Why does the Bible say 'after these things'? Joseph's good looks are not a 'thing', so 'things' must refer to what Joseph did to make himself handsome: he washed, combed his hair, smartened himself up, so that Potiphar's wife, who had hardly been aware of him before, began to take notice. Or it may be that 'these things' refers to what the lady did: she surprised him unawares and talked seductively to him, and even, some versions allege, changed her clothes three times a day in order to get herself noticed. 'In both cases,' concludes Kugel, 'the midrashist has invented something that was not in the Bible itself, and yet, to the midrashic way of thinking, the invented material is practically there, the phrase "after these things" inviting the interpreter to supply the missing information.'

The modern reader will find this puzzling. 'And it came to pass after these things' is, after all, a common transitional phrase in the

Bible: first X happened (Joseph was sold into slavery and ended up in Potiphar's household), and then ('after these things') Y happened (Mrs P tried to seduce him). But the midrashist reads with an eagle eye for detail and little common sense. Even more baffling, to our eyes, is the interpretation of Genesis 32: 4: 'Thy servant Jacob saith thus, I have sojourned with Laban and stayed there until now.' The Hebrew for 'I have sojourned' is *garti*, the numerical value of whose letters (every Hebrew letter doubles for a number) is 613, indicating that 'I have sojourned with Laban, yet observed the 613 precepts of the Torah and did not learn from his wickedness.' This is crazy, we feel. Jacob lived before any Torah was ever thought of, and, besides, the Bible is just not encoded like that. That, the interpreter would reply, just shows how little you know about it.

Ginzberg is not interested in the principles and procedures of midrash, only in gathering together the end products. James Kugel is interested in both. He concurs with Fishbane in his view that 'the interpretation of the Bible goes back virtually as far as the oldest text within it', but he recognises that a decisive change came about as a result of the Babylonian Captivity, so that the later books of the Bible, particularly Chronicles, have to be seen as powerful retellings and reinterpretations, suited to the spirit of the times, of many of the early portions of the Bible. Kugel also recognises that an even more crucial change occurred in the first century of the Common Era, when, as a result of the canonisation of the Bible, the Bible itself became the subject of meditation, not God's word or the events in the life of the community. At that point, the prophet was replaced by the sage as the leader of the community, and we had entered a phase that was to last until the Enlightenment.

Thus the Bible of Jews and Christians from the first century on was never simply the Bible, but the Bible with its commentaries and interpretations. In his massive *Traditions of the Bible: A Guide to the Bible as It Was at the Start of the Common Era*, Kugel follows the Torah or Pentateuch, the most sacred portion of the Bible for Jews and of the Old Testament for Christians, and shows, by means of examples culled from a huge variety of sources – pseudepigrapha, sermons, apocalypses, midrash, the New Testament and the Fathers of the Church – just how the Bible would have been understood then and for centuries to come. And yet this raises questions which neither he, nor fine scholars such as Fishbane and Schwarz, are really willing to address. Chief among these is this: Is it really so obvious that there is an essential continuity between the Bible and the later legends and tales? After all, the fact that the Bible was understood in a certain way centuries after it had been written does not mean that that was how the writers themselves conceived it.

Here, for example, is how the Bible tells the story of Jacob's encounter with the angel:

> And he rose up that night, and took his two wives, and his two women servants, and his eleven sons, and passed over the ford Jabbok. And he took them and sent them over the brook and sent over that he had. And Jacob was left alone; and there wrestled a man with him until the breaking of the day. And when he saw that he prevailed not against him, he touched the hollow of his thigh; and the hollow of Jacob's thigh was out of joint, as he wrestled with him. And he said, Let me go, for the day breaketh. And he said, I will not let thee go, except thou bless me. And he said unto him, What is thy name? And he said, Jacob. And he said, Thy name shall be called no more Jacob, but Israel; for as a prince hast thou power with God and with men, and hast prevailed. And Jacob asked him, and said, Tell me, I pray thee, thy name. And he said, Wherefore is it that thou dost ask after my name? And he blessed him there. And Jacob called the name of the place Peniel: for I have seen God face to face, and my life is preserved. And as he passed over Penuel the sun rose upon him, and he halted upon his thigh. (KJV, Gen. 32: 23–33)

As the story is recounted in Ginzberg, Jacob, as he is about to cross over, sees a herdsman with sheep and camels. The man suggests that they should cross over together and help each other carry over their animals. Jacob agrees on condition that his possessions be transported first. In the twinkling of an eye they are on the other side. But when Jacob tries to carry the stranger's animals over, no matter how many he carries, some are always left behind. Finally Jacob realises that it is no human companion he has to contend with and leaps on the 'man' in anger. But the 'man' is none other than the archangel Michael, and when Jacob grapples with him he touches the earth with his finger and a fire bursts forth. Another legend retold by Ginzberg takes up the story. After the struggle with the 'man', dawn breaks. 'The dawn on that day was of particularly short duration. The sun rose two hours before his time, by way of compensation for having set so early on the day on which Jacob passed Mount Moriah on his journey to Haran, and to induce him to turn aside and lodge for the night on the future Temple place.' In fact, the sun shone with the same power as it had during the six days of creation, and it cured Jacob of his limp, while Esau and his princes were all burnt by the terrible heat, as, at the end of days, the heathen will be consumed.

The Bible story is both utterly mysterious and quite natural. The men of the Bible live under the same constraints of time, place and gravity as we do. This makes the sudden appearance of the 'man' all the more shocking. Thereafter the story moves forward rapidly yet unhurriedly, never looking back and never commenting on itself or delivering a moral. The midrashic tales, by contrast, are full of fairy-tale and folklore elements; they ruin the pace of the story by elaborating charming but irrelevant folklore motifs; they are frequently proleptic (the future Temple place) and divide mankind clearly into the Good (Jacob) and the Bad (Esau, the heathen).

Though Kugel states that interpretation of the Bible is to be found in its earliest strands, he admits that in the hands of the later interpreters 'the Bible took on a new, and sometimes radically different significance'. But even though he proceeds to lay the evidence before us, he is unwilling, like Fishbane and Schwarz, to acknowledge that the Bible was doing something utterly different. Instead, like them, he finds refuge in the concept of the hermeneutic:

> We like to think that the Bible, or any other text, means 'just what it says'. And we act on that assumption: we simply open up a book – including the Bible – and try to make sense of it on our own. In ancient Israel and for centuries afterward, on the contrary, people looked to special interpreters to explain the meaning of a biblical text. For that reason, the explanations passed along by such interpreters quickly acquired an authority of their own.

But the fact that all reading requires interpretation does not mean that the Bible means what these storytellers and interpreters say it does. After all, from the start the Bible turned its back on the myths and epics of the surrounding cultures. The legends that spring up in its wake only testify to the fact that if you try to throw myth and folklore out of the door, they creep back in through the window. It does no service to the Bible to try to pretend otherwise, and one wonders if there is still a hint of the motive imputed to Ginzberg by Kugel – that is, the desire to reassert pride in the Jewish tradition – in the efforts of scholars like Fishbane and Kugel to find continuity where none exists.

Of course, the rabbis did frequently come up with real insights. A remark such as the one that 'As Absalom lived by his hair so he died by his hair' alerts us to the ironies and pathos of Absalom's life and death. Robert Alter frequently turns to such rabbinic insights to help his own work of defining the unique nature of the narratives of the Hebrew Bible. But, by and large, immersion in these later rewritings only serves to bring out the gulf that separates the Bible from them. The reprinting of Louis Ginzberg's great collection ought to help us grasp more fully the uniqueness of the Hebrew Bible precisely by making clear how different it is from 'the legends of the Jews'. As well, of course, as making available to the general reader once more that wonderful store of legends which is the Jewish contribution to the folktales of the world.

1 A review of Louis Ginzberg, *The Legends of The Jews*, translated by Henrietta Szold and Paul Radin, with a new foreword by James L. Kugel, 6 volumes (Baltimore: Johns Hopkins University Press, 1998).

Two Resurrections

It seems that as Cervantes was approaching the end of the second part of Don Quixote he learned of the publication of a book entitled *The Second Volume of the Ingenious Gentleman Don Quixote of La Mancha.* The author of this work has never been identified, though the book was published under the name of Alonso Fernandez de Avellaneda, a native of the town of Tordesillas. Since the second part of the authentic *Don Quixote* makes much of the fact that many of the people Don Quixote and Sancho Panza meet have already heard of them because of the fame of Part I, this further testimony to their existence was surely welcomed by Cervantes, though he takes every opportunity to insult it and its author for purveying a scurrilous and inauthentic account of his hero. What the success of Part I did was to make Cervantes' task in Part II that much easier, for instead of having to go on inventing adventures for his two characters and intercutting this with playful references to Cide Hamete and his translation of the purported original, he could now fall back on the theme of the Knight and his squire being recognised for the gullible fools they are and having those who come across them play on this gullibility for their own amusement.

The most extended treatment of this theme concerns a duke and duchess who welcome the two into their castle and set up elaborate shows with a view to seeing how foolishly they behave. Thus Sancho is finally given the governorship of an *insula* that he had so long craved, and this allows Cervantes to meditate, as Rabelais had before him, on the nature of the wise ruler in a world in which authority is starting to come under question. But it is not just the Duke and Duchess who set about manipulating the two simpletons for their own amusement – everybody tries to get in on the act.

One of the duchess's maids, the beautiful Altisidora, pretends to be in love with Don Quixote and serenades him at night, to the delight of her fellow maids:

O you, who lie in your bed,
Between sheets of Holland linen,
Soundly and deeply asleep
All night long and until the morning,
O brave Knight, the most courageous
Ever born in great La Mancha,
More modest, more chaste, more blessed
Than the fine gold of Arabia!
Hear this melancholy maiden.

The Don is appalled. He has sworn allegiance to Dulcinea de Toboso and though he feels sorry for the lady he knows that knights often find themselves in this plight and have to remain steadfast. He is happy to console her with a song of his own ('Often the power of love / can madden a maiden's soul [...] Dulcinea of Toboso: / she is painted on my soul's / tabula rasa, and never / can she ever be erased.'), but that is as far as he will go, though the lady pretends to faint when he passes by and various tricks are played upon him to make him see the error of his ways.

Eventually Don Quixote and Sancho leave the castle and make their way to Barcelona, where more adventures await them, including a challenge to a joust from a mysterious Knight of the White Moon, who defeats Don Quixote and orders him as penance to return to his village and live there for a whole year. Ruefully Don Quixote accepts, since this is what the rules of Knighthood require, and sets off with his squire. Now we learn that the Knight of the White Moon was none other than his old friend and neighbour Bachelor Samson Carrasco who, desperate at his friend's continuing madness, has devised this plan to get him to come back home. One more major adventure, however, awaits Don Quixote.

He and Sancho are captured by bandits and taken in silence, as dusk falls, to a castle. As they enter the main courtyard they see that it is decorated in such a manner as only to increase their bewilderment. All around are burning torches and hundreds of lamps which turn the night almost into day.

> In the middle of the courtyard a catafalque rose some two *varas* off the ground, entirely covered by a very large canopy of black velvet; around it, on the steps, candles of wax burned in more than a hundred silver candelabras; displayed on the catafalque was the dead body of a damsel so beautiful that her beauty made death itself beautiful. Her head, crowned with a garland of fragrant flowers, lay on a brocade pillow, and her hands, crossed on her bosom, held a branch of yellow triumphant palm.

A stage has been erected on one side of the courtyard, with two seats, on which two people with crowns and sceptres are sitting, and on the steps leading up to it are two other seats, to which Don Quixote and Sancho are led, still in utter silence. Now two more figures appear, recognised by Don Quixote as the Duke and Duchess, his recent hosts, and they take their place beside the two apparent kings. At this moment Don Quixote realises that the dead body on the catafalque is none other than the maiden who had fallen in love with him, Altisidora.

Now Sancho's cap is removed and a cone-shaped hat such as those worn by penitents is put on his head, and a garment of black buckram decorated with flames is placed on his shoulders. Soft music is now heard, coming apparently from underneath the catafalque, and next to the pillow of the corpse appears a handsome youth dressed in Roman fashion, who proceeds to sing a song, accompanying himself on the harp:

> Until Altisidora 'turns to life,
> killed by the cruelty of Don Quixote;

until, in the enchanting court, the ladies
begin to wear cloth made of rough goat's hair [...]
I shall sing of her beauty and affliction
more sweetly than that famed singer of Thrace.
    And yet I do not think that this sad duty
ends for me on the day that my life ends [...]
And when my soul, freed of its mortal shell,
is led across the dark infernal Styx,
it will celebrate you still, and with that song
it will halt the waters of oblivion.

Now one of the two kings speaks up, ordering him to stop and explaining to the assembly that the lady 'is not dead as the ignorant world thinks, but alive on the tongues of Fame, and in the punishment that Sancho Panza, here present, must undergo in order to return her to the light she has lost.' This, it turns out, is Minos, and now his companion, Rhadamanthus, judge of the shades of the dead, announces what Sancho must undergo: twenty-four slaps on the nose and twelve pinches and six pinpricks on his arms and back, 'for the welfare of Altisidora depends on this ceremony.' And this, despite his protestations, is what ensues. Finally he breaks free of his tormentors and shouts: 'Away, ministers of hell! I'm not made of bronze! I feel your awful tortures!' 'At this point,' says the narrator, 'Altisidora, who must have been tired after spending so much time supine, turned to one side, and when the onlookers saw this, almost all of them cried out in unison: "Altisidora is alive! Altisidora lives!"' Altisidora sits up on the catafalque and the flageolets and flutes begin to play, while every voice rings out: 'Long live Altisidora! Altisidora, long may she live!' All rise to their feet, while Altisidora, looking Don Quixote in the eye, says: 'God forgive you, cold-hearted knight, for because of your cruelty I have been in the next world for more than a thousand years, it seems to me; and you, the most compassionate squire on earth, I thank you for the life I possess!'

The narrator now explains how and why the deception was practised, and 'Cide Hamete goes on to say that in his opinion the deceivers are as mad as the deceived, and that the duke and duchess came very close to seeming like fools since they went to such lengths to deceive two fools.' But the episode is not quite over. Altisidora enters Don Quixote's room that night, and they have a long conversation about what happened to her when she died:

> 'To tell the truth,' responded Altisidora, 'I probably didn't die completely because I didn't enter hell, and if I had, I really couldn't have left even if I'd wanted to. The truth is I reached the gate, where about a dozen devils were playing pelota, all of them in tights and doublets [...], and what amazed me most was that instead of balls they were using books, apparently full of wind and trash, which was something marvellous and novel [...]'

But as the conversation develops, with Sancho also throwing in his pennyworth, Altisidora suddenly grows enraged at Don Quixote's solemn reiteration that Dulcinea is his only love and that he pities her for her mad passion for him, and suddenly bursts out:

> Good lord! Don Codfish, with a soul of metal, like the pit of a date, harder and more stubborn than a peasant when he has his mind set on something, if I get near you I'll scratch out your eyes! Do you think by any chance, Don Defeated, Don Battered, that I died for you? Everything you saw tonight was pretence; I'm not the kind of woman who would let herself suffer as much as the dirt under her fingernail, much less die on account of nonsense like that.

Don Quixote never replies to this, and other events deflect attention from what she has just said, but there is no doubt that her words make a deep impression on him and help lead to his eventual understanding, on his deathbed back in his village, that he has been mad for a long time, so that he dies, at least, freed from the obsession that had ruled his life.

Episodes like this one of Altisidora would seem to signal the end of the Middle Ages, with their miraculous saints' lives and other tales of fantasy and magic. In the new world which Cervantes both bears witness to and helps usher in, those who believe in such things are shown to be living in a world of their own – mad. And yet at the very same time as Cervantes was writing the second part of his novel another writer, equally great, equally aware of the follies of such imaginings, was writing a play that would challenge Cervantes' challenge to the beliefs of the waning Middle Ages. Shakespeare had used the theme of the dead who are not really dead in a number of comedies, notably *The Comedy of Errors* and *Much Ado About Nothing*, but even here it was never quite in the purely ironical spirit of Cervantes, and, even in the early *Comedy of Errors,* was hedged about with a sense of mystery. In his great tragedies the dead do indeed return, but only to haunt the living, whether by urging them to do something, as in *Hamlet,* or in silent accusation, as do Duncan and Banquo in *Macbeth*. Something new seems to emerge in the course of *King Lear*. As that extraordinary play progresses through a series of bewildering changes of direction the bond between Lear and Cordelia, shattered by Lear's folly in the opening scene, comes to seem the most important thing in the play, and the climactic scene in which he is finally reunited with her in death is the most frightful and desperately painful moment in a play which has not lacked for either fear or pain. And that bond of father and daughter is one that seems to preoccupy Shakespeare above all in his final period, the period of *Pericles*, *Cymbeline*, *The Winter's Tale* and *The Tempest*. What appears to be at stake here is not just family bonds and not just the relation between the generations, but the mystery of resurrection, presented to us as something other than either magic or religious dogma but as connected with the roots of ordinary life.

The Winter's Tale deals with not one death but three. Leontes, seized by a mad jealousy, accuses his loving wife Hermione of betraying him with his best friend, and refuses to even listen to her denials. His actions call down the wrath of the gods upon him and he learns in rapid succession that his son has died and then that his wife, whom he had imprisoned, has also died, giving birth to a baby girl. Struck down with remorse, he becomes a recluse for the next sixteen years. The baby girl is entrusted to a faithful servant to be cast out to sea, but she, of course, survives, and returns with her young lover, who is none other than the son of that Polixenes whom Leontes had accused of betraying him with his wife. The reunion of father and daughter, unlike the parallel one in *Pericles*, which forms the climax to that play, is passed over quickly and we are only told about it at second hand. 'There might you have beheld one joy crown another,' says one Gentleman of the court to another,

> So and in such a manner that it seemed sorrow wept to take leave of them, for their joy waded in tears. There was casting up of eyes, holding up of hands, with countenance of such distraction, that they were to be known by garment, not by favour. Our king, being ready to leap out of himself for joy of his found daughter, as if that joy were now become a loss, cries, 'O, thy mother, thy mother!' then asks Bohemia forgiveness; then embraces his son-in-law; then again worries he his daughter with clipping her; now he thanks the old shepherd which stands by, like a weather-bitten conduit of many kings' reigns. I never heard of such another encounter, which lames report to follow it, and undoes description to do it.

And what, asks the other, became of the faithful servant to whom the child had been entrusted? 'Like an old tale still,' answers the other,

> Which will have matter to rehearse, though credit be asleep and

not an ear open. He was torn to pieces with a bear: this avouches the shepherd's son; who has not only his innocence, which seems much, to justify him, but a handkerchief and rings of his that Paulina knows.

All is ready then for the last scene. The wife, Hermione, who, like Cervantes' Altisidora, had seemingly died out of love for her husband, though not quite in the way Cervantes meant, has had a statue put up in her stead, and this statue the faithful Paulina is now going to unveil to the King and his court. Paulina says:

As she liv'd peerless,
So her dead likeness, I do well believe,
Excels whatever yet you look'd upon,
Or hand of man hath done; therefore I keep it
Lonely, apart. But here it is: prepare
To see the life as lively mock'd as ever
Still sleep mock'd death.

She draws a curtain and, says Shakespeare's stage direction, 'discovers Hermione standing like a statue.' All exclaim at its truth to life, but Leontes is puzzled: 'But yet, Paulina, Hermione was not so much wrinkled, nothing / So aged as this seems.' 'Not by much,' answers Paulina, brushing off his remark. Perdita, the newly found daughter, tries to kneel and kiss her hand, but Paulina pushes her back: 'O patience! / The statue is but newly fix'd, the colour's / Not dry.' Leontes seems so upset by the vision that Paulina suggests drawing the curtain again:

I'll draw the curtain:
My lord's almost so far transported that
He'll think anon it lives.

'O sweet Paulina,' answers Leontes,

Make me to think so twenty years together!
No settled senses of the world can match
The pleasure of that madness. Let't alone.

And as now he makes to kiss it she moves the action into a new dimension:

Either forbear,
Quit presently the chapel, or resolve you
For more amazement. If you can behold it,
I'll make her statue move indeed; descend,
And take you by the hand: but then you'll think
(Which I protest against) I am assisted
By wicked powers.

When Leontes agrees to this, she explains the rules:

It is requir'd
You do awake your faith. Then all stand still:
Or – those that think it is unlawful business
I am about, let them depart.

And when Leontes tells her to proceed, she goes on:

Music, awake her; strike!
'Tis time; descend; be stone no more; approach;
Strike all that look upon with marvel. Come!
I'll fill your grave up; stir, nay, come away:
Bequeath to death your numbness; for from him
Dear life redeems you. You perceive she stirs:

'Hermione comes down', says the stage-direction.

Start not; her actions shall be holy as
You hear my spell is lawful. [*To Leontes*] Do not shun her

Until you see her die again; so then
You kill her double. Nay, present your hand:
When she was young you woo'd her; now, in age,
Is she become the suitor?

Leontes: O, she's warm!
If this be magic, let it be an art
Lawful as eating.

As they embrace the others exclaim. Paulina presses on with her manipulation of events:

That she is living,
Were it but told you, should be hooted at
Like an old tale: but it appears she lives,
Though yet she speak not. Mark a little while.
[*To Perdita*] Please you to interpose, fair madam, kneel
And pray your mother's blessing. [*To H*] Turn, good lady,
Our Perdita is found.

And, finally Hermione speaks, for the first time since the scene of her trial in Act II:

You gods, look down,
And from your sacred vials pour your graces
Upon my daughter's head! Tell me, mine own,
Where hast thou been preserv'd? where liv'd? how found
Thy father's court? For thou shalt hear that I,
Knowing by Paulina that the Oracle
Gave hope that thou wast in being, have preserv'd
Myself to see the issue.

Like Cervantes, Shakespeare is at pains to make us see the machinery behind the apparent miracle. Like him he is, in these last plays, as realistic as he is in his tragedies: Mamillius, the son of Leontes and Hermione, is dead, and he will not be brought back to life. Hermione is twenty years older. Nothing will take her suffering or that of Leontes away from them. And yet, where Cervantes was content to leave it at that, Shakespeare is not. Paradoxically, the fact that this is a play may help. I say paradoxically because one might think that it would, on the contrary, make his aim completely unrealisable. But that is to reckon without great art. Shakespeare, who could prick the pretensions of both a Falstaff and a Hotspur with a lethal dose of reality, has understood that the only way to make his resurrection work is to stress again and again how the rediscovery of Perdita is a wonder that even the old story-tellers would be ashamed to recount, and is also at pains to stress that in this final scene what we are witnessing is nothing more than an actress stepping down from a pedestal. Like Sophocles in his last play, *Oedipus at Colonus*, the ordinary is here imbued with wonder. The fact of death is wondrous, mysterious, beyond our human comprehension, yet the most ordinary thing in the world: we all experience it. The fact of love is wondrous, mysterious, beyond our mortal comprehension, yet it is the most ordinary thing in the world: we all experience it. That we can walk and embrace is the most extraordinary thing in the world; yet we all experience it. All it requires to recognise it is that we awake our faith, and, perhaps, that music be playing.

Medieval Matters[1]

A FEW YEARS AGO I travelled to Germany with the painter Timothy Hyman to look at medieval art. After an hour in the extraordinary Germanisches Nationalmuseum in Nuremberg, Tim turned to me and said: 'What a difference it would make to London if even one of these rooms was transported there.'

That was then. Today, all of a sudden, London is flooded with medieval art: the medieval and Renaissance galleries at the V&A have opened, revealing unsuspected riches; a fascinating and highly intelligent exhibition of medieval reliquaries recently filled the main exhibition space of the British Museum; and ambitious exhibitions of medieval illuminated manuscripts have been seen in Cambridge and London.

A subtler change has also been making itself felt in the world of scholarship. Gone are the days when the Middle Ages were regarded as Dark, mired in superstition and waiting for the light of the Reformation and Enlightenment to shine again as it had in ancient Greece and Rome; the days when medieval art was seen, in all its manifestations, as merely the crude approximations of the glory that lay round the corner in the Renaissance. That mindset – though not entirely eradicated, especially in the popular imagination, and in the occasional gallery caption – is now rightly understood as having been merely the propagation of the polemics of the Renaissance and the Reformation themselves. Today scholars happily straddle the divide between the fourteenth and the seventeenth centuries, and they approach the period more in the spirit of anthropologists than of polemicists, seeking to understand and to help us to understand what made these societies tick, and to help us shed our post-Enlightenment and post-Romantic notions of what art should be.

Forty years of feminist and postcolonial studies have also helped shape the scholarship of the period. Apologists for the Middle Ages are no longer card-carrying Catholics, as blind to the anxieties and dark areas of the period as churchmen so often were at the time. Cathars and other heretics, and especially Jews, are beginning to be seen not just as problems for the authorities, but as vehicles for the confusions and doubts besetting the Christian majorities. And scholars are discovering that in the field of manuscript production, for example, Christian and Jewish workshops often worked hand in hand, both in the German- and in the Spanish-speaking lands.

Jewish art historians have of course long dominated the field. But as Jas Elsner notes in *Judaism and Christian Art: Aesthetic Anxieties from the Catacombs to Colonialism*, until the war and for some time after, they were adept at mimicking the tone of the dominant culture in which they were working. One would not know that Panofsky and Gombrich had Jewish roots, nor does it seem to matter. But in the aftermath of the war and with a growing understanding of the nature of the Holocaust, not to speak of the foundation of the state of Israel, such innocence was simply no longer possible. Running through all three of the books under review is a deep awareness of all these shifts and a sophisticated understanding of what they imply, neatly encapsulated in the quote from Susannah Heschel with which Marcia Kupfer introduces her fascinating essay in the volume on Judaism and Christian art. Christianity, notes Heschel, took over the central Jewish theological concepts 'of the Messiah, eschatology, apocalypticism, election and Israel, as well as its scriptures, its prophets and even its God', while denying the continued validity of those ideas for Judaism. But in so doing

> Christianity was unable to erase it; Judaism is taken within, becoming the unwilling presence inside the Christian realm, a presence that is deeply troubling and gives rise to a variety of strategies within Christian theology to contain, redefine, and finally, exorcise its presence.

Christianity was the religion of the Incarnation, of the Word made flesh. From the start it was fighting on two fronts: both Jewish literalism and Gnostic symbolism had to be shown to be misguided, a misunderstanding of the nature of reality. The Gnostics were incapable of seeing this, clinging to the mistaken idea that no God would allow himself to suffer as Jesus had suffered; the Jews were incapable of seeing this, mired as they were in a literalist mindset and insisting that Jesus was simply a man. Yet Jesus, if the Son of God, was also a Jew, and his coming had been foretold by Jewish Scripture. St Paul struggled to articulate the paradoxes of the new religion, and St Augustine and the Church Fathers after him elaborated in encyclopedic fashion on his writings. But the balance was always delicate, and throughout the history of Christianity there has always been pressure to clarify, along with the repeated discovery that all attempts to clarify only further endanger the balance.

Caroline Bynum has made her name as the pre-eminent historian of the body in the late Middle Ages. The titles of her many books testify to her range and interests: *Wonderful Blood*, *Metamorphosis and Identity*, *Holy Feast and Holy Fast*. She is happy to see herself as both anthropologist and sociologist and makes no bones about her indebtedness to researchers in those fields, especially Alfred Gell and Bruno Latour. But she is firm that she is first and foremost a historian of late medieval *mentalités,* and not a 'scholar of the body' – that would be too general a field for her. Her new book, *Christian Materiality: An Essay on Religion in Late Medieval Europe*, is merely a further instalment, but it in fact provides a marvellous introduction to the 2011 *Treasures of Heaven* exhibition at the British Museum, of which a splendid catalogue (*Treasures of Heaven: Saints, Relics, and Devotion in Medieval Europe,* edited by Martina Bagnoli and Holger A. Klein) is still available. That exhibition, in stark contrast to the usual crowd-drawing blockbuster, was not only designed to show visitors some remarkable and little-seen artistic treasures, but also to introduce them to a fascinating and alien mode of thought. As Bynum points out, Muslims and Jews, when they think of holy places, think of places sanctified by some sacred event which occurred there and is recorded in their scriptures. Christians, though, from the earliest times, went on pilgrimages to enter the presence of (to try and touch, even to take away a portion of) the dead body of a saint, or of Jesus himself. Reformers in the sixteenth century could laugh at this and make snide remarks about the number of pieces of the holy cross which had been found adding up not to a tree but to a forest, but the *Treasures of Heaven* exhibition – like Peter Brown's wonderful examination of the earliest pilgrimages, *The Cult of the Saints* (already thirty years old) – is not here to scoff but to understand and to try to convey what such a cult of relics meant to those who engaged in them.

We are shown reliquaries in the form of an arm and hand, said to contain the arm of St Louis of Toulouse; in the form of a bust, said to contain the head of Saint Balbuina; as well as simpler, box-like containers, often exquisitely carved or enamelled. One of the most fascinating exhibits is not an object but a photograph of the Sainte-Chapelle in Paris, which was built by Louis IX to house the Crown of Thorns. Seeing it we realise suddenly that it is not so much that many reliquaries were made in the shape of a church, but that churches themselves were first and foremost reliquaries. At that moment the ubiquity of the cult of relics in Western Christendum is driven home to us.

Caroline Bynum frequently discusses the very objects we were able to see in the exhibition. But her book brings out how very much stranger medieval culture was than either the exhibition or the catalogue makes out. This is inevitable. A major exhibition, no matter how sophisticated, clothes everything in a certain aura of respectability; Bynum is determined to move beyond this. What she wants to do is to explore the paradoxes of an incarnational religion, in which body is seen to be at once immortal and corruptible, at once whole and fragmented. Thus the catalogue to the exhibition describes the reliquary of Thomas Becket's blood, from the Metropolitan Museum in New York, in typical museological fashion, giving us some historical background about Becket's martyrdom and pointing out that the 'dramatic use of niello lends a cold, graphic immediacy to the scenes' on the box, which it then goes on to describe. After that it discusses the possibility that the box contained two phials of Becket's blood, which depends on the deciphering of a damaged inscription on the reverse, and which is 'impossible to confirm due to lack of documentary evidence'. Bynum, on the other hand, highlights the simulated ruby on the lid, about which the exhibition catalogue is silent, and has this to say about the object:

> Reliquaries – especially those of the later Middle Ages – explore and expose materiality in complicated ways. Denying the corruption of the flesh by displaying the body as hard, apparently dead bone, they simultaneously sublimate partition and deadness by sheathing such stuff in the gold and gems explicitly associated in Scripture and sermon with the life of the heavenly Jerusalem. For example, in the reliquary of Thomas Becket's blood, the blood itself (which is presumably a few rusty, dried flakes) is hidden in a casket, not displayed, but a large jewel has been constructed on the top by backing rock crystal with red foil to evoke the redness of blood. The stuff of the jewel is palpable and shouts out living redness, but it plays visually with its own physicality; it is neither the blood in the container nor the ruby it appears to be.

Bynum is fascinated by such play between perception and conception. What she makes clear is the sheer oddity of much late medieval visual culture. One striking example is a woodcut of the Wounds of Christ with symbols of the Passion, c. 1490, now in the National Gallery of Art in Washington. The wound in Christ's side, shaped like a mandorla, fills the page from top to bottom, with Christ's head and hands appearing above it and His feet below, so that the wound stands in for the body. On either side is a scroll. That on the left reads:

> This is the length and width of Christ's wound which was pierced in his side on the Cross. Whoever kisses this wound with remorse and sorrow, also with devotion, will have as often as he does this, seven years indulgence from Pope Innocent.

That on the right refers to the cross inscribed within the wound, and reads:

> This little cross standing in Christ's wound measured forty times makes the length of Christ in his humanity. Whoever kisses it with devotion shall be protected from sudden death or misfortune.

Bynum notes that what gives the image power is that it purports to be an accurate measure. This is a protective amulet against disaster, but 'it is also Christ himself', for, to the culture to which it belongs, to measure is somehow to own. The woodcut thus becomes a kind of contact relic.

In the later chapters of her book Bynum turns to the most famous examples of such ambiguity: statues which moved, paintings of saints who descended from the walls to perform miracles, communion wafers which bled. The question of whether Christ is literally present in the wafer – and, if so, how He can be in so many places at once and yet be standing on God's right hand, whole and perfect – was one which of course had always troubled Christianity and would continue to do so in the centuries of the Reformation. The Church was torn: to allow miracles such as statues moving or wafers bleeding was to cede power from the centre to the periphery – to the local site of the miracle. But to suppress such ideas altogether was to deny the central plank on which Christianity was founded.

Miracles occur when sceptics dismiss the image as mere image or the wafer as mere matter. Such scepticism forces the miraculous nature of the Christian dispensation to break out into the open, so to speak. And this is where the Jew enters. As is well known, Christian anxieties about the eucharist and anxieties about the Jews in their midst fed off each other throughout the later Middle Ages. Jews were accused of killing Christian children and using their blood to make the Passover matzos, and of desecrating the Host. The authorities reacted in contradictory ways, sometimes squashing such rumours in the interests of peace and sometimes fomenting them in order to get rid of the Jews in their cities or lands. But, as Bynum points out, the Jew, like the Christian sceptic, was an ideal vehicle for the projection of the notion that Hosts could bleed, could be violated, were more than mere bread.

Neither Bynum nor the contributors to the Kessler and Nirenberg volume wish to play down the historical facts of persecution and pogroms, but they are mainly concerned to understand the way in which, as Jaś Elsner says, 'The role of Judaism […] is […] as an empty vessel to be filled with a complex nexus of Christian projections'. Looking at the art of the West through this lens yields some remarkable results, whether it be the analysis of an early Christian sarcophagus of the Red Sea crossing or of Delacroix' Jewish Wedding in Tangier (though the latter suffers because here, as in the Bynum volume, the illustrations are all in black and white). Particularly fine are Sara Lipton's study of the twelfth-century portable altar from Cologne, known as the Eilbertus altar, and Richard Neer's study of Poussin's *Christ and the Woman Taken in Adultery*. Situating the making of the Eilbertus altar in the midst of the debate amongst Christian theologians about the value of images, Lipton writes:

> Jewish prophets appear as venerable and authoritative witnesses to the antiquity, sanctity, and efficacy of luxurious matter and corporeal vision. Their function is not to rehabilitate the Jew as a spiritual witness, but to rehabilitate the realm long associated with Jews (the external […] image-saturated world so inimical to early Cistercians) as a valid part of Christianity […] That is,

> the witnessing Jew appears *in* art in order to provide historical, scriptural, and epistemological justification *for* art, and to justify the very artworks in which he appears.

Neer, for his part, provides a dazzling analysis of how we as viewers are asked by Poussin to read the barely legible Hebrew writing that Christ has inscribed in the dust at his feet. The Hebrew is almost but not quite decipherable, so we 'end up in much the same situation as the Pharisees in the picture: pointing, puzzling, and conversing'. But 'just as the Pharisees point at the ambiguous text, so Christ points to the adulteress.' Yet if the woman is a text of sorts, she still has a figural meaning. As the medieval *Glossa Ordinaria* put it: 'The woman taken in adultery signifies the Synagogue, which according to the tradition of the Fathers adulterated the law of Moses.' Look harder, though, and you see that behind the woman Poussin has placed a mother and child, at whom Jesus seems to be pointing no less than at the other woman. Except that Poussin's genius lay in confusing us as to what is behind and what is before through his manipulation of pictorial space. Thus: 'For one sort of viewer [...] the picture is a kind of nonsense, a contravention of Scripture and the rules of history painting. For another, however, it is exactly the violation of those rules that reveals the ineffable conditions of sense under the New Covenant.'

But Jews did not merely sit back and let the Christian majority treat them as figures, important but secondary, in their own cosmic drama. In what is perhaps the finest essay in *Judaism and Christian Art*, Marcia Kupfer tells the story of the early-fifteenth-century Spanish Alba Bible. In the 1320s Luis de Guzmán, grand master of the military order of Calatrava, commanded Rabbi Moses Arragel of Guadalajara to produce a Castillian translation of Hebrew Scripture. The richly illustrated volume that resulted has long been seen as an example of the Golden Age of Spain and of amicable Christian-Jewish relations. Kupfer is more sceptical. Far from being a fine example of *convivencia* (at the very moment when that model was falling apart), she argues, 'the commission symbolised and advertised Jewish subservience to Christian overlords'. Rabbi Moses, however, had his own agenda, and in determining what it was Kupfer focuses on a single image, that of Abraham circumcising himself on folio 37r. (Genesis 17: 9–27). This she sees as the site of a kind of silent struggle between two visions. Christianity and Judaism diverged on the fundamental matter of religious initiation, baptism versus circumcision. Yet for both faiths blood symbolism is central:

> The salvific power of Christ's blood shed on the cross guarantees the spiritual remaking of the person in baptism [...] Less generally well known is that from c. 800 rabbinic sources and Jewish custom began strongly to associate circumcision blood with atonement, sacrifice, and redemption.

By 1300 this had received powerful expression in the most famous enterprise of Castilian kabbalists, the *Zohar*. The image in Alba of Abraham in a garden, holding his huge penis with his left hand as, with his right, he wields the knife and his blood spurts in a red torrent over his knees, would not only have reminded Jewish readers of the first circumcision, it would have pointed back to the glory days of the Temple, and forward to messianic deliverance. For as the midrash explains:

> The Holy One, blessed be He, said: By the merit of the blood of the covenant of circumcision and the blood of the Paschal lamb ye shall be redeemed from Egypt, and by the merit of the covenant of circumcision and by merit of the covenant of the Passover in the future ye shall be redeemed at the end of the fourth kingdom.

The 'fourth kingdom' (Dan 2: 40, 7: 23) in rabbinic tradition most often stood for Rome – that is, Christianity. The image in Alba would thus be 'read' differently by Christian and Jewish users of the manuscripts. To the Christian it might show the crude, fleshy, even animal-like aspects of Judaism (the enormous bloody penis), while to the Jewish viewer it would call to mind the end of persecution and the salvation of the nation.

The works with which Marc Michael Epstein in *The Medieval Haggadah* is concerned did not need to deploy such ambiguity, though, as he shows, the 'authorship' (as he calls the combination of patrons, rabbinic advisers, scribes, and illuminators) had one eye always focussed on a Christian viewer. They consist of four medieval *haggadot*, one from Germany (Mainz, probably) and three from Spain. A *haggadah* is the book used during the *seder* ritual of Passover, somewhere between an order of service and a theatre prompt book, for this celebration of the central episode in Jewish history takes place not in a synagogue but in the home, around the table set for an evening meal, with unruly children and uninterested adults among the participants (haggadah manuscripts frequently show signs of spilt wine, evidence of home use).

'In each and every generation each one has the obligation to view himself as if he had come out of Egypt', the text enjoins us. But unlike the Mass, where the issue of what exactly is meant by 'remembrance' in Jesus's 'this do in remembrance of me' (Luke 22:19) was an issue that would divide theologians and eventually entire communities and even nations, the dialogic nature of Judaism means that the meaning of the injunction is merely explored, different views dramatised, and the unity of the community affirmed, as all are reminded that what happened then is relived now and will come to pass again in the future, in the messianic time of 'next year in Jerusalem'.

Marc Epstein, who is quite as sophisticated a scholar and as acute a reader of images as Bynum and the contributors to the Kessler and Nirenberg volume, moves comfortably between large theoretical issues and minute detail. Throughout, he posits the principle that the 'authorship' of these works knew exactly what they were doing and that, if we are puzzled, it is much more likely to be because *we* have lost the ability to read them than because *they* were ignorant or careless.

In the so-called Birds' Head Haggadah, probably from Mainz around 1300, he explores the vexed question of why birds' heads should be substituted for human ones, and dismisses explanations which adduce parallels from cultures near and far, whether the zoocephalic gods of the ancient Near East or animal-headed saints from the European Middle Ages. Instead, in a move parallel to that made long ago in relation to Green Men by John Burrow in his groundbreaking book on *Sir Gawain and the Green Knight*, he argues that we must find the answer in how the birds' heads function *within* the manuscripts, not in some notion of a universal unconscious. I am not entirely convinced by his answer, but the principle is surely right. He follows this up with a persuasive argument about how the narrative sequence of the manuscripts, which deviates considerably from the story as given in Exodus, makes precisely the point the authorship wishes to make. On the way he develops a number of fascinating topics, suggesting, for example, that the falling manna in the shape of communion wafers, and the quails descending in the form that the dove so often takes in Christian iconography (fol. 22v), are an assertion that it is the bread of the Jews, given them by God to assuage their very real hunger, that is the true bread, not the purely symbolic bread of the Christians.

Then, in a dazzling analysis of the so-called Golden Haggadah, created in Catalonia around 1320, he shows how the 'authorship' wanted us to read diagonally and chiastically *across* the folio (there are four images to each folio) and sometimes across bifolia, rather than steadily from right to left. He also shows how carefully the book is constructed, with six pages devoted to Genesis, six to Exodus, and two to the transition from one to the other, and he points out the multiple parallels between the two sets of six. Epstein also argues persuasively that the 'authorship' was particularly interested in women, not only providing us with more images of women than in any other *haggadah*, but also, towards the end, at the climactic song of Miriam, devoting a whole quarter-page image to the women around Miriam (they don't figure at all in the Birds' Head Haggadah), frieze-like, and bigger (two and a half centimetres where the norm for figures filling the three-centimetre space is two and a quarter). Whether this was in order to stress the Jewish family and Jewish fertility in contrast with the unnaturalness of Christian asceticism, or because the manuscripts were commissioned by or were a present for a woman, we will never know. One of the strengths of this book is Epstein's insistence that he is opening up possibilities, not providing answers.

His third section examines the so-called 'sister' manuscripts, the 'Rylands Haggadah' and 'British Library Oriental 1404', both Catalonian, c. 1330–40. They are called 'sister' because the Rylands appears to be a fairly close copy of the British Library manuscript, but Epstein questions this. There is no such thing as a literal illustration, he rightly insists, and there is no such thing as a mere copy: all art takes a stand of some sort, whether consciously or not. With painstaking detail he goes on to show how very much the two manuscripts differ. BL Or. 1404, which initially appears cruder, is nevertheless, he argues, much more sophisticated in its conception. Thus in Rylands the Israelites number anything from eight to fifteen when in a crowd, but in BL Or. 1404 always add up to twelve, denoting the twelve tribes of Israel. And in confirmation of this, when the text has the choice between describing them as *ha'am* (the people) or as *b'nei yisrael* (the children of Israel) it consistently chooses the latter, whereas Rylands moves haphazardly between the two. Moreover, he discerns, there is in Rylands an animus towards the Egyptians and a kind of glee on the part of the triumphant Israelites, quite lacking in the more restrained BL Or. 1404. Was this because the latter emerged from pietistic circles which saw amity with Christians as important? Again, we do not know – Epstein merely highlights the issues.

He ends with a magnificent excursus on the way these manuscripts play with Christian iconography. He has already shown how the Birds' Head Haggadah uses the depiction of the manna and the quails to make a theological point; now he takes the image of a Jewish 'voyage to Egypt', that of Moses, his wife and two sons, and contrasts it with the better-known parallel Christian voyage to Egypt of Joseph and Mary with the infant Jesus. In the image of Moses' journey Moses' two sons are shown, suggesting fertility (a motif reinforced by the tree seemingly growing out of Moses' head in the Golden Haggadah), in contrast to the sterility of Christ (Christians would of course say that Jesus' spiritual progeny enormously outnumbered the sterile and flesh-bound Jews). But note the ass in BL Or. 1404, with its prominent member (the Christian ass is tactfully sexless) and contorted neck as it turns to look back. The same ass, Rashi argued (he is attempting to explain why it is described in Exodus 5: 20 as *ha-hamor, the* ass, not just *an* ass – though the English translations I've consulted all ignore the article and give 'an ass', proof of how little translations are to be trusted), that accompanied Abraham and Isaac to Mt Moriah at the *akedah*, and that the Messiah will ride as he enters Jerusalem at the end of days (Zechariah 9: 9). In the image in BL Or. 1404, Epstein argues, the ass appears unwilling to advance, just like the Hebrew people, who are often referred to in the Bible as being like asses, reluctantly being pushed and prodded towards redemption. 'This advance,' says Epstein, 'is constantly in danger of being forestalled by Abraham's potential lack of faith, by Moses' self-doubt, by humankind's evil or indifference.' And the donkey (which in the Golden Haggadah is to be found prominent in the very first image of God's naming of the beasts), 'moves slowly, determinedly, with plodding perseverance, inexorably through history toward personal, national, and finally, universal deliverance.' This is very fine, reminding one of the mixture of humanity, learning, and perception that characterised the writings of the greatest of medieval art historians, Meyer Schapiro. And Yale have done Epstein proud: every page with an image on it, in each of the four *haggadot,* is reproduced in colour, and whenever an image is discussed it is reproduced, again in colour, on the page in which he is talking about it. One could not ask for more.

All three of these volumes testify to the new-found sophistication of medieval studies. Their authors have moved beyond polemics as they have moved beyond historicism and formalism. The key questions are no longer, Where does this come from? and, What has influenced it? But rather, What is it for? and, How does it function? 'I explore these texts in order to ferret out slippages and silences, unconscious inconsistencies and contradictions,' writes Bynum, and the subtitle to the Penn volume points to the same intent: 'Aesthetic *anxieties* from the catacombs to colonialism'. This emphasis on filling in silences, examining the anxieties of artists and cultures, is splendid, but there is a danger that with such an agenda something vital to medieval art will be overlooked. One of the most moving rooms in the Germanisches Nationalmuseum in Nuremberg houses ten small wooden painted sculptures of the Virgin and Child dating from the twelfth and thirteenth centuries. Mostly the Virgin is seated, with the child on her lap. I had first been drawn to them when I saw three examples in the Diocesan museum in Brixen in the Südtirol (Bressanone in Alto Adige). They are simple, modest works but they exude an overwhelming sense of peace and wonder, the same sense as is conveyed by such medieval lyrics as 'I sing of a maiden' – the result I think of our sensing that for the carver and his audience there was no gap between an ordinary mother and child and the Mother of God and her child. No hint of anxiety here, and worth a hundred treatises on Incarnational theology. Bynum reproduces one of these sculptures, but her main interest in it is that there is a hole at the back where relics could be inserted. No doubt this is important, but focussing on it ignores the primary effect of the work. It is an effect which Ruskin and Proust understood to be central to much medieval art, and they found the words to convey it. A critic and scholar who could combine the learning and sophistication of the modern medievalist and Ruskin and Proust's sense of the wonder of medieval art – now *that* would be something.

Medieval Matters

1 A review of the following three books:

Judaism and Christian Art: Aesthetic Anxieties from the Catacombs to Colonialism, ed. Herbert L. Kessler and David Nirenberg (Philadelphia: University of Pennsylvania Press, 2011).

Caroline Walker Bynum, *Christian Materiality: An Essay on Religion in Late Medieval Europe* (New York: Zone Books, 2011).

Marc Michael Epstein, *The Medieval Haggadah: Art, Narrative, and Religious Imagination* (New Haven and London: Yale University Press, 2011).

The Tallith and the Dishcloth[1]

THERE IS A FAMOUS DEPICTION of the Last Supper by the thirteenth-century Sienese artist Pietro Lorenzetti in the lower church in Assisi. Christ and the Apostles are gathered in a circular chamber, defined by elegant pillars, but what is striking is Lorenzetti's expansion of the scene. To the left, by the door, two men converse, probably the master of the house, elegantly dressed, and his head servant. The door seems to lead to a kitchen, depicted within a high narrow oblong. Here, next to a roaring fire where presumably the food has been cooked, a cat is warming itself, while a dog is licking a dirty plate, and a scullion is bending forward as he wipes another dish and empties its contents into the dog's plate; another, better-dressed servant, leans over him, apparently engaging him in conversation. Earlier art historians enthused about Lorenzetti's way with perspective and domesticity, but recently scholars have begun to explore the symbolic content of the scene. The fire, they say, shows the Old Testament sacrifice, a lamb killed and eaten for Passover, while next door we see the new sacrifice instituted by Christ, himself the Passover lamb, in order that Christians may come to a new and purely spiritual sacrifice, ritually re-enacted in the partaking of the wine and bread of the mass.

A closer look brings a shock to our liberal sensibilities, happy to go along with the abstractions described so far, but balking perhaps at certain aspects of the medieval imagination. For what is this dishcloth with which the scullion is wiping the crockery? It is nothing other than the tallith, the Jewish ritual shawl. This domestic kitchen, then, with its cosy cat and dog, is the stinking physical world of the Old Testament, for St Bonaventura tells us that those who want real flesh as opposed to the spiritualised flesh of the Lamb of God are dogs who must be excluded from the eucharistic banquet. This is strong stuff to emanate from so noble a painting, but it is indubitably there. Or is it – quite? For what is the other servant, the one who bends over the scullion, pointing to, if not to his own prayer shawl, this time correctly covering his shoulders? Does not the emphatic gesture of his left hand suggest that he is reprimanding the scullion for desecrating this piece of ritual clothing, asking that it be reinstated in some sense, reminding us, the viewers, that it stands for the very world out of which Jesus emerged? After all, is it not this very same shawl that we see worn with pride by the Virgin's father in another painting by Pietro Lorenzetti, the Nativity, now in the cathedral museum in Siena?

Steven Kruger does not mention these paintings by Lorenzetti, but their complex arguments and ambiguities are precisely what his fascinating new book, *The Spectral Jew*, explores. For the Christians of the Middle Ages, the Jews represented a problem: the Jew was the Old Man of St Paul, who had been overcome and transcended by the New Man ushered in by Christ. The Jews were defined by their blindness in refusing to see that Christ was the Son of God, and this blindness was a sign of their carnality, their irredeemable physicality. In this they were like women, an Other *against* whom the medieval Christian male defined himself. But there was a paradox, the seed of an anxiety: for Jesus himself was a Jew and it was out of Judaism that Christianity had come. Hence the desperate need to make Jews see the light, to convert them, to make them confess that they had been wrong and the followers of Jesus right all along. Their refusal to be converted was of course a sign of their blindness, their stubbornness, but it left just the trace of a suspicion that perhaps they knew something that was hidden to Christians. Kruger shows that this paradox – this source of anxiety, already present in St John's Gospel and the Pauline epistles – deepened after 1096 and the first crusade, as Christians became more aware of the Jews in their midst (and the Muslims at their borders), as their scholars began to learn about Jewish traditions and, in Spain, as Jews came to prominence in many professions. For not only were individual

Jews clearly intelligent and thoughtful men, hardly the stereotypes of the Gospels, but it turned out that Judaism itself was not a single monolithic religion, stuck in its stubborn denial of Christianity, but a continuously evolving entity. In the great disputations which took place, mainly in Spain, in the later Middle Ages, it was most often Jewish converts who were selected to make the Christian case, and they did so now by arguing not just with the Old Testament but with the Talmud. These disputations were, however, always rigged, for the power lay with the Christians who had called them into being and dictated the rules by which both parties had to abide. The outcome was in effect decided beforehand, and the argument of the Christians was often contradictory to the point (for us, with hindsight) of absurdity: the Talmud, the Christians argued, was a pack of lies from beginning to end; but it also, amazingly, recognised the divinity of Christ, even though the Jews refused to see this.

In response, as Kruger shows, the Jews, constrained to appear under threat of death, to them and their communities, retreated into silence, refusing to damn themselves out of their own mouths, maintaining the final freedom of the oppressed; but of course by this token they gave the Christians the impression that they had no answer to their probing questions. At least in John 8 both sides are given equal weight: the Jews find it absurd that anyone should think any man the son of God, the Christians think the Jews are being wilfully blind in refusing to see that Jesus is precisely that. In Tortosa, in 1413, by contrast, Pope Benedict XIII opened the proceedings by saying: 'It is a known thing with me that my religion and faith is true, and that your Torah was once true but was abolished.' The frightening thing about this is not only that he believes it but that he *has* to believe it or he could no longer call himself a Christian. And surely Christians will have to go on believing it, however much they call for interfaith dialogue. At a time like the present, when another Benedict sits on the papal throne and the secret Other is no longer primarily the Jew but the Muslim, Steven Kruger's book should be of interest not only to scholars of medieval culture and theology but to every thinking person, whatever his or her own faith or lack of it.

1 A review of Steven F. Kruger, *The Spectral Jew: Conversion and Embodiment in Medieval Europe* (Minneapolis and London: University of Minnesota Press, 2006).

The Hebrew Poetry of Medieval Spain [1]

We seem to live, intellectually and emotionally, in sealed-off universes. Peter Dronke, polymath and medievalist, began his wonderful little 1968 book on the medieval lyric: 'This book is intended as an introduction to medieval lyric, secular and sacred, in both the Romance and the Germanic languages.' The reader could be forgiven for imagining (as I did) that what followed was an introduction to the entirety of the poetry of Europe in that period. Yet, though on re-reading I find that Dronke was clearly not unaware of the rich trilingual culture of medieval Iberia, his book passes over in silence a vast body of magnificent work in Arabic and Hebrew, written first in Spain and Portugal, and then (when those countries grew increasingly antagonistic to the Arabs and Jews in their midst) in Provence and Gascony. Meanwhile, readers of Hebrew poetry who probably have never heard of Arnaut Daniel or Walther von der Vogelweide, know the work of Shmuel HaNagid, Shelomo Ibn Gabirol, Moshe Ibn Ezra and Yehuda Halevi as well as readers of English know Milton or Keats, and even those who do not read poetry are familiar with many of their works, which figure prominently in the liturgies of Judaism.

Though there have been several translations of the work of these poets (who lived and worked between the end of the tenth and the middle of the twelfth century) into English – notably Gabriel Levin's beautiful selection of Yehuda Halevi, *Poems from the Diwan* – Peter Cole has in the past decade been establishing himself as the leading English language translator of this great body of work, with a selection of the poems of Shmuel Hanagid appearing in 1996 and one of the poems of Ibn Gabirol (dedicated to Gabriel Levin) in 2001. The present volume crowns his efforts. Not only does he give us samples from the work of fifty-four (yes, fifty-four) poets, but he embeds these in a dense thicket of commentary: a general introduction of twenty pages (with twenty-two pages of notes); introductions to each of the poets; notes to the poems, including the multitude of biblical references and comments on word-play impossible to reproduce in English; discussion of the form and prosody; scholarly information on provenance, attribution and so on (many of these poems were found by accident in the twentieth century, and some are still turning up); and, to conclude, a fascinating glossary of terms, such as '*adab*: A central term in classical Arabic – and, by extension, Hebrew – literature, *adab* connotes both learning in its fullness as a way of life and the signature style of the cultured person. It refers at once to disciplines of the mind and soul, good breeding, refinement, culture, and belles-lettres. Similar to the Greek notion of *paideia*.'; and, '*Vidu'i*: A section of the liturgy recited on fast days and days of penitence, especially between the New Year and the Day of Atonement. Sometimes incorporated into larger *piyyutim*. See, for example, Ibn Gabirol's *Kingdom's Crown* and Avner's "The Last Words of My Desire".'

As all this suggests, the book is a treasure trove, a labour of love and great erudition, which will open up to the reader a world of poetry and culture as rich as anything in human civilisation. Of course, no matter how good the translation and how full the notes, there is no substitute for the original. However, since readers of Hebrew are few and far between and a dual language edition would have made an already-bulky volume impossibly large and massively increased its price, Princeton University Press has sensibly solved the problem by providing the Hebrew originals online.

Many of the poems Dronke dealt with are anonymous; the poems in this anthology, on the other hand, were written by poets who were known and respected and the outlines of whose biographies, in most cases, are well known. We have to think of court poets like Chaucer and Gower, or of circles of friends like those around Guido Cavalcanti or John Donne. And the range is astonishing.

There are stylised love poems close to the Arabic, such as the mid-tenth-century 'A Fawn Sought in Spain' by Yitzhak Ibn Mar Shaul:

> A fawn sought in Spain
> works wonders with desire,
> and through it he controls
> all male and female creatures.
> Formed like the moon –
> his height adds to his splendor;
> his curly hair is crimson
> against his cheeks of pearl

There are powerful poems lamenting the loss of sons or brothers or patrons; religious poems which, perhaps unsurprisingly, remind one more of the Psalms than of other European religious lyrics of the period; there are extraordinary kabbalistic poems that remind one of Blake's Prophecies ('The name of the first warrior-king is Qadari'el, / and the name of the second is Magdi'el; and the name of the third / is Alfi 'el: and the name of the warrior-king you saw / at the beginning of that vision is Turi'el'). Many are acrostic poems, and a number work with constraints that would have delighted Raymond Queneau and Jacques Roubaud (himself the editor of a wonderful anthology of Provençal poems). Some form part of those poetic slanging matches earlier cultures were so fond of, like the *tensos* of the troubadours and the *flytings* of Dunbar. A large number are slight and witty, such as the many flea and fly poems, or Halevi's 'When a Lone Silver Hair', which is worth comparing to Herbert's 'The Harbingers':

> When a lone silver hair appeared on my head
> I plucked it out with my hand, and it said:
>
> 'You've beaten me one on one –
> but what will you do with the army to come?'

Cole is rightly proud of his inclusion of a recently discovered poem by a woman – the wife of the first poet in the anthology, Dunash Ben Labrat, who is credited with having first combined the Hebrew language and Arab poetic forms – but equally surprising is a poem that wittily flies in the face of the daily prayer that has always been a problem to liberal Jews, where the supplicant ends by thanking God for not having made him a woman. Here the author, Qalonymos Ben Qalonymos, who was renowned as a translator from both Arabic and Latin, ends his prayer by begging God: 'If only you would make me a female.' Amazingly, there are even poems about writer's block, such as this one by Shem Tov Ardutiel (late thirteenth century), who also wrote epigrams in Spanish and was much admired by Antonio Machado, from what sounds like a remarkable work, called *The Battles of the Pen and the Scissors*:

At night he says: 'Tomorrow I'll write,'
but there's nothing at all to back up his words;
the heaven's frost laughs in his face,
and the cackling of mocking ice is heard.

What a modern reader might find most surprising is the sexual explicitness of quite a few of the poems. Some time in the early twelfth century Yosef Ibn Tzaddik, a *dayyan* or religious judge as well as a poet, sent a poem of consolation to his friend Avraham Ibn Ezra, who, as Cole says, 'found himself in a most uncomfortable situation when his bride's menstrual period began just after the wedding ceremony but before the marriage could be consummated.' Playing with a number of biblical motifs, Ibn Tzaddik writes:

Take up this poem and let it console you,
bridegroom of blood who resembles a ram
perched on a cliff above a stream,
        where its thirst can't be quenched.

Delight in the doe of your desire.
So beautifully formed and fine to behold;
Look as you will, but do not touch her.

Ibn Ezra replies in the same Hebrew meter and with the same Hebrew rhyme:

The rivers of Eden flow along
        gently before me, and I am thirsty,
and like a man looking up at the sky,
        all I have is what I can see.
But a poem has come to offer me comfort –
        its words woven like the finest embroidery –
and the signs it mentions are already here
        and this is what they mean for me:
hugging and kissing, thigh over thigh,
an arm across shoulder and nape –
though now from that place where the milk runs full
        I turn as the Nazirite turns from the grape.

Sometimes the poet is utterly direct, like the early-fourteenth-century Todros Abulafia:

The day you left was bitter and dark,
        you finest thing, you – and when I think of it,
it feels like there's nothing left of my skin.
        Your feet, by far, were more beautiful,
                the day they mounted
        and wrapped my neck in a ring.

My feeling is that Cole is better at these occasional poems than at the great religious poems for which the major poets of the period are best known. It may be that the Hebrew of such poems is simply too alien to come across adequately in contemporary English, or that his Poundian orientation makes him respond more easily to the informal than to the grand and the hieratic. Or it may just be that I myself need more time to enter into them. However, by surrounding them with this sea of fascinating, more occasional verse, and by setting them in the rich context of his scholarship, he has performed an enormous service and produced a book which is by turns moving, charming, and funny. No one after this will be able to write a book on medieval poetry without taking the Hebrew and Arabic poets of Spain into account.

The title of this anthology is taken from a remark by the leading modern Palestinian poet, Mahmoud Darwish: 'Andalus [...] might be here or there, or anywhere [...] A meeting place of strangers in the project of building human culture [...] It is not only that there was a Jewish-Muslim co-existence, but that the fates of the two people were similar [...] Al-Andalus for me is the realisation of the dream of the poem.' One need not be a starry-eyed idealist to say: Hear hear!

1 A review of *The Dream of the Poem: Hebrew Poetry from Muslim and Christian Spain 950–1492*, translated, edited and introduced by Peter Cole (Princeton and Woodstock: Princeton University Press, 2007).

Sacred Trash[1]

At least once a month, from the ages of five to fifteen, I would take the little train from suburban Maadi to Cairo and back, a twenty-minute journey either way. Today the line is electrified and goes underground as it reaches Bab-el-Louk Station in Cairo (not far from Tahrir Square), but it still stops at Mari Girgis, or St George, on the way. This is where the Coptic Church stands, visible from the train, in what was once the centre of Old Cairo. Right next to the grand Coptic Church, though invisible from the train, is the tiny synagogue of Ben Ezra.

The synagogue once housed a remarkable treasure trove of written material, thrown any old how into a small room high up above the women's gallery, and handed over, quite unlawfully, in 1898 by my grandmother's great-uncle, Moise Cattaoui, then head of the Cairo Jewish community, to a Cambridge scholar to take back to England. The story of that transaction, of the cache that was shifted and of the scholars who subsequently deciphered it, has been told many times, but never so well as by Adina Hoffman and Peter Cole in *Sacred Trash: The Lost and Found World of the Cairo Geniza*.

The room that housed the material was known as a *geniza*, from the Persian *ganj*, meaning 'hidden treasure'. In the Talmud, the word usually implies concealment: any writing that seemed heretical should, it was felt, be *ganuz*, hidden away. Gradually that came to include manuscripts that time or human hand had rendered unfit for use, but which could not be thrown out due to their sacred content and so required removal to a safe place that would allow them to decay of their own accord. In Old Cairo the ban was extended even further and soon any piece of writing thought to include the name of God, and finally anything in

Hebrew, was thrown into the upstairs room, there gradually to expire.

And so it remained for the better part of a thousand years, as Cairo shifted northwards, as the synagogue of Ben Ezra became a backwater and as Egypt lost its place at the centre of a thriving Mediterranean culture. But in the nineteenth century, material that had lain hidden for centuries in the Geniza, preserved by the dry climate of the region, began to surface, and stray items started to be sold to Western buyers in the markets of the region. In 1896, Agnes Lewis and Margaret Gibson – widowed Scottish sisters resident in Cambridge and remarkable scholars of Arabic and Syriac – bought a few such fragments on their way through Cairo. Back home they showed them to their friend Solomon Schechter, Cambridge's Reader in Rabbinics, who at once grasped their significance. What he had in his hand was a Hebrew fragment of the apocryphal book known as Ecclesiasticus or Ben Sira, which until then had been known only in Greek and Syriac versions. As it happened, Schechter was at that very moment engaged in fierce controversy with his Oxford counterpart, D. S. Margoliouth, over whether the book was Jewish at all. The idea that he was actually holding in his hand something that proved he was right and his rival wrong was almost too much for him. He had to go and see for himself.

Schechter set off for Cairo in the autumn of 1897. Establishing himself there, he gained the good will of the Grand Rabbi and the heads of the Jewish community and was at last allowed into the Ben Ezra synagogue. Wading waist deep in paper, he began to sift, and for four weeks worked in appalling conditions, but with growing excitement. The small room teemed with insects undisturbed for generations, while every movement raised clouds of dust – 'Ich full of spots bin', he wrote in his charming bilingualism to his wife. He left the printed matter alone and concentrated on the manuscripts; there he uncovered, often stuck together, fragments of letters, bills, contracts, poems, biblical and Talmudic material, and much else besides. He filled four trunks and, since he was beginning to arouse the suspicions of the Egyptian authorities, decided that was enough. With the help of Lord Cromer, the de facto ruler of Egypt, Schechter shipped the trunks to Cambridge.

When news got out that the university had acquired this material some were sceptical. As late as 1913, Margoliouth wrote: 'About a score of years ago the University of Cambridge was presented with the contents of a huge waste paper basket, imported from Egypt where such stores abound. The material contained in these repositories is almost always valueless, like the gods of the gentiles unable to do good or harm, and so neither worth preserving nor worth destroying.' But history has proved Margoliouth wrong. Schechter's discoveries in the Geniza opened up an entire civilisation and showed Cairo to be the hub of a vibrant culture in which Jews and Arabs successfully intermingled for hundreds of years.

For over a century, scores of extraordinary scholars, mainly Jewish, mainly Eastern European, but almost all working in London, Cambridge or New York, have given their lives to deciphering, integrating and understanding what Schechter uncovered. Biblical and Talmudic material has emerged; innumerable poems have been added to the corpus of early medieval Hebrew literature; philosophical and religious controversies of the period have been elucidated; and the multitude of letters, legal documents, memos and lists have enabled scholars like S. D. Goitein to build up a detailed picture of Eastern Mediterranean Jewish society in the early Middle Ages. *Sacred Trash* is a celebration of their labour.

Peter Cole is a poet and translator of distinction. His wife Adina Hoffman has written a remarkable biography of a contemporary Palestinian poet. Both are deeply involved in the cultural politics of the Middle East. Through Ibis Editions, their small press based in Jerusalem, they have brought out numerous works about the Levant in the belief that literature is essential for an 'understanding between individuals and peoples, and for the discovery of common ground'. In this book they have demonstrated just that, giving us a wonderfully passionate and lively account of a civilisation we could not have imagined existed and of the men and women whose enthusiasm and dedication has brought it to light.

1 A review of Adina Hoffman and Peter Cole, *Sacred Trash: The Lost and Found World of the Cairo Geniza* (New York: Nextbook/Schocken, 2011).

Claudel and the Bible[1]

FOR ONCE, Auden got it wrong. Time has not pardoned Paul Claudel; it has not even been kind to him. It is today almost impossible to imagine that, as poet and playwright, he once held a place in France comparable to that of Yeats and Eliot in England, Rilke in Germany, or Montale in Italy. Even in his native country, he is now more revered as a monument than admired as a living presence, his poetry unread, his plays largely unperformed, his peculiar brand of Catholic traditionalism totally out of favour.

Though he died only in 1955, he was born as long ago as 1868, so that he belongs to the generation of Péguy and Bergson, and his immediate poetic precursors were Rimbaud and Mallarmé. In the course of his long life he poured out a seemingly endless stream of poems, plays, essays on poetics and on painting and meditations on theology and the Bible. His Collected Works run to twenty-six volumes, and that does not include the letters. Yet all the while he was pursuing an active career as a diplomat, which took him to China, Japan, Prague, Copenhagen, Rio and, eventually, as Ambassador, to Washington and Brussels. At once more worldly and more religious than his main literary rivals, untainted by the political events of the 1930s or by Vichy, he should have emerged, at the time of his death, as one of the great European writers of the first half of the century. But while the controversy which surrounds Eliot or Mann is a sign of their continuing vitality, Claudel has simply faded into obscurity.

'As far as I'm concerned I'm done with drama and profane poetry', he wrote to Stanislas Fumet, the founder and director of the liberal Catholic review *Temps Present*, from Washington in 1930. 'I shall devote my last years almost exclusively to thinking about Sacred Scripture. It is time to place the Bible once again on its rung as the Word of God, and what would be a word which did not address itself to us?' Now Michel Malicet and his team have culled the Collected Works and the Claudel archives for these biblical meditations and issued them all (up to 1946, but the editors say nothing about a second volume) in one enormous tome: almost 1,400 large pages of text and 500 of notes. Only the first fifty pages of *Le Poète et la Bible* are drawn from the years 1910–30, the rest belong to the following sixteen years, for the majority of which Claudel had retired to the family home in Brangues, and when the political events of the times forced him into an agonised questioning of God's role in history.

Claudel's *bêtes noires* are the atheism of the nineteenth century and the liberal Protestant theology of his time. The growth of rationalism has led to the disappearance of 'the ancient moral and symbolic tradition of interpretation so long pursued by the Fathers and Doctors of the Church'. What we need is something different from philological and textual quarrels: we need to take God at His Word, to deliver ourselves totally and naively to the Word of God as it is given us by the Church, to love it, to re-speak it in ourselves and, following the instruction given by the angel to St John on Patmos, to swallow it, to make it pass right through our bowels by way of the teeth, the tongue and the taste buds.

> If instead of attaching ourselves to [...] the gross critique of texts, to pseudo-historical fantasies, to gratuitous and in most cases inept hypotheses about the psychology and intentions of the redactors, we humbly admitted with the Church and the Fathers that the Bible is the Word of God and that the Holy Spirit is the constant inspirer who, from end to end, has guided the pen and mobilised the vocation of the diverse writers, what an enlargement of the mind that would be!

His Catholic faith, his reading of the Church Fathers and his poet's response to literature thus led him to a rediscovery of forgotten ways of reading the Bible, ways which scholars like Jean Danielou and Henri de Lubac were beginning to bring to the attention of the academic world, but to which Claudel found his way instinctively. At times, he is as critical of contemporary Catholic teaching as he is of Protestant scholarship, and one of his essays was even refused permission by the Church to appear, but by and large he forms part of a renaissance of Catholicism in France which has its roots in tradition and is very different from its manifestations in Britain (though Claudel did translate Chesterton's *Orthodoxy*).

A good example of Claudel's method of using the Bible to read the Bible is his little essay on Psalm 28 (29 in the Authorised Version). He starts with a meditation on David dancing before the Ark and being derided by his prudish wife, Michal. What we need, says Claudel, is a 'dancing commentary' to this great poem in praise of God's power. Since the Vulgate superscription (not in the Hebrew or the AV) is 'Psalmus David in consummatione tabernaculi', he turns at once to an examination of the making of the tabernacle in Exodus 25ff. And what, he wonders, is the significance of the two 'sets' of sheets, each formed of five pieces and joined together by fifty gold rings and fifty cords of hyacinth (26: 3–6)? Are they not the sky and the earth, the Old and New Testaments, Sacrifice and Grace? Sky and earth lead him back to Genesis 1, and then, by way of Isaiah and the giving of the tablets of the law, he returns to the Psalm and its striking image: 'The voice of Yahweh over the waters! Yahweh over the multitudinous waters!' Then, via Revelation and Hebrews, back to Exodus and the making of the tabernacle, until he reaches the climactic verses of the Psalm, which describe Yahweh sitting enthroned over the Flood as King for ever: The waters of sin have overwhelmed us, but they are counterbalanced by the waters of abounding grace which, as Romans 5: 20–21 reminds us, are more powerful than death. Mary, the Mother of God, whose name in Latin is 'the sea', inhabits the ocean and an ocean of grace flows from her breast. Thus is the ancient figure of the Ark consummated.

In the essay on Isaiah 7–12, we see Claudel bringing his experience as a diplomat to bear on the story of the confrontation of King Ahaz of Judah and the prophet Isaiah. Ahaz, faced by threats from two petty kings and with the might of Assyria looming in the background, wants reassurance, but Isaiah only warns him that the time for negotiation is over and that a cataclysm is about to engulf him. Ahaz wants a sign? He shall have one: a virgin is with child and will soon give birth to a son whom she will call Immanuel. The land will be ravaged and the people taken into exile, but one day a remnant shall return, Yahweh will dry up the gulf of the Sea of Egypt, and the people will walk dry-shod as they once did in the escape from Egypt.

Claudel brushes aside the problem of the Hebrew word *alma*: is it to be translated virgin or maiden? The Church says the former, and sees in this a prophecy of the birth of Christ; modern scholarship insists on the latter. But how can that be right, since what is at issue is a miraculous event? What the entire passage shows us is the House of David, in the person of Ahaz, rejecting what God offers it, but the informed reader will know that what the Jews reject the Gospels will offer to mankind.

Claudel is here at his most patristic and traditional. He gives us an insight into how the Bible was read for centuries, and makes us see the sense and richness of such a reading. But how far can a non-Catholic go along with him? Take his interpretation of Isaiah 7: 15: 'On curds and honey will he feed until he knows how to refuse evil and choose good.' The tree of Good and Evil stood in the Garden of Eden, says Claudel, but it is only with the Crucifixion that mankind really understood the meaning of what it is to choose good or evil. The tree of the Cross is prefigured in the tree of the Garden, but is foretold here by the prophet. If everything in the Bible is significant and all is written through God's inspiration, then, of course, such a reading makes sense, and *figura* is not some special technique of interpretation but a certain vision of the world and of history.

Like the Church Fathers, Claudel moves with ease between figural and moral allegory: the tree of the Garden of Eden prefigures the Cross, but the obdurate Pharaoh of Exodus is Human Reason; Sarah in the Book of Tobit is the Human Soul in Exile, her seven husbands who die before they sleep with her are the Seven Deadly Sins, the miraculous fish which restores Tobit's sight is Jesus Christ; St Peter's boat is the Church, while the 'daughter of Abraham', bent in two, in Revelation, is the Synagogue.

For Claudel, a number of Old Testament books, such as Leviticus and Numbers, are 'dead letters', and he tends to favour the Psalms, the Prophets, and the later books such as Job and Ruth, and apocryphal books such as Tobit. His introduction to a now forgotten book on Ruth by a French cleric provides us with the fullest exposition of his method. Since Bossuet, he says, the traditional interpretation of Scripture has been lost. We need to live the Bible once again, not use it to tell us about the history or mythology of the Ancient Near East. Yet, as with his reading of the Book of Tobit, when he finally gets down to it, he can only allegorise. Or rather, he moves between a poetic retelling of the events narrated and a sense that, when we ask 'what it all means', the only answer can be allegorical: Elimelech – who comes out of Bethlehem, the House of Bread, and whose name means The King God – is Jesus Christ, who is driven by hunger for the souls of men and who dies *extra muros*; Naomi, his wife, is the Church; their two sons are the missionaries who seek new churches in the midst of the pagan enemy; and Ruth, of course, who chooses to enter the House of Bread, is Faith. The notion that there might be a third way, one which takes the story seriously and stays with it, drawing out its non-allegorical implications, a way which has led Martin Buber, Robert Alter, Jan Fokkelman, Meir Sternberg and others to open up the Bible for us afresh, seems never to cross Claudel's mind, as it never crossed that of St Augustine or St Gregory; the pull of allegory, the sense that Christ explains everything if only we open our eyes, is just too strong.

This means that Claudel's way of reading is naturally apocalyptic, and the two longest pieces in *Le Poète et la Bible*, amounting between them to more than 200,000 words, are in fact attempts to respond to the challenge of the Book of Revelation. In 1928, following an invitation by a publisher, Claudel began to write about Revelation, though he had been thinking about that book ever since his conversion in 1895. *Au Milieu des vitraux de l'Apocalypse* was the result, the title referring to the fact that as the sunlight brings to life the images in a stained-glass window, so his commentary will bring the images of Revelation to life. It begins as a series of conversations with his daughter, then moves into letters from his diplomatic post at Washington, first to his daughter and then to his friend Agnes Meyer. The loose form suits the poet admirably, but the book was never finished, and was only published after his death. In 1940, sitting in his chateau in Brangues, with the Germans in Paris and France in disarray, he returned to the project more systematically, but the result is less convincing, both because the form does not suit his essentially intuitive response to the text and because the pressure of external events drove him to do what he had earlier resisted, which is to draw precise parallels between the text and current events. In a companion piece, 'Prophecy and Birds', he half laughs at himself for this, citing one of Dostoevsky's characters 'who imagines that the star Absinth which falls on the earth to poison it signifies the spreading network of railways'; but he himself goes on to find references in the biblical account, not just to Hitler and Stalin and the collapse of the dollar, but even to the Maginot Line.

Both works, though, are essentially much more profound than that. Once again, Claudel's poetic instinct and deep study of the Church Fathers lead him to a reading of the Bible that is more akin to that of Spenser and Milton, as rediscovered by Northrop Frye, than to that of modern scholarship or theology. Moving with assurance from the diatribes of Isaiah and Jeremiah against Babylon and Tyre to Ezekiel's vision of the Heavenly City, Claudel brings out the coherence and power of the apocalyptic mode in the Bible at large. This may not be 'imaginative literature' in the accepted sense of the term, but its nearest equivalent in our own day is Thomas Mann's own anguished meditation on history and evil in the great novel he was writing far away in America at exactly the same time: *Doktor Faustus*.

But it is here too that Claudel's traditional Catholicism leads him to strike the most awkward notes. Not only does he sometimes sound like an Ayatollah – as when he equates Satan with Luther, Voltaire, Robespierre, Hugo, Renan, Hitler, and Stalin – but there is something profoundly disturbing about the way he deals with a topic he not only cannot avoid but rightly feels the need to tackle head-on: the Jewish question. Indeed, at the very moment war was breaking out, in August 1939, he devoted an entire essay to this topic, 'Moab', which is very much of a piece with his work on Revelation. Visiting Palestine in 1906, Claudel had been struck by the great red escarpment that juts out into the Dead Sea on its eastern flank and which, according to the Bible, was once inhabited by the Moabites. His argument in the 1939 essay is that this people, at first an enemy of the Hebrews, comes to be identified, in the course of the Bible, with the Hebrews themselves, in so far as they rejected their prophets and turned to the worship of idols. The remnant who chose to listen, on the other hand, found their fulfilment in the Church. Is it not significant that the Hebrew alphabet goes from Aleph to Taw, that is, from the beginning of the world to the Tree of the Cross, while that of the Church goes from Alpha to Omega, from the Beginning to the End? Claudel recognises that the Jewish people have stood, in the course of their history, for opposition to tyranny and for elevated moral values, but how, he wonders, have they not paid attention to Job's cry, 'I know that my Redeemer liveth', and not understood that Jesus Christ is that Redeemer? 'And you, Israel, new Moab', he cries out, 'do not stand any longer petrified in the contemplation of Jerusalem, of the seat of your ancient glory. It is nothing but a tomb and a ruin. *Surrexit non est hic.*' Convert! he pleads, return to the fold. Let it be thus! he concludes.

Reading 'Moab', I was reminded of those Christian-Jewish disputations of the Middle Ages, in which there was indeed debate but no meeting of minds: 'I have not sent for you in order to prove which of our religions is true,' said Pope Benedict XIII at the Tortosa disputation, 'for it is perfectly known to me that my religion is true and that your religion has been superseded.' The origins of such an attitude are, of course, already to be found in the New Testament, notably in John 8. It is disconcerting, though, to find it still there, unaltered by the rhetoric and deeds of the Nazis, in the mouth of a humane and intelligent man like Claudel. It raises the question of whether Christianity can ever really recognise the Jews without giving up its essence.

The editors have undertaken a mammoth task in annotating these infinitely varied and wide-ranging texts. They give us every manuscript variant and a wealth of notes, as well as often essay-length introductions to the different items. Yet their work leaves much to be desired. The notes are often arbitrary, many references are allowed to pass without identification, and the indexes are woefully incomplete. At times, when the editors berate Claudel for his waywardness, they sound like the very pedants he himself criticises, while at others they indulge in sideswipes at those they consider inferior to their man which are reminiscent of Claudel himself at his most bigoted, as when they remark that next to him even Proust and Gide appear 'maquillés et fardés de poudre de riz' ('made-up and with too much rice powder'). The sad truth is, though, that Proust and even Gide have lasted a good deal better than Claudel.

1 A review of Paul Claudel, *Le Poète et la Bible, Volume I: 1910–1946*, edited by Michel Malicet with Dominique Millet and Xavier Tilliette (Paris: Gallimard, 1998).

'Like a Bad Russian Novel': Eliot in His Letters[1]

IN THE FINEST of his early quatrain poems Eliot, playing on the Elizabethan use of 'nightingale' as a term for a prostitute, describes a louche meeting in a seedy bar in ambiguous terms: we feel that anything might be about to happen, or nothing.

The host with someone indistinct
Converses at the door apart,
The nightingales are singing near
The convent of the Sacred Heart,

And sang within the bloody wood
When Agamemnon cried aloud,
And let their liquid siftings fall
Upon the stiff dishonoured shroud.

Agamemnon's great cry, as Klytemnestra cuts him down in the bath, thrice repeated in Aeschylus, and used (in Greek) by Eliot as his epigraph, is what the modern protagonist (and so the modern poet) is incapable of uttering (perhaps, after all, this is just a nightmare from which he will soon awake), yet nightingales sing today as they sang then and as they will go on singing in ages to come, and let their 'liquid siftings' fall indifferently on Agamemnon and on Sweeney. Something of the pathos and horror of that scenario hovers over this third volume of Eliot's letters, as it does the second, covering between them the years after the publication of *The Waste Land*, 1923–27.

On the surface life goes tediously on. Eliot is now firmly ensconced as a publisher at the new firm of Faber & Gwyer and as the editor of the literary magazine, *The Criterion* (*The New Criterion* after January 1926). The bulk of the letters in this bulky volume consist of his handling of the day-to-day affairs of *The Criterion* and, to a lesser extent, of Faber & Gwyer. By the standards of Keats, van Gogh, Lawrence or Beckett, this is tedious stuff, but it has its own kind of fascination. Eliot was an excellent editor – courteous, firm, persuasive when contributors were reluctant, emollient when, as frequently happened, they took umbrage, keeping his hands firmly on the reins yet letting his chosen contributors have their say even when he disagreed with them. And always keeping his eyes firmly fixed on his goal, that of producing a first-class literary review with a visible European presence. To that end he woos Ortega y Gasset, Valéry, Montale and many others, usually successfully, tries to get debates going on such topics as West v East, and to publish chronicles of what is going on not only in the different European countries, but in art, music and drama. Throughout he relies on a few henchmen, above all Herbert Read, though it is he who always leads. And, it must be said, in comparison with today's journals, the standards he sets are high indeed.

He also has to deal with the transition, much debated but finally accepted by all, from a quarterly to a monthly, and with the volatile and opinionated part-owner, Lady Rothermere – no easy task. This culminates in a visit to her home in Switzerland in the Autumn of 1927, where an unholy row ensues. 'In brief,' he writes to Richard Aldington, 'we have fallen out completely with Lady Rothermere, who, it appears, dislikes the *Criterion* intensely and who wishes to withdraw her capital from it immediately. We at first intended to shut up shop at once, but a number of people have objected and interposed so that a small collection has been made in order to run the January number at least, while a few people are scurrying about to see if the capital which has been withdrawn can be replaced from other sources.' Such are the travails of a literary editor, and anyone who has tried to run a literary journal or has an interest in the cultural health of a modern democracy will read these letters with appreciation of Eliot's unflagging energy, goodwill, realism and vision.

But of course the immense effort he put into the journal, and into his duties at Faber & Gwyer were not only the result of an ingrained Puritan work ethic, but also a way of keeping at bay the horrors that were besetting his private life. Already in a letter to Middleton Murry from mid-April 1925, printed in *Volume II*, he had written:

> In the last ten years – gradually, but deliberately – I have made myself into *a machine*. I have done it deliberately – in order to endure, in order not to feel – *but it has killed* V[ivien]. [...] But the dilemma – to kill another person by being dead, or to kill them by being alive? Is it best to make oneself a machine, and kill them by not giving nourishment, or to be alive, and kill them by wanting something that one *cannot* get from that person? Does it happen that two persons' lives are absolutely hostile? Is it true that sometimes one can only live by another's dying?'

The confusion and turmoil caused by Vivien's growing anxieties and instability, which had lasted for some ten years, starts, in the years covered by this new volume, to recede a little. Vivien seems to accept that there is something seriously wrong with her, and to spend more and more time in what are euphemistically called 'rest-houses', either in the South of France or outside Paris, and Eliot officially announces that she is convalescing or 'recovering', while the two of them and those closest to them know that something is coming to an end, to the relief, at least, of Eliot himself.

Nevertheless, it is a shock to be confronted by Vivien's own letters. One of the strengths of these volumes, as many commentators have noted, is the inclusion of letters to or merely connected with, as well as from, Eliot – though these are necessarily even more selective and dependent on choices made by the editors than are Eliot's own letters. 'Dear Tom,' she writes in January from a rest-home in Sussex, 'Do you wish your wife to be the boon companion of your masseur. I shd like an answer.' In April she writes to Ottoline Morrell: 'I am in great trouble, do not know what to do. In great fear. I wish I could see you.' In July, this, to Middleton Murry:

> You sent me the necessary words: 'Keep calm & quiet.' I managed to for that day, but you know, I *can't*. Something awful has happened to me. I can't help myself & I can't ask God to help me. I don't ask Tom to help me now. I am quite alone & I have nothing at all inside. It is absolutely dark. I must speak to you honestly, for there is no one else who wd at the same time understand & not be *hurt* by it.
>
> I can't keep calm & quiet, John. It's no use. Why does Tom love me? You know I love Tom in a way that destroys us both. And it is *all* my life. Nothing remains.

One's heart goes out to her in her pain and confusion – but one can also see how impossible such confusion – and often delusion – must have been for her husband to deal with. On the other hand it is not always like this. His brother Henry writes to their mother: 'On the last evening we were in London Tom and Vivien and Theresa and I went to a hotel in Kensington to dinner and had such a jolly time. We then danced a while, Vivien was in fine humor and very nice.' Partly this is dictated by the fact that both sons felt it was imperative to keep any problems from their mother, and partly it was that in the early months of 1926 Vivien was so volatile, almost normal one day and determined to make the best of things, deep in depression and terror the next. By September Henry is writing to his brother: 'The doctors of Paris agree that there is no trace of mental disease proper, and that the delusions are projections of a state of emotional anguish. To this I would add, as my opinion, that the state of emotional anguish is self-induced, voluntarily and deliberately. It is not melancholia, which is something more involuntary. It is something which Vivien herself could put a stop to at any moment, by an effort of will.' His enormous letter ends: 'My final advice, with regard to the whole matter, is simply, *forget*. The elasticity of your nature will tend to pull you back to the norm. Do not be too much together, mix with people, and relax and regain strength – you as well as she.' Advice well-meant, of course, but, like all such advice, useless. 'You are in some sort of purgatory,' Eliot writes to Middleton Murry. 'I am perhaps thoroughly damned.' But on the whole he remains guarded, Old Possum, even to his closest friends, even to his brother. Only the news of his mother's grave illness in August 1927 causes him to open up and reveal his deepest feelings and thoughts, and then the shock of such a letter is immense precisely because he has remained so buttoned up throughout.

> Dearest mother, your letter made me very sad; you speak as if you would perhaps never see me again either here or elsewhere. In the first place I hope to come to America and spend a month with you next winter, and in the second place I have a much more positive conviction than you have that I shall see you in another life. It is rather too soon perhaps to talk of that! but I somehow have a much firmer conviction than you have, and I wish that you felt as I do; for although I am sure of seeing you at least once more in this life, yet as either of us, or anybody, might suddenly be taken away by some accident, I should like to feel that you felt sure as I do of our meeting again. I feel that the 'future life', or our future meetings, may not be in the least like anything that we can imagine; but that if it is different we shall then realise that it is right and shall not then wish it to be like what we can now imagine.

Clearly, profound changes have been taking place in Eliot since the writing of *The Waste Land*. These have been well documented, but it is fascinating to see him in the course of these letters moving slowly towards the Anglo-Catholicism to which he committed himself in 1927. It is part of the transition from the confusion and anguish of the previous years to a more settled and considered life, accepting and incorporating his relations with Vivien into a larger vision, though whether it was a change in their relationship which led him to embrace the Anglican faith or the other way round is a moot point – no doubt it was a dialectical process. And at the same time as he was negotiating to be baptised he was also arranging to become a British citizen – doing his best to keep both manoeuvres from the papers and to remain invisible as much as possible.

His poetry was changing too. As he was to say much later: 'I thought my poetry was over after 'The Hollow Men', and it was only because my publishers had started a series of "Ariel" poems and I let myself promise to contribute, that I began again. And writing the "Ariel" poems released the stream, and led directly to *Ash Wednesday*.' But he was very clear that this new direction was in no way a repudiation of the old. As he wrote to William Force Stead in January 1927: 'One may change one's ideas, sentiments and point of view from time to time; one would be rather atrophied if one did not; but change of mind is a very different thing from repudiation [...] One might as well repudiate infancy and childhood.' Critics and biographers love to work with abrupt and violent changes of direction, but one of the pleasures of reading an artist's letters, especially as leisurely a collection as this is proving to be, is that one gets far closer to the tiny, seemingly random, changes that lead eventually to something quite new.

Taking up more time than his poetry (he claimed to Conrad Aiken that he had written 'The Journey of the Magi' 'in three quarters of an hour after church time and before lunch one Sunday morning, with the assistance of half a bottle of Booth's gin') was the preparation of the Clark Lectures at Cambridge (one a week for eight weeks on 'The Metaphysical Poetry of the Seventeenth Century with Special Reference to Donne, Crashaw and Cowley'), the reviewing he did (mainly for the *TLS*), and his ambitious project to write three volumes tracing the transition from the medieval to the modern world, a project he quickly dropped but whose central themes continued to haunt him. Here we can see him exploring the historical and cultural dimensions of his move towards Anglo-Catholicism in essays on Lancelot Andrews, Machiavelli, Seneca and the Elizabethans, Dante and Donne; and in epistolary conversations with Mario Praz and the German translator of *The Waste Land*, the great cultural historian Ernst Robert Curtius, as well as with friends like Read and Murry, and churchmen like Lord Halifax. To the Bishop of Oxford he explains:

> I admit that I am not primarily a Thomist. I am an Aristotelian and my interest in St Thomas is partly in St Thomas as a reviver of Aristotle. I feel that St Thomas is a witness: if the Aristotelian could be so magnificently revived in the thirteenth century, then I feel that it can be revived again in the twentieth century [...] You say that you cannot see how the scholastic theory can be expressed in terms of recent psychology. The fact that it cannot be expressed in terms of recent psychology is to me a point in its favour. What I am interested to do is to examine the basis of modern psychology, for I think that it rests on wholly unwarranted assumptions.

Of course this takes us back to many of the essays published in *The Sacred Wood* (1920) and to many of Eliot's most famous pronouncements about the dissociation of sensibility in the seventeenth century and the unified sensibility of earlier eras. These have unfortunately become reified, in large part because of Eliot's popularity and the central role of so many of his pronouncements in the academic study of English in the fifty or so years after they were adumbrated. Seeing them being worked through again in different forms here as Eliot struggled to make sense of what was for him self-evident but extremely difficult to articulate, we are made aware of how much this was a living issue for him (and should be for us, for it has not gone away). His sense of the inadequacy of romantic attitudes to the self and of modern psychology to make sense of the world and of how liberating an immersion in traditional and pre-individualistic cultures could be for himself as both poet and confused individual, is at the root of all his art and thought. In the early years it led to a powerful ironic and apocalyptic voice; now, he finds it leading him towards a vision of a possible twentieth-century reinvention of pre-Renaissance culture, one which is bound up with his recognition (as he saw it) of the inadequacy of the attitudes in which he had been brought up and an embracing of Anglo-Catholicism. In July 1926 he writes to his brother Henry: 'Unitarianism is a bad preparation for brass tacks like birth, copulation, death, hell, heaven and insanity: they all fall within the classification of Bad Form. It often seems to me very bizarre that a person of my antecedents should have had a life like a bad Russian novel.'

As the editors point out, part of this is repeated word for word in (or taken from) the 'Fragment of an Agon' that he was working on at the time:

> Birth, and copulation, and death.
> That's all the facts when you come to brass tacks:
> Birth, and copulation, and death.

But simply to note this is to deflect the thrust of the letter, which is that the system of values in which he had been raised was simply inadequate to cope with the world in which he found himself. Many years later William Golding was to write in a similar vein about the inadequacy of the liberalism in which *he* had been raised to prepare him or his generation for Hitler and the evil of Nazism. For Eliot, Anglo-Catholicism was simply more realistic than either the religion of his fathers or the atheism of men like Bertrand Russell. 'I have just read your little pamphlet on Christianity,' he writes to the latter in June 1927. 'With some sadness. All the reasons you advance were familiar to me, *I think*, at the age of six or eight;

and I confess that your pamphlet seems to me a piece of childish folly. But I was brought up as an Atheist, and you were evidently brought up, and in my opinion remain, an Evangelical. Why don't you stick to mathematics?' Such vehemence is unusual in these largely urbane and polite letters, but what Russell stood for clearly riled Eliot. To Aldington he writes: 'Read any of the more recent philosophical works of Bertrand Russell, and see what a dark age of gross superstition we still live in. The middle ages were a period of scientific superstition, this is an age of philosophic superstition.'

The problem with such views, so strongly held, is that they can lead to superstition quite as easily as Russell's. Too often in these letters we find Eliot lapsing into purely automatic and unthinking sneers at Communists and Jews, who of course take on the garb of secular cosmopolitanism, the very opposite of what Eliot is slowly inching his way towards as his ideal of organic nationhood underpinned by Faith. 'The "foreign agitator", sometimes Russian and often Jew, is no longer confined to America,' he writes to his mother. 'He is conspicuous in England and still more so in France. But France is in a far worse way than England [...] In France, several of my friends (of the royalist party) might at any time be shot at by some communist fanatic, and even in case of death, the chances are 100 to 1 that the assassin would escape with a light punishment.' This borders dangerously on extreme right-wing fantasy.

The championing of Maritain and Father d'Arcy is one thing; of Maurras and *Action Française* quite another. Eliot always remained loyal to Maurras, writing as late as 1954 to William Force Stead: 'I do owe Maurras a good deal, and retain my admiration for him', which could be read either as a brave refusal to ride with the wind or as a wilful burying of his head in the sand.

Eliot was not only corresponding with his royalist friends in France and making plans to enter the Church of England, he was also manoeuvring to take up British nationality. Stephen Spender, in *Eliot* (1975) was to quote Vivien as saying that for him 'becoming an English citizen and being received into the English Church' was but a single step, and in March of 1950 an article in *Time* reported him as saying: 'Here I am, making a living, enjoying my friends here. I don't like being a squatter. I might as well take the full responsibility.' To his brother, in October 1927, he merely says: 'At the moment I am waiting (PRIVATE AND CONFIDENTIAL) for my British Passport, as I have applied for Naturalisation and been accepted, having pulled a few strings with the Home Secretary. If this shocks you I will present you my reasons; in any case, don't tell mother.'

One wonders if the embracing of Nation, King, Church, and Tradition in this wholehearted way was the result not just of the personal crisis in his life brought about by his marriage to Vivien, but of a crisis that went back to the traumas of the war and the devastation it left behind, and even, perhaps, to Eliot's sense of always having been a 'squatter'; the St Louis boy feeling himself in the Harvard inhabited by the ghosts of his ancestors to be no less of an outsider than Kafka in Prague or Pessoa in Lisbon. The animus against Gerontion, whose 'house is a decayed house / And the jew squats on the window sill, the owner / Spawned in some estaminet in Antwerp' – is this not an animus against himself? Is this not where the power of this poem, like *Prufrock* before it, comes from? But where Borges recovered with pride the Jew in his past and used it to probe the limitations of an Argentinian cultural nationalism, Eliot went in the opposite direction, feeling that what he had to do was eradicate the squatter for ever, bury him in a new, nationalist identity.

Fortunately, he did not entirely succeed. Mary Colum, the wife of Padraic Colum, who knew Eliot in those years, wrote later:

> He was not in the least like any Englishman I ever knew, yet that he was of clear English descent one could not but realize; one felt that England was his homeland; he needed it, not for his happiness, but to fulfil whatever dream of life he had [...] Nevertheless, Eliot looked a little alien in London; he was very carefully dressed, not

> in the *dégagé* British manner, but in the deliberate American way; his handsome face and figure had not at all the British look; he seemed to be aware of his own alienness, for he told us of the remark of a French writer of immediate American-Spanish ancestry: 'All of us born in North or South America feel more at home with each other than we do with anybody in Europe.'

Clearly, whatever changes to his personality the embracing of Church and State would bring about were not yet visible. His friends worried for him. 'Dear friend T. S.', wrote Lady Rothermere. 'I am so sorry you won't come & see me here [at Fribourg in Switzerland]. You would so enjoy it – (& you don't enjoy much in your life – it's rather like *The Criterion* – a bit dry! That's what's wrong with your work, lack of emotion in your life). Oh, dear, what am I talking about – I think my illness must have upset my brain!! – Forgive me cher ami & believe me always to be your friend (& in spite of all!) admirer.' That, of course, could be dismissed; less easy, though, when the correspondent was Geoffrey Faber, the man who had brought him into Faber & Gywer, and asked him to be godfather to his son. In a remarkable letter in which he discusses in turn the lack of philosophical awareness in contemporary historians, the joys of fishing and the language of Shakespeare, Faber turns at last to more personal matters. First he ventures some remarks about the poetry:

> You have, as a poet, reached a curiously marked position in contemporary literature. It is the combination of your very modern-seeming obscurity, with sincerity & power, which has done this for you. But unless you now, having achieved your position, set yourself to write less obscurely, you will not go any further. You will remain in literary history – a sort of ossified specimen of genius destroyed by an impossible fashion, which itself created.

As if this wasn't bad enough, he goes on to criticise Eliot's way of life:

> I do think that, for whatever reason, you are putting yourself in some danger by the rigidity of your way of life. It is not right that you should chain yourself to a routine – it will cramp your mind, & ultimately be fatal to you both as poet & critic, if for no other reason than that it will divorce you further & further from the common man. I cannot help at times suspecting that the difficulties are, to some extent, of your own forging.

That last phrase interestingly echoes Henry's equally well-meant comment about Vivien. And though Faber ends by asking Eliot to 'forgive me if I am being cruelly unjust, out of sheer ignorance,' this must have been a devastating letter to receive. On the one hand it seemed to show that even one of his closest friends (and his own publisher!), really had no idea what his poetry was about; on the other it resembled the kind of well-meaning letter an addict to drink or drugs will get from his friends: For your own sake, change your way of life. The answer to that is always: Thank you very much, I wish I could, but this is the one I'm saddled with.

Eliot tried replying, penning a letter three days later: 'I feel impelled to try and pull out a few of the spines that the friendly porpentine has discharged into me,' he begins. 'If anyone asked me what I take to be the good things of life,' he goes on, 'I should say, primarily, heroism and saintliness.' Then he goes into a long disquisition on the love of God, but stops short, realising he is not really saying anything: 'All this may seem to you a fanatical and puritanical Catholicism.' He tries again, with talk of his love for good food and drink being one with his love of God, then switches to discussing the sense of horror that occasionally comes over him at

> the sudden realisation of being separated from all enjoyment, from all things of this earth, even from Hope; a sudden separation and isolation from *everything*; and at that moment of illumination, a recognition of the fact that one can do without all these things, a joyful recognition of what John of the Cross means when he

> says that the soul cannot be possessed of the divine union until it has divested itself of the craving for all created beings.

Did Eliot not feel that the sense of 'a sudden separation and isolation from everything' comes across as a good deal more real and powerful than 'the recognition of the fact that one can do without all these things', followed by the somewhat dutiful reference to St John of the Cross? Or does my question merely reflect my inability to follow him along the mystical religious route?

Certainly his poetry, right through to the end of *Little Gidding*, owes its strength to the constant play of light and dark that runs through it and that must, of necessity, be lacking in the linear exposition of philosophical or religious 'positions'. And this may explain why the only really uninhibited letters in this volume are addressed to the one person Eliot must have felt was as well read as he was, as great an artist (for he must have had a sense of his own worth, however modest his public pronouncements), as aware as he had become of the terrors as well as the joys of life: Virginia Woolf. 'My dear Virginia,' he writes in May 1927, 'If you are back in London, as I hear from George Rylands, and if and when convenient, I think you might invite me to tea. If so, I shall bring you a new gramophone record.' In June: 'I am free for tea on Wednesday or Thursday or for dinner on Wednesday. And if any of those times suited you I should be glad to show you what little I know about the Grizzly Bear, or the Chicken Strut.' The Grizzly Bear, the excellent notes explain, was a pre-war dance craze. Irving Berlin wrote a song to words by George Botsford (1910) that went: 'Out in San Francisco where the weather's fair, / They have a dance out there, / They call the "Grizzly Bear". / All your other lovin' dances don't compare, / [...] Listen my honey, do, / And I will show to you / The dance of the grizzly Bear.' Woolf replied: 'I shall pin you down to dinner. I enjoyed my tea party the other day very much, and I think it should be repeated. We might dance.' Perhaps one reason why both of them were able to go on writing so extraordinarily well was that, despite the views they held and the bundle of prejudices they, like all of us, carried with them, they remained close to the child and the adolescent in themselves, ever responsive to the physical pleasures of dancing and writing.

This is a wonderful volume. The notes are copious but always to the point, and include not only extracts from later letters we might have to wait a long time for, but also invaluable accounts of how his contemporaries saw Eliot at the time, including a hilarious and horrifying description by Osbert Sitwell of dinner at the Eliots'. It is a pity, therefore, that it is marred by a total failure to have a competent person check the French quotations. *La Trahison des clercs*, for example, is frequently referred to as *Le Trahison des clercs*. This is not merely annoying, it makes it impossible to know when Eliot's not always perfect French is at fault and when this is merely a copy-editing error. Surely Faber, for the publication of the letters of their most important author, could have made sure this kind of thing did not occur?

1 A review of *The Letters of T. S. Eliot, Volume 3: 1926–1927*, edited by Valerie Eliot and John Haffenden (New Haven and London: Faber & Faber, 2012).

Boris Pasternak[1]

To HIS DYING DAY Vladimir Nabokov maintained that *Doctor Zhivago* was a piece of pulp fiction about, as he put it in the afterword to the Russian version of *Lolita*, 'a lyrical doctor with penny-awful mystical urges and philistine turns of speech and an enchantress straight out of teenage romances'. This was not just sour grapes because the Nobel Prize had gone to a Russian novel that was not his own. Though in 1941 he was recommending Pasternak's poetry to Edmund Wilson, back in Berlin in 1927, writing under his émigré name of V. Sirin, he had reviewed a volume of Marina Tsvetaeva's poetry and had this to say about Pasternak's invidious influence on her:

> In Russia there is a fairly talented poet called Pasternak. His verse is convex, goitrous and goggle-eyed, as though his muse suffered from Basedow's disease. He is crazy about clumsy imagery, sonorous but literal rhymes and clattering metre. His syntax is really depraved [...] It is difficult to enthuse about Pasternak; he has a rather poor knowledge of Russian, expresses his thoughts clumsily and the incomprehensibility of much of his verse is not at all explained by the profundity or complexity of the thought itself [...] To imitate such a poet is a fearful thing. One fears for Marina Tsvetaeva.

Today, as the world celebrates the centenary of Pasternak's birth and the anniversary publications pour off the presses, such remarks seem like *lèse-majesté*. Ever since the publication in the West of *Doctor Zhivago* in 1958 the idea has taken root in the West that he is the towering figure of twentieth-century Russian literature, and that that literature, boasting as it does Blok, Mayakovsky, Akhmatova,

Mandelstam, Tsvetaeva, Brodsky, and many others, has been second to none in the world. Although, as Peter Levi admits in his new biography, Pasternak's reputation in the West has been fuelled by anti-communism, the question today seems to be less whether or not Pasternak was a major writer than whether, with his enormous output of poetry, autobiography and even fiction, he is or is not *the* major writer of the twentieth century.

Yet we should not, I think, dismiss Nabokov's remarks as merely spiteful or silly. After all, Anna Akhmatova, who loved Pasternak and his poetry, was not much taken with *Doctor Zhivago* either. She found the figure of Lara ridiculous and held that much of the novel must have been written by Pasternak's then mistress, Olga Ivinskaya. Re-reading the novel after twenty-five years I found myself in substantial agreement with both Nabokov and Akhmatova.

Lara, we are told, is 'the purest being in the world'. 'She moved,' says Pasternak, 'with a silent grace, and everything about her – voice, figure, gestures, her grey eyes and her shining hair – was fitting and harmonious.' Twenty pages later we learn that 'she had for him the unique charm of the incorporeal. Her hands astonished him like a sublime idea. Her shadow on the wall of the hotel room had seemed to him the outline of innocence.' The 'him' referred to here is the villainous Komarovsky, the rich and powerful protector of Lara's mother, who soon seduces the innocent girl. The young Yuri Zhivago, by one of the many coincidences of the novel, finds himself in the same room as the depraved adult and the pure child:

> Meanwhile the girl and the man were enacting a dumb-scene. Not a word passed their lips, only their eyes met. But the understanding between them had a terrifying quality of black magic, as if he were the master of a puppet show and she were a puppet obedient to his every gesture.

This vision inflames the sensitive youth: 'He had once again experienced the irresistible attraction of this wild, desperate girl.'

The attraction persists, and many years and two revolutions later, Zhivago, having abandoned his wife and child, is living with Lara in a remote town in the Urals:

> Coming home at night, hungry and tired, he found Lara [...] cooking or washing. In this prosaic, workaday aspect of her being, dishevelled, with her sleeves rolled and her skirts tucked up, she almost frightened him by her regal beauty and dignity, more breath-taking than if he had found her on the point of going to a ball.

This is the world of historical romance: a beautiful doomed love, heroism, death, world-shaking historical events. True to the genre, the most amazing coincidences occur. School friends from Moscow find themselves fighting each other in the wastes of Siberia; Zhivago keeps meeting Lara's husband; Lara appears as a nurse at the front at the very place where Zhivago himself has been sent; when Zhivago and his family arrive in the Urals, who should be there but Lara? One would think Russia was the size of Lichtenstein. As a result the one scene of real literary merit, when Mme Fleur and the dying Zhivago pass each other by without ever knowing it, is greatly weakened.

Pasternak insisted at the end of his life that the only work of his of any lasting value was *Doctor Zhivago*, and although Christopher Barnes is right to warn us in the first volume of his new biography against reading the early life as though it had to lead up to the novel, both he and Evgeny Pasternak, the writer's son, give plenty of evidence that Pasternak was already turning something like it over in his mind in the 1920s and 30s. What he wanted to do, he said later, was to give a panoramic picture of Russia in the first forty-five years of the century. But he wanted to do more than that. The novel has a number of themes, not to say messages. One, which was of course stressed in the West when the novel first appeared, was to show the ideals of the Russian Revolution turning sour, the monster devouring its children. But that theme is subsumed in another, rather Dostoevskian one, that of Christian redemption.

Zhivago's uncle adumbrates that theme in the opening pages of the novel:

> This ancient world ended with Rome [...] Heavy, spokeless wheels, eyes sunk in fat, bestialism, double chins, illiterate emperors, fish fed on the flesh of learned slaves [...] And then, into this tasteless heap of gold and marble, He came, light-footed and clothed in light, with his marked humanity, his deliberate Galilean provincialism, and from that moment there were neither gods nor peoples, there was only man – man the carpenter, man the ploughman, man the shepherd.

But it was not only the Romans for whom Jesus came to redeem the world. Also quite early in the book Pasternak puts these words into the mouth of Misha Gordon, Zhivago's Jewish friend:

> Their [the Jews'] national idea has forced them, century after century, to be a people and nothing but a people – and the extraordinary thing is that they have been chained to this deadening task all through the centuries when all the rest of the world was being delivered from it by a new force which had come out of their own midst!

The Jews, it seems, had the chance to redeem themselves but let it go, preferring instead to cling to their absurd and outdated practices, hugging their martyrdom to themselves:

> In whose interests is this voluntary martyrdom? Who stands to gain by keeping it going so that all these innocent old men and women and children, all these clever kind, humane people, should go on being mocked and beaten up throughout the centuries? [...] Why don't the intellectual leaders of the Jewish people ever get beyond facile *Weltschmerz* and irony?

Of course the speaker is an impressionable boy, who admits to being influenced by Zhivago's uncle. But years later, in the Urals, the same sentiments are voiced by none other than that paragon of perfection, Lara herself. Indeed, she goes one step further. Haven't you noticed, she says to Zhivago, that when Jews are beaten and killed in pogroms, even though, if you are an intellectual, half your friends are bound to be Jews, 'we don't only feel sorry and indignant and ashamed, we feel wretchedly divided, as if our sympathy came more from the head than from the heart and had an aftertaste of insincerity.' Why? Because they had the chance to see the light and refused to do so, the chance to 'rise above themselves and dissolve among all the rest', yet clung to their individuality:

> Of course it's true that persecution forces them into this futile and disastrous pose, this shame-faced, self-denying isolation, which brings them nothing but misfortune. But I think some of it also comes from a kind of inward senility, the fatigue of centuries. I don't like their ironical whistling in the dark, the workaday poverty of their outlook, their timid imaginations.

It might be argued that this is meant to show up Lara's appalling bigotry, but no one who has read the novel can imagine that this is how Pasternak wants us to see it. The anti-Semitic clichés are simply the reverse of the Christian ones which are meant to resound throughout the book. I say Christian clichés but Pasternak's Christ, though he has his roots in the Gospels and in the Russian Church, is also a figure of late Romanticism. He is the pale Galilean who takes upon himself the suffering of humanity to redeem man, starting with the fallen woman, Mary Magdalene, and extending to the whole of mankind, but especially to Russia. Zhivago's poems, which form the last chapter of the book and have been hailed as its ultimate triumph by its champions, contain two versions of that *fin-de-siècle* Mary Magdalene, but open with a version of *Hamlet* which manages, under the influence of the same clichés, to identify Hamlet with Christ and both, implicitly, with their author, Zhivago/Pasternak:

> The noise is stilled. I come out on the stage.
> Leaning against the door-post
> I try to guess from the distant echo
> What is to happen to my lifetime.
>
> The darkness of night is aimed at me
> Along the sights of a thousand opera-glasses.
> Abba, Father, if it be possible,
> Let this cup pass from me.

It could be argued that Pasternak was after all only voicing prejudices and attitudes common to the epoch and that not too much should be made of this. Two factors, though, militate against this charitable view. The first is the date of *Zhivago*. Though the hero dies in 1929, the book was in progress from 1940 to 1955, and the bulk of it was written in 1945–47, at the very time, in other words, when the scale of the Nazi atrocities against the Jews must have become known even in the Soviet Union. What might have seemed merely bad taste in Dostoevsky or Swinburne becomes something far more shocking in Pasternak.

The second factor is Pasternak's own Jewishness. It is this which makes it essential for anyone writing about him to face up to the implications of the speeches of Gordon and Lara. The two English biographers do indeed touch on the issue, though with a certain gingerliness on the part of Christopher Barnes and with a heavy-handed lack of understanding of the real issues involved on the part of Peter Levi. As for his son's account of the second part of his life from 1930 to 1960, now issued in English translation, it seems to perpetuate the spirit of Pasternak's own memoirs in trying to draw a veil over the whole issue without going quite so far as to deny outright that Pasternak was a Jew. Thus Evgeny tells us that his father 'was born and bred into a family of professional artists', and leaves it at that. Later he tells us that in 1935 'the clouds of Fascism were gathering over Europe and Pasternak was appalled by its inhuman manifestations; he saw it as a "reactionary footnote to the history of Russia"', without saying that it was eventually to force his grandparents and their two daughters to find refuge in England. Most damaging, for both him and his father, he quotes a letter from Pasternak to his cousin Olga, written in 1949, without making any comment on the state of mind it reveals. Pasternak has been boasting to Olga about Maurice Bowra having included a chapter on him in *The Creative Experiment*, alongside Apollinaire, Mayakovsky, Eliot, and Lorca, but goes on to lament his 'present downfall' in the Soviet Union, both on the official plane and evidently, *vis-à-vis* the public itself. He goes on:

> What I am in fact worth, in the final count, if the barrier of blood and origin has remained unsurmounted (all that there remained to surmount) – and may mean something, albeit in intimation; and what a pretentious nonentity I must really be if I end up the focus of a narrow, private popularity cult among the most oppressed and unhappy members of the Jewish intelligentsia. Or, if it be so, then I ask for nothing; and who am I or what point is there in bothering about me when the heavens turn aside from me so readily and so fully.

What this shows is that even as late as his sixtieth year Pasternak was obsessed with 'surmounting' what he took to be the 'barrier of blood and origin' that stood, as he thought, between him and acceptance as a legitimate Russian writer. Yet the reader will search in vain in his son's book for any awareness that this was ever an issue.

Peter Levi's book gives every indication of having been put together in a hurry. Andrei Sinyavsky appears as Sinyovsky, Saint-John Perse as the Joycean Persse, Valéry Larbaud acquires a hyphen, Peter France's 1982 book on modern Russian poetry is listed in the bibliography as appearing in 1952. Levi's adulation of Pasternak knows no limits ('of all the poets of this century in any European language he is the most invigorating, the most interesting, and has the most to say'; 'he was the greatest of all Shakespeare's translators in any language'; *Doctor Zhivago* 'is certainly a work of genius'). Levi acknowledges Pasternak's anti-Semitic remarks but his comments on them are either beside the point or as offensive as his hero's. 'I was told in Russia,' he remarks of Pasternak's growing estrangement from his parents, 'that the trouble was Boris's "abandonment" of Judaism, but Leonid was not Orthodox', so he is only half-inclined to believe this. But Orthodoxy has nothing to do with it. Leonid, the son of a synagogue cantor and a simple country-woman, grew up a child of the Enlightenment. Tolstoy, who greatly admired his painting, once jokingly told him that he, Tolstoy, was more Jewish than he was. But, as he said in his memoirs, 'Although I believed in God, but did not in practice belong to any religious denomination, I would never have considered baptism as a means of facilitating my progress in life or of raising my social status.' In 1918–19 he wrote a book on Rembrandt and the Jews which was published in Berlin when he settled there shortly after. One does not have to be Orthodox, only to have a sense of solidarity with one's persecuted brethren, to resent one's son's active repudiation of his Jewish roots. Later, after quoting a passage from *Zhivago* about the *Weltschmerz* of Jewish intellectuals, Levi remarks: 'These two or three passages of powerful polemic are difficult to answer.' They may seem difficult for Levi to answer, but to me they seem perfectly simple. It is a form not only of anti-Semitism but also of the kind of sloppy thinking that informs all racism to think of people in terms of essences and generalities, and Pasternak's increasing tendency to do just that cannot but cast doubts on the qualities of his mind and spirit.

Again, of course, the dates are all-important. Both Mandelstam and Wittgenstein were Jews who, at one tine or another, spoke the language of European anti-Semitism. But poor Mandelstam was murdered in 1937 and Wittgenstein, from the early 1930s on, never again generalised about 'the Jews'. He went further. In 1937 he confessed to friends that he felt guilty about the fact that he had never declared himself a Jew and might have led people to believe that he was not. Wittgenstein's family had been Protestant for two generations; Pasternak's had never been anything but Jewish, yet in another letter to Olga, about *Zhivago*, dated 1946, which Levi paraphrases, we learn: 'The book was to settle accounts with Judaism, and with every kind of nationalism'. 'Settle accounts' is chilling, but Levi, like Evgeny, seems unaware of what it is he is telling us.

Barnes' biography is a completely different matter. It will surely remain the authoritative life for many years. It is written with sensitivity and care (though I was surprised to find him referring to Rilke as an Austrian poet, and he surely means the *second* Temple on page two). He is never quite prepared to criticise his subject, but he does provide us with enough information to make up our own minds. Levi, for example, gives it as a fact that the boy's Russian Orthodox nanny baptised him; Barnes reserves judgement, saying we have only Pasternak's own word for this. He admits that Pasternak 'always played down the importance of his racial origins', and argues that in the first part of his life he 'was not overly concerned by his racial and religious status', and that it was only later 'that he became more self-conscious about his position.' 'Position' is a little quaint, but Barnes promises to discuss the matter more fully in the second volume. We can only wait.

Barnes draws a sympathetic picture of Boris's parents, the highly gifted painter and his much wealthier concert-pianist wife; of their circle of artistic and intellectual friends in Moscow, to which the family had moved from Odessa, where both Leonid and Boris were born; of the impact of Tolstoy, who became a friend of the family; and then of Scriabin, whose flamboyant personality persuaded Boris, at thirteen, that he should become a composer. However, though he played the piano well, he preferred to improvise rather than work at his technique either at the keyboard or at composition. His brother noted at the time that he soon lost interest in what he could not master easily, that he always wished to do what lay well beyond him, and that he was a poor loser. Barnes notes that 'his autobiographies several times drew a veil over episodes and personalities when his interest in them had been exhausted or disappointed.' So he gave up music and took up philosophy, which led him to Marburg and Hermann Cohen in 1912 (Eliot was there two years later), but then abandoned that as well and returned to Russia. He had already begun to write and publish poetry, and from then on he never stopped, earning his living, except for brief periods, solely by his pen, and, in his early years, as involved as any Western poet in the cliques and journals of the day.

A childhood accident had left one leg shorter than the other and this exempted him from active duty in both wars. Like most of his class he welcomed the February revolution; like some, he also welcomed the October revolution, seeing it in Nietzschean terms as a triumph of the ruthless will. The rest of his life shows him struggling to come to terms with this ruthlessness, adapting more easily than some, such as Akhmatova and Mandelstam, but less easily than others. After 1936, under constant attack from Party ideologues but stubbornly refusing to toe the line, he more or less retired to his house in Peredelkino, getting by on translations, mainly of Shakespeare.

In his youth Pasternak fell idealistically in love with a number of women, including his cousin Olga, who, like the others, shrugged him off. She confessed she found him in this mood 'difficult [...] unpleasant, and – I don't like saying this of him – repulsive.' Their friendship, however, survived. In 1922 he married a young Jewish artist, Evgenya Lurye, and the following year Evgeny was born. By 1928, though, the marriage was failing. Akhmatova said it was because Pasternak couldn't stand his wife's bohemianism; Levi suggests that 'part of the trouble was her Judaism'. It is true that when her mother died he wrote to Olga: 'For the first time in my life I saw how they [*sic*] bury Jews, and it was awful.'

In 1930 he met Zinaida Neigauz and her pianist husband. He

seems to have been attracted by her efficiency and by the fact that as a child she had been forced into an affair by her forty-five-year-old cousin: 'Zina is intimately close to me in having fully paid as a woman and a human being for the right [...] to pass judgement on life and the soul and its history and sufferings,' he wrote. 'She is just as foolish, as stupid, as elemental as I. Just as pure and holy in her consummated depravity, just as sombre.' Though he calls her a beauty, the photographs, which reveal a charming Evgenya and Olga Ivinskaya, do not bear him out, and what one learns of her does not seem endearing. She refused, for example, to let Boris see the Mandelstams at home when they returned from their first exile, so that he had to meet them at the station.

In 1943 he met Olga Ivinskaya, twenty-two years his junior, and till the end of his life she and Zinaida fought over him. Akhmatova felt he wouldn't be able to face a second divorce, and she was right. He died with Zinaida still in charge, though Olga later wrote a memoir in which she claimed that Boris had known almost at once that his second marriage had been a mistake, and that it was really Zinaida's husband he loved, and that mainly for his piano-playing. Clearly Lara is modelled in the first instance on Zina, on whom Pasternak has superimposed some of Olga's traits.

A life like any other, then, full of those little hypocrisies, little heroisms, big ambitions, big mistakes, and unresolved contradictions which make up the existence of most human beings well enough off to be able to think of other things than where the next mouthful is to come from. It has none of the emblematic quality of the life of Kafka or Wittgenstein, none of the tragedy of the life of Mandelstam. Its interest has to lie in its being the life of a major artist.

I have said what I think about *Doctor Zhivago*. But what of the poetry? Joseph Brodsky, among others, has rightly warned against judging Russian poetry by translations. Yet from the verse quoted in these three biographies, and from the new translations offered by Andrei Navrozov and the reprint of the late poems, translated (much more ably, it seems to me) by Michael Harari, I have to say that to a reader fairly well acquainted with Modern European and American poetry the claims made for them seem grotesquely overblown. Though we are told that Pasternak found his true voice when he repudiated the symbolism of Blok and Bely, the differences, in translation, seem less great than the similarities. All his life Pasternak seems to have worked in a mode which was basically that of the late nineteenth century, writing personal lyrics on personal subjects. Levi, who insists, as we have seen, that Pasternak was a better poet than Rilke, Eliot, Yeats, Valéry, and Auden, does suggest at one point that a poem of Pasternak's reminds him of Edward Thomas, and occasionally mentions Hardy. That seems more like it. Here, for example, is the end of an early poem, described by Levi as 'particularly clean and fine':

The earth is black under the thaw
and the wind furrowed with bird-cries
and certainly and suddenly
verses drip weeping from my pen.

And here is a stanza from a very late poem:

What is the evil I did,
murder or robbery?
I made the whole world weep
for my beautiful country.

I can see that other translations could make something rather different of these poems, but what is undeniable, it seems to me, is that the poet who wrote such lines remained untouched by European Modernism – by which I mean not typographical play *à la* Apollinaire or the glorification of speed and violence *à la* Marinetti, but that reticence, that questioning of the whole concept of selfhood; that shedding of such romantic locutions as *weeping*, *longing*, *swooning*; that doubt before the possibility of poetry itself, which characterises the work of Eliot, Stevens, Rilke, and Valéry.

But then that is perhaps precisely why Pasternak is so popular both in the Soviet Union and in the West. As far as Russia is concerned one thinks of the passion aroused by Aragon's poetry in France during the Second World War: it gave people then what Valéry, for example, could never have given them, though today Aragon strikes us as merely an interesting minor poet. As far as England is concerned one hears poets speaking enviously of the thousands of copies sold by poets in the Soviet Union, and it is true that one cannot imagine Stevens or Eliot ever being recited on street corners. But the comparison should perhaps be with a poet who *has* sold in bulk: John Betjeman. Of course with Pasternak there is the added spice for Western readers that he was the Victim of Soviet Oppression. Unfortunately, the fact that those who criticise a writer are bigoted, foolish, and wrong does not always mean that the writer is magnanimous, wise, and right. Or a very good artist.

1 A review of the following five books:

Christopher Barnes, *Boris Pasternak: A Literary Biography, I: 1890–1928* (Cambridge: Cambridge University Press, 1990).

Peter Levi, *Boris Pasternak: A Biography* (London: Century Hutchinson, 1990).

Evgeny Pasternak, *Boris Pasternak: The Tragic Years 1930–60*, translated by Michael Duncan with poetry translated by Ann Pasternak Slater and Craig Raine (London: Collins Harvill, 1990).

Boris Pasternak, *Second Nature: Forty-six Poems*, translated by Andrei Navrozov (London: Peter Owen, 1989).

Boris Pasternak, *Poems 1955–1959 and an Essay in Autobiography*, translated by Michael Harari and Manya Harari (London: Collins Harvill, 1989).

György Kurtág: *Samuel Beckett What is the Word*

THE QUIET AND RETICENT Hungarian composer György Kurtág (born 1926) has emerged in the last twenty years as one of the great artists of the post-war era. This is rather surprising when one recalls how diffident and faltering were his first steps in composition, how marginal he has been for much of his life, stuck away in Communist Hungary, and how modest his music-making has been, with no operas and no vast choral and orchestral works to his name. It is, though, perhaps this very modesty, this marginality, that has made him such a potent artistic force in our confused, fragmented and disillusioned world.

On his first visit to Paris, to study with Olivier Messiaen, in 1957–58, in the wake of the Soviet invasion of Hungary, he experienced a kind of breakdown and found that he could no longer compose. As had happened to Hofmannsthal's fictitious Lord Chandos sixty years earlier, the creative act, which had until then seemed so natural to him, suddenly became impossible. He no longer knew how or where to start, or how to go on. He fell into a depression. He was saved from this, he says, by a wonderful psychologist, Marianne Stein, who helped him recover by suggesting he go back to the most primitive building blocks and simply put down one note and then, if possible, another. One note, after all, is a noise; two notes are already a composition. At the time, too, he encountered the music of Anton Webern and the writings of Samuel Beckett, then just beginning to make his name as an artist of international stature.

Kurtág followed Stein's advice and, very gradually, began to recover. He returned to Hungary and has remained there ever since, producing music characterised by its extraordinary brevity and concision, by his startling ability to convey a totally realised world with a unique character in tiny pieces that often last no more than half a minute. In the decades that followed he began to string these pieces together, as in his work for piano, *Játékok* (*Games*), which he is constantly expanding and performs with his wife Márta (some of the pieces are for two, some for four hands, some are transcriptions of Bach, many are tiny memorials to friends who have died), or the *Kafka Fragments* for violin and soprano, which consists of dozens of tiny settings, sometimes of a mere phrase of Kafka's, which together build up to a major work lasting fifty minutes. Like Britten, Kurtág is a great reader with a sure instinct for what texts to set, though where Britten turned to predominantly English and Romantic material, Kurtág, the Central European, has shown a preference for the great writers of European Modernism, Hölderlin, Kafka, and Beckett.

Beckett died in 1989 and in 1990 Kurtág set his last work, *What is the Word?*, for voice and piano, rewriting it the following year for soloist, chamber ensemble, and five other voices. In the first, *opus 30a*, he uses a Hungarian translation, in the second, *opus 30b*, the soloist sings the words in Hungarian but the five other vocalists utter snatches of the piece in Beckett's English translation of his French original. Beckett's work consists of 57 lines, the longest comprising eight words, the shortest, one. Here is how it opens:

folly –
folly for to –
for to –
what is the word –
folly from this –
all this –
folly from all this –
given –
folly given all this –
seeing –

And it ends:

folly for to need to seem –
to glimpse afaint afar away over there what –
what –
what is the word –
what is the word –

As in all of Beckett after the great crisis of 1945–50, when he gradually realised that the 'dark he had struggled to keep under', as he wrote to a friend, was actually what he had to write *about* rather than escape *from*, a voice searches for the right formulation, does not find it, and gives up, but in the meanwhile the search has become the work. To read such pieces is not to enter another world, it is to enact a desperate movement in the inner reaches of one's being and to find, at the end, that the enactment of failure has led not to triumph but to a quite physical sense of release. One can see why the reading of Beckett in the moment of crisis in the fifties freed Kurtág from the terrible sense of blockage that had overwhelmed him and helped him back on the path to composition. For blockage, Beckett seems to be saying, is not a chance calamity that has befallen you but a part of what it means to be human, and it cannot be overcome but only acknowledged, accommodated. And one can see why, given this personal sense of debt, Kurtág should have turned, in his sixties, at the height of his powers, to this beautiful last work of Beckett's.

But there is more. Kurtág had got to know one of the most famous pop singers in Hungary, Ildikó Monyók. A tragedy had overwhelmed Monyók. She had been involved in a terrible car accident which had, for seven years, left her unable to speak. However, gradually, she was, quite literally, beginning to find her voice again. Perhaps remembering his own crisis and recovery, Kurtág determined to write something for her that would help her back onto the stage. That is when he decided to set Beckett's own drama of a voice in search of language.

And it worked. Singing the piece (if singing is the right word), Monyók literally rediscovered her stage voice. 'She can say syllables but not words. She can say words but not make sentences,' Kurtág explained in his rudimentary English. 'But when she *performs* being able to say only syllables, only words, then something happens.' The wonder of art is that it is infinitely repeatable. I have heard her live and I have heard her on CD (*György Kurtág, Portraitkonzert Salzburg 10.8.1993*, WWE 2CD 31870). Each time the ritual is repeated (and, as with all genuine rituals, the outcome is always in doubt) the agony of the effort to bring into being that most common and most precious of human possessions, speech, is almost too much to bear, until, with the final failure, the silence at the end of the piece, comes the realisation that actually the ritual has worked. For Beckett. For Kurtág. For Monyók. And perhaps for each of us.

'The Itch to Write': Beckett's Early Letters[1]

WHATEVER ONE FEELS about the ethics of publishing the personal letters of an artist after their death, there is no doubt that among the glories of nineteenth- and twentieth-century art must be numbered the letters of Keats and van Gogh, of Kafka and Lawrence. Though they were among the greatest artists of their day there are others equally great, such as Wordsworth and Cézanne, Proust and Eliot, whose letters, though of course occasionally moving, and interesting because of who they were, would never figure in anyone's list of the ten or twenty greatest books of the era. The letters of Keats and van Gogh certainly would. And so, on the evidence of this first volume of his letters, would those of Beckett.

Beckett was a prolific letter-writer. The editors have transcribed more than 15,000 letters written in the course of sixty years, from 1929, when he was twenty-one, till his death in 1989. Of these they plan to give us some 2,500 complete and to quote in the notes from a further 5,000. Some letters we might have found significant or moving we will never see, for when Beckett gave the editors his blessing he specified that he only wished to have published letters which would 'have a bearing on my work', and one can surmise from the editors' introduction that they had to fight long and hard with the executors to make their sense prevail of what 'had a bearing' and what did not. This suggests that we will never see, even if they exist, the equivalent of Kafka's *Letters to Milena* and *Letters to Felice*.

But we still have quite enough to be getting on with. And though many of these have been in the public domain for years – some of the letters to Thomas McGreevy were quoted by Deirdre

Bair in her 1978 biography – the effect of reading them all together is completely different from reading extracts in a biography. For biography, no matter how tactfully it is written, has the effect Sartre described years ago, of imposing a false teleology on its subject, making us see early setbacks and failures entirely in the light of later triumphs, and of giving a shape and meaning to the life which it did not have for the one who lived it. Letters, on the other hand, are so moving, heart-rending even, because we live each moment with the writer and time takes on the dimension it has in our own lives of being more like a well into which we are perpetually though exceedingly slowly falling than like a well-lit road along which we are travelling, with our destination clearly visible ahead. Of course the editorial decision to publish Beckett's letters in four heavily annotated volumes rather than the one volume in which we read the letters of Keats or Wallace Stevens rather weakens their impact, and the publication of a first volume of four, stopping in 1940, with no dates set for the other three, is frustrating, to say the least. But we should be thankful for what we have. It is already a rich enough feast.

By 1929 Beckett had already spent some time in Italy and Germany, where he had relatives, and, after a dazzling early career reading French and Italian at Trinity College, Dublin, had just settled into a two-year post as exchange Lecteur at the École normale supérieure, where his predecessor, Thomas McGreevy, a much older man who had served in the First World War, and who was still living in Paris, had introduced him to many of his friends, including James Joyce and Richard Aldington. In the next few years he returns to Dublin, takes up and then renounces an academic job at TCD; writes a little book on Proust, a great many poems, some of which are published, some stories, including the masterpiece 'Dante and the Lobster', which are published under the title *More Pricks than Kicks*, and a novel, *Murphy*; tries to settle in London and undergoes a course of analysis with Wilfred Bion; experiences the death of his father and later of a favourite dog; tries to settle in Dublin; undertakes a six month long trip to Germany to study the art in its great museums; and, at the end of the decade, finally settles in Paris where he meets and begins to live with Suzanne Deschevaux-Dumesnil, though almost at once the war which had been threatening for so long finally breaks out, and in June 1940, along with a large part of the population of Paris, the pair flee the capital in the face of the advancing Germans. If at the start of the decade Beckett was known in Dublin circles as a highly promising academic with an illustrious career ahead of him, by the end of it he was known to a small coterie of Irish and French intellectuals as a bohemian writer of obscure verse and almost equally obscure fiction, a shy hard-drinking man of remarkable learning and a savage and witty turn of phrase. Had the war engulfed him as it engulfed so many of his contemporaries it is doubtful if we would now be reading his collected letters.

But that of course makes the letters of these years all the more precious and all the more interesting. Beckett, by all accounts, was the most courteous of men, and it seems that even at the height of his fame he still tried to answer as courteously as he could the hundreds of letters he received. But the sixty-year-old smiling (or, more often, in the photos we have of him, scowling) public man now knew where his interests lay: after spending the mornings on his correspondence he would devote the afternoons to his own writing. But in the thirties there was no public man, and we have to see the letters as merely one of many ways in which the ambitious, confused and tormented young writer attempted to understand who he was and what it was he really wanted, out of life and out of art. These early letters, in other words, are, like the early poems and stories, *essais*, the trying out of a voice, a tone, even, at times, as we will see, a language.

There are, of course, some letters to publishers and to agents, but even these are hardly run-of-the-mill. Having been informed that an American publisher had shown an interest in *Murphy* but wanted him to cut it, he first of all responded as authors always do that he had already cut everything superfluous and did not see how anything further could be done on that score. Some months later, though, he writes to his agent: 'Is there no further news about Quigley. I mean Murphy? [...] The last I remember is my readiness to cut down the work to its title. I am now prepared to go even further, and change the title, if it gives offence, to Quigley, Trompetenschleim, Eliot, or any other name that the publishers fancy.'

Already in the first letter to McGreevy, in the Summer of 1929, from Kassell, where he was staying with his father's sister Frances and her Jewish husband Abraham Sinclair and his two cousins Peggy and Morris, we catch the authentic Beckettian note and sense that we are going to enjoy ourselves. The subject, as will so often be the case in the years to come, is the placing of a piece of his writing, and the tone is both bitter and funny:

> My dear McGreevy, the abominable old bap Rusell duly returned my MSS with an economic note in the 3rd person, the whole in a considerably understamped envelope. I feel slightly paralysed by the courtesy of this gesture. I would like to get rid of the damn thing anyhow, anywhere (with the notable exception of 'transition'), but I have no acquaintance with the less squeamish literary garbage buckets. I can't imagine Eliot touching it – certainly not the verse. Perhaps Seamus O'Sullivan's rag would take it? If you think of an address I would be grateful to know it.

This might remind readers of two other ambitious and irreverent young men writing to each other for support and to try out their literary skills, Amis and Larkin. But what follows most certainly will not. After quoting two lines of Dante in Italian to make the witty point that his sunburn makes trying to sleep as uncomfortable a procedure as faced the city of Florence, 'that can find no rest on her bed of down but with turning seeks to ease her pain', he goes on to comment on Proust, which he was reading with a view to fulfilling a commission to write a short book about him:

> I have read the first volume of 'Du Coté de chez Swann', and find it strangely uneven. There are incomparable things – Bloch, Françoise, Tante Léonie, Legrandin, and then passages that are offensively fastidious and almost dishonest [...] Some of his metaphors light up a whole page like a bright explosion, and others seem ground out in the dullest desperation [...] His loquacity is certainly more interesting and cleverly done than Moore's, but no less profuse, a maudlin false teeth gobble-gobble discharge from a colic-afflicted belly. He drank too much tilleul. And to think that I have to contemplate him at stool for volumes!

This ability to tear into what he dislikes but not let it blind him to what is admirable in a work or artist is to remain typical of Beckett. He is never taken in by a reputation but he is always alert to what is fine and important. 'I feel that Beethoven's Quartets are a waste of time,' he writes to McGreevy in February 1931. 'His pig-headed refusal to make the best of a rather pettifogging convention annoys me. And why do they go on playing that bloody Mendelssohn!' Three years later, in a letter to his cousin Morris Sinclair in which he is trying out his French, he writes: 'Je n'ai jamais pu me reconcilier avec la Symphonie Pastorale ou j'ai l'impression que Beethoven a versé tout ce qu'il y avait de vulgaire, de facile et d'enfantin (et c'était beaucoup), pour en finir avec une fois pour toutes.' The Seventh Symphony, on the other hand, and the cavatina of the Quartet, op.130, moved him deeply. In the great letter he wrote (in German) to Axel Kaun in 1937, he comments on the way 'the sound surface of Beethoven's Seventh Symphony is devoured by huge black pauses, so that for pages on end we cannot perceive it as other than a dizzying path of sounds connecting unfathomable chasms of silence', a response to the work that he clearly felt touched on something very important, for it appears, in almost exactly the same words, in the discarded novel, *Dream of Fair to Middling Women*.

The same fierce individuality is evident in his response to

literature. 'Am reading [Balzac's] *Cousine Bette*. The bathos of style and thought is so enormous that I wonder is he writing seriously or in parody.' 'Read Cecil's Life of Cowper, *The Stricken Deer*. Very bad. But what a life! It depressed & terrified me. How did he ever manage to write such bad poetry?' '[...] Goethe's *Tasso*, than which, except for some good rhetoric, anything more disgusting would be hard to devise.' 'So I was reduced to reading [Mauriac's] *Le Désert de l'Amour*, which I most decidedly do not like. A patient, tenuous snivel that one longs to see projected noisily into a handkerchief.' But then: 'I'm reading the 'Possedés' in a foul translation. Even so it must be very carelessly and badly written in the Russian, full of clichés & journalese: but the movement, the transitions! No one moves about like Dostoievski. No one ever caught the insanity of dialogue like he did.'

The letters reveal how hard Beckett worked to educate himself once he had decided the academic life was not for him. He reads Descartes and his disciple Geulincx (in Latin), he reads Leibnitz and Spinoza, Kant and Hegel, Schopenhauer (a great favourite), as well as Ariosto, Tasso, Schiller, Goethe, Fielding, Jane Austen, George Eliot and any amount of minor writers in French, Italian, German, and English. But 'educate himself' is hardly the right phrase. Beckett read avidly, passionately, looking for what could stimulate his own work, and finding it in places that might surprise us. Jane Austen, he tells McGreevy, 'has much to teach me'; he is enchanted with *Joseph Andrews* – *Jacques le fataliste* and *The Vicar of Wakefield* rolled into one, he thinks – and picks out for comment 'the ironical replies and giving away of the show pari passu with the show', while 'the very short chapters are an idea'.

At some point in the thirties Beckett toyed with the idea of becoming an art dealer. His comments on works of art are therefore slightly different from those on music and literature. He spends hours in the National Gallery in Dublin, relaying to McGreevy (who would later become Director of that gallery), what the new Director has done with the rehang and commenting in detail especially on his beloved Dutch and Flemish masters. In London it is the same with the National Gallery, and in Paris he will often drop in to the Louvre to examine this or that work or artist he has grown interested in, duly reporting his impressions back to McGreevy. Among the most surprising and fascinating letters are those Beckett sent back to family and friends when he undertook a six month long trip to Germany, from September 1936 to April 1937, in order to study the art on view there. He travelled from Hamburg to Berlin via Hannover and Brunswick; to Leipzig, Dresden, and on to Munich, via Bamberg and Nuremberg. Everywhere he goes he tries to see all that is on show and much that isn't, for under the Nazis some art had begun to be withdrawn as 'decadent'. Beckett badgers directors to give him access to these pictures in the vaults, makes friends with (usually Jewish) patrons and collectors, who invite him to their houses and introduce him to some of the artists who can no longer show freely, and these in turn give him introductions to friends and fellow artists in other cities. The weather is bitter and Beckett is depressed both by his health and by the Nazification of Germany. Finally, exhausted, giving up plans to visit Stuttgart, Colmar and Frankfurt, he flies home. The visit not only tells us a great deal about Beckett, but it is an invaluable – and surprising – record of the state of German museums and art galleries in the thirties, and it includes descriptions – for Beckett in his letters describes at great length what he is seeing – of paintings that have since disappeared, the victims either of Nazi looting or Allied bombing.

By the end of the decade friends were showing him paintings they had purchased with queries about provenance and authentication. But Beckett could no more become an art dealer than he could become a lecturer in French, a commercial pilot, a teacher of Italian in South Africa, a student of Eisenstein or any of the other careers he briefly toyed with but either resigned from when they became a reality (the Lectureship in French) or simply left to drift in the realm of possibility. For there was really only one thing he wanted to do, and that was to write. Even the letters about art, though they sometimes consist simply of lists of what he has seen, are in the main concerned with the same thing as the letters about music, philosophy and literature: the attempt to understand what it was he felt he wanted to do and how the art in question could help him. Hence his passion for the unlikely trio of Watteau, Cézanne and Jack Yeats.

On 14 August 1937 he writes to McGreevy about Jack Yeats, whom over the years in Dublin he had got to know and like, and whose little painting 'Morning' he bought when he could ill afford it and treasured ever after:

> What I feel he gets so well, dispassionately, not tragically like Watteau, is the heterogeneity of nature & the human denizens, the unalterable alienness of the 2 phenomena, the 2 solitudes, or the solitude & loneliness, the loneliness in solitude, the impassable immensity between the solitude that cannot quicken to loneliness & the loneliness that cannot lapse into solitude. There is nothing of the kind in Constable, the landscape shelters or threatens or serves or destroys, his nature is really infected with 'spirit', ultimately as humanised and romantic as Turner's was & Claude's was not & Cézanne's was not.

On the same day he had written to his aunt Cissie Sinclair on the same theme:

> The way [Jack Yeats] puts down a man's head & a woman's head side by side, or face to face, is terrifying, two irreducible singlenesses & the impassable immensity between. I suppose that is what gives the stillness to his pictures, as though the convention were suddenly suspended [...] a kind of petrified insight into one's ultimate hard irreducible inorganic singleness.

Three years before he had written to McGreevy from London:

'What a relief the Mont Ste Victoire after all the anthropomorphised landscape – van Goyen, Avercamp, the Ruysdaels, Hobbema, even Claude...' Ten days later he comes back to it, and this time you feel he is struggling to articulate something that is buried very deep within him:

> What I feel in Cézanne is precisely the absence of rapport that was all right for Rosa or Ruysdael for whom the animising mode was valid, but would have been false for him, because he had the sense of his incommensurability with life of such a different order as landscape but even with life of his own order, even with the life – one feels looking at the self-portrait in the Tate, not the Cézanne chauve but with the big hat – operative in himself.

He struggles a little longer to express this but ends with a shrug: 'Comprends pas'.

And not surprisingly. He will never understand, but in the work that comes so naturally after the war, especially in the last great plays, *Footfalls* and *Rockaby*, he will discover how to embody it. At this point, though, little comes naturally. In 1930 he writes to Charles Prentice at Chatto, who had been enthusiastic about his little Proust book and to whom he had promised to add a few pages: 'I have added nothing to Proust. I can't do anything here – neither read nor think nor write. I must apologise for the absurdity of the entire proceeding. I expected more generous rifts in the paralysis.' To McGreevy from London, two years later: 'I haven't tried to write. The idea itself of writing seems somehow ludicrous.' When a poem or story does come it seems to be unrelated to himself or his will: 'I'm enclosing the only bit of writing that has happened to me since Paris and that does me no particular credit as far as I can judge.' What he loathes is the arbitrariness, the meaninglessness of it all. In a wonderful letter to McGreevy of 18 October 1932, which deserves to stand with Hofmannsthal's fictional Lord Chandos Letter of 1902, he writes:

> I'm in mourning for the integrity of the pendu's emission of semen, what I find in Homer & Dante & Racine & sometimes Rimbaud, the integrity of the eyelids coming down before the brain knows of grit in the wind.

Lacking that, what is writing but self-indulgence? And yet he cannot stop himself: 'I dribble malgré moi and knowing I do & oughtn't to is no help.' And, six months later: 'This writing is a bloody awful grind. I did two more "short stories", bottled climates, comme ca, sans conviction, because one has to do something or perish with ennui.' A year later, to his cousin, he writes, the French helping him to speak of things he would otherwise keep buried: 'Malgré ce que je t'ai écrit touchant l'impossibilité de travailler, je viens de me livrer a des efforts d'enragé pour écrire ce que personne ne veut entendre.' ('Despite all I've written to you concerning the impossibility of writing, I've just been struggling like mad to produce what no one wants to hear.') And he will even confess to McGreevy: 'I get frightened sometimes at the idea that the itch to write is cured.'

This whole complex and tormenting web of contradictory urges is very reminiscent of Kafka. And the parallels go further. Like Kafka, Beckett is always complaining of his body: his teeth are bad, his neck hurts, he has pleurisy, his feet are giving him hell. Like Kafka, he is paralysed and bored. Accidia hangs heavily over him, and as Kafka blamed Prague, so Beckett blames Dublin: 'This tired abstract anger – inarticulate passive opposition – always the same thing in Dublin.' Kafka went to see Rudolf Steiner and Buber but the sages couldn't help him; Beckett undergoes a course of psychoanalysis with Bion in London, and feels better for it, but soon confesses that it has changed nothing. With his father dead his mother grows more and more possessive, and getting away from Dublin becomes getting away from Mother. The years of these letters are not just years of literary apprenticeship but years in which we see him constantly attempting to settle elsewhere – London, Paris – and coming back with his tail between his legs and even, occasionally, with relief, to the horrors and boredom of Dublin, where neither his mother nor his brother understand what he is up to but where at least he has a room of his own and does not have to struggle every day to make ends meet. Towards the end of the decade, though, he can look at his relationship with his mother a little more dispassionately: 'I don't wish her anything at all, neither good nor ill. I am what her savage loving has made me, and it is good that one of us should accept that finally.'

As with Kafka, everything hinges on the writing: what he is doing may be rubbish, it may be pure self-indulgence, no one may be interested in reading it, but it is the only thing he is sure he wants to do:

> Frank came back from his 10 days in Donegal last Tuesday [...] When he heard Heinemann had turned down the book [*Murphy*] he said: 'Why can't you write the way people want', when I replied that I could only write the one way, i.e. as best I could (not the right answer, by the way, not at all the right answer), he said it was a good thing for him he did not feel obliged to implement such a spirit in 6 Clare St. [his office]. Even mother begins to look askance at me. My departure from here is long overdue.

But if that is not the right answer, what is? In a wonderful letter of July 1937 to a German friend, in German, he tried to find an explanation:

> It is indeed getting more and more difficult, even pointless, for me to write in formal English. And more and more my language appears to me like a veil which one has to tear apart in order to get to those things (or the nothingness) lying behind it. Grammar and style! To me they seem to have become as irrelevant as a Biedermeier bathing suit or the imperturbability of a gentleman. A mask. It is to be hoped the time will come, thank God, in some circles it already has, when language is best used when

> most efficiently abused [...] Or is literature alone to be left behind on that old, foul road long ago abandoned by music and painting? Is there something paralysingly sacred contained within the unnature of the word that does not belong to the elements of the other arts? Is there any reason why that terrifyingly arbitrary materiality of the word surface should not be dissolved, as for example the sound surface of Beethoven's Seventh Symphony is devoured by huge black pauses, so that for pages on end we cannot perceive it as other than a dizzying path of sounds connecting unfathomable chasms of silence? An answer is requested.

We will never know if an answer came from Axel Kaun, for Beckett did not keep the letters he received. But an answer did come, years later, from Beckett himself, not in the form of a philosophical or aesthetic treatise, but in that of fiction and plays, in an abundance which would have astonished the thirty-one year old author of this letter. What Beckett was to learn in the decade that followed was that the things he grumbled about to McGreevy and others was not something that had to be resolved before he could begin to write properly, they were precisely what he had to write about. How he came to understand this is presumably what the next volume will reveal.

We can grasp the dynamics of it though even in these letters. We hear the voice of what we recognise as the authentic Beckett either when he trusts his interlocutor, as happens with McGreevy, and so is prepared to confess his confusions, or when he writes in a language not his own, as in the letter to Kaun or one or two to Morris Sinclair. The rest of the time, and especially in the letters to women he was interested in, he is often brilliant, nearly always funny, but we feel, as we do with many of the early stories and poems, that he is trying too hard, that he is simultaneously showing off and protecting himself. What this makes us see, as well, is that, very unlike Kafka in this, Beckett had a deep unconscious confidence in his own use of language. And not just language. The letters show us how warmly he could respond to landscape, to people, and to animals. Cycling and walking in the countryside round Dublin were nearly always a pleasure, and, here and there, we get glimpses of the gentle and considerate (if desperately shy) man he was. Apart from the miracle of his transformation from a minor bohemian artist into probably the greatest writer of the second half of the twentieth century, what later volumes will no doubt show is how he managed, better than any other artist I can think of in our age, to preserve his human qualities even in his years of fame.

1 A review of *The Letters of Samuel Beckett, Volume I: 1929–1940*, edited by Martha Dow Fehsenfeld, Lois More Overbeck, George Craig, and Dan Gunn (Cambridge: Cambridge University Press, 2009).

Why Write Fiction?

THE IMMEDIATE RESPONSE to the question in my title might well be: Why not write fiction? After all, everybody seems to be doing it, and (in Britain and the US at any rate), for those lacking in confidence, more and more 'creative writing' courses are springing up all the time.

But a little thought is enough to make you hesitate. Though there have never been so many novels published as there are today, and though every other novel is hailed as a masterpiece, there is a countercurrent in our culture which suggests that fiction is essentially trivial and worthless, a pleasant way to pass the time on a beach or a railway journey, but no more; if you want to read something serious and worthwhile you should read one of the equally large number of excellent books of history, biography or popular science. And if you want to get close to experience you might be better off watching documentary films or immersing yourself in street culture, rap, hip-hop and graffiti, for this is where the real life is to be found. Or so argues the American critic David Shields, whose manifesto, *Reality Hunger*, clearly caught the mood of a disaffected intelligentsia and has proved enormously popular. Yet it hasn't succeeded in stemming the flow of novels or the enrolment at creative writing courses. And how could it? We all of us seem to have the need to tell stories, to ourselves if not to others, and some have even argued that man is a storytelling animal, that our species defines itself by precisely this capacity. So, once again: Why *not* write fiction?

Listen now to another voice. It is the voice of Hamm, in Beckett's *Endgame.* Hamm is terrified by the sense that something nameless is 'taking its course', something he cannot grasp but is constantly aware of. 'Something is dripping in my head [...] Splash, splash, always on the same spot.' 'Perhaps it's a little vein,' he thinks, 'a little artery.' Then he pulls himself together: 'Enough of that, it's story time, where was I?' He ponders for a moment, then plunges in: 'The man came crawling towards me, on his belly. Pale, wonderfully pale and thin, he seemed on the point of— no, I've done that bit.' He pauses, then resumes: 'I calmly filled my pipe – the meerschaum, lit it with... let us say a vesta, drew a few puffs.' Suddenly he can't go on with the farce and lets out a scream: 'Aah!' 'Well, what is it you want?' he asks himself, but of course nobody answers him, and after a while he returns to his story: 'It was an extraordinarily bitter day. I remember, zero by the thermometer.' He develops this for a while, then stops and tries another tack: 'It was a glorious bright day, I remember, fifty by the heliometer'. He stops, tries again: 'It was an exceedingly dry day, I remember, zero by the hygrometer. Ideal weather, for my lumbago.'

What Beckett is dramatising here is a quite different view of the notion that man is the storytelling animal. What he is showing is that we may indeed have an innate capacity to tell stories, but that far from this being the royal road to truth it is simply a way of *avoiding* the truth, of avoiding the sense that something nameless is taking its course, that our lives are passing us by, that we are moving inexorably towards a death we do not understand or want and certainly do not know how to cope with.

In such a situation it is not the *difficulty* of telling stories that is frightening but, on the contrary, the *ease*. Hamm can tell a story about bad weather, good weather, storms or calm. All he has to do is say, 'I remember it was a fine day', or, 'I remember it was a cold day', and we are off. But what does that do to the feeling that something nameless is taking its course, something that needs to be dealt with that otherwise will drive him mad? This, it seems to me, is the paradox that lies at the heart of all modern art: the need to speak of that which cannot be uttered, together with the recognition that the utterance perverts or destroys the thing that needed to be spoken of.

In his book *Modernism as a Philosophical Problem*, Robert Pippin, referring to an article by Max Weber, alerts us to a historical change that is very relevant here. 'Tolstoy had noted', he remarks, 'that in pre-modern times, or times oriented around the centrality of nature and not historical time, the prospect of death was much easier to bear. The cycle of life and death had (or was experienced as having) a regular and predictable pattern. After some stretch of time, if one were fortunate enough to have lived into middle age, one could console oneself with the thought that one had basically seen all that life had to offer. The cycle of birth, growth, work, love, reproduction and death had run its course. What more there was to see would likely be only a repetition. Even the great events on the world stage, wars, famine and so forth, were themselves the return of the eternal troubles of the human heart, were themselves repetitions. With the advent of a historical consciousness, though, and so some belief in the uniqueness of historical events, especially the unrepeatability of historical moments, it was impossible to avoid the crushing sense that death was completely meaningless, occupied no place in any natural cycle; was an event without possible consolation [...] One's death became a mere ending at some arbitrary point; there would always be something, probably an infinity of distinct and unprecedented events, to "miss".'[1]

It is this sense of missing out, of dying before one has properly lived one's life, that distinguishes the modern world from what went before – whether one believes 'the modern world' began in the Renaissance, the Reformation, the eighteenth or the nineteenth century. It is this that is at the heart of the modern artist's sense that making art is something more than a pastime or even a profession, but something more akin to a religious vocation, though one fraught with paradox and confusion.

Here are some examples.

'I have only to let myself *go*!' Henry James confides to his notebook in 1891. 'So I have said to myself all my life – so I said to myself in the far-off days of my fermenting and passionate youth.

Yet I have never done it. The sense of it – of the need of it – rolls over me at times with commanding force: it seems the formula of my salvation, of what remains to me of a future.' This desire to let go, by writing to get close to the pulse of life, is expressed again and again by him, bearing witness to the fact that though he knew by then that he could write novels and stories that would find favour with the public, this no longer satisfied him. Though he always began work with a sense of excitement, he ended all too often with a sense of failure, the sense that he had, somehow, by writing, lost that initial grasp of what was really important.

We see much the same pattern in Kafka's journals. On 23 September 1912 he notes: 'This story, "The Judgement", I wrote at one sitting, during the night of 22–23. From ten o'clock at night to six o'clock in the morning, I was hardly able to pull my legs out from under the desk, they had got so stiff from sitting. The fearful strain and joy, how the story developed before me, as if I were advancing over water. Several times during the night I heaved my own weight on my back. How everything can be said, how for everything, for the strangest fancies, there waits a great fire in which they perish and rise up again. How it turned light outside the window'. This was to remain the happiest memory of his writing life. For most of the time, and more and more as his brief life unfolded, he only felt a sense of failure, so much so that by the end he felt that his art was perhaps a kind of trap, set by the devil to keep him from the true path: 'Writing sustains me,' he writes to Max Brod in 1922, 'but is it not more accurate to say that it sustains this kind of life? By this I don't mean, of course, that my life is better when I don't write. Rather, it is much worse then and wholly unbearable and has to end in madness [...] Writing is a sweet and wonderful reward, but for what? In the night it became clear to me, as clear as a child's lesson book, that it is the reward for serving the devil.'

In 1926 Virginia Woolf confided to *her* diary: 'I enjoy almost everything. Yet I have some restless searcher in me. Why is there not a discovery in life? Something one can lay hands on and say:

"This is it"? My depression is a harassed feeling. I'm looking – but that's not it – that's not it. What is it? Shall I die before I find it?' It is this that forces her to abandon established and accepted forms of the novel and grope for something else, something as yet non-existent. 'I have an idea that I will invent a new name for my books to supplant "novel". A new ___ by Virginia Woolf. But what? Elegy?' The excitement at capturing the elusive truth she referred to as catching a momentary glimpse of the fin of a large fish before it vanished again beneath the waves is palpable in her diaries, though the end of each effort to capture it invariably leads to depression and despair. It was during one of these bouts of depression, after finishing what some believe to be her finest book, *Between the Acts*, and with Hitler's forces seemingly set to invade England at any moment, that she drowned herself.

Let me evoke one more great modernist author, a poet this time – Paul Celan. In the introduction to a volume of his prose, his admirable English translator, Rosemarie Waldrop, writes: 'He always finds himself face to face with the incomprehensible, inaccessible, the "language of the stone". And his only recourse is talking. This cannot be "literature". Literature belongs to those who are at home in the world. He can only talk in a simple – deceptively simple – way: circular, repetitive, insisting on the very gap between him and the world, between him and nature. He can only hope that out of his insistence will come a new language which can fill the gap and include the other side. "Reality must be searched for and won."'

'He always finds himself face to face with the incomprehensible, the inaccessible [...] And his only recourse is talking.' Is this not true also of James, Kafka and Woolf? Are not their diaries ways of talking? But it is the next sentences that are crucial: 'This cannot be "literature". Literature belongs to those who are at home in the world.' Of course that is a melodramatic way of talking. The works of these writers are, after all, still classed as literature. But I think what Waldrop is suggesting is that while these are, in one sense, stories that they write, and novels, and poems, they are not quite stories and novels and poems as they have been understood for generations. What we call them – novels, anti-novels, elegies – is less important than the recognition that there is something odd about them, that they exist in the margins of, and as a challenge to, the very notion of story, novel and poem.

More than that. They exist as a challenge to the very notion of Truth, of a truth that can be found and put into words. This is what is dramatised in what is perhaps James's greatest story, *The Turn of the Screw*. In that story the innocent young woman who has been hired to look after two orphaned children who seem to be in some mysterious way in league with the ghosts of two sinister former employees of the country house where they reside, makes it her mission to draw the truth out of them. In the chilling last scene she finally succeeds in getting the little boy to drop his mask of innocence and to utter the words she has been waiting for: 'Peter Quint – you devil!' With that he falls into her arms: 'I caught him, yes, I held him – it may be imagined with what a passion; but at the end of a minute I began to feel what it truly was I held. We were alone with the quiet day, and his little heart, dispossessed, had stopped.'

It is as though Miles could not both speak and live; it had to be one or the other. But of course James has, better than almost anywhere else in his work, by tracing the tension between utterance and annihilation, managed to bring *his* story to its triumphant conclusion – it is terrible, but it is releasing, even cathartic, in a way the classic ghost story never is. It is terrible in the way of ancient tragedy.

But you no sooner say one thing about a modernist work than you need to say the opposite. We can say that James and the others enter realms the classic novel and poem never could, but we also have to remember Kafka's terrible story of the Hunger Artist, with his insistence that he would willingly have eaten the food that other people eat, only he found that such food simply did not agree with his stomach. It is not that *another* kind of food will satisfy him. There *is* no other kind of food. The choice is between eating or starving. Of course we could say that Kafka, by writing this story, shows that he was prepared to eat. Kafka recognised this. That is why he called writing the temptation of the devil. And why we feel he is wrong in doing so, but have to understand *why* he said it.

There is something terrifying, apocalyptic even, about Kafka, and even about the total dedication to their art of the other great modernists. It is not by chance that both Woolf and Celan, so absolute in their lives, ended them by suicide. But there is also something grand and noble in their dedication, and a cause of celebration as well as of horror.

★

I hate the word 'postmodernism' and what it stands for. It seems to me to reflect an attitude of both cynicism and despair, and its products give me no more solid food than is given me by most of the novels that win the Goncourt and Booker Prizes. I firmly believe that the great artists of the second half of the twentieth century are merely continuing the work done by the first great wave of modernists. At the same time I recognise that there is a slightly different 'feel' to the work of those born in the twentieth century and coming to full flowering after World War II – Beckett, Borges, Duras, Robbe-Grillet, Spark, Bellow, Hofmann, Bernhard, Perec.

These are more modest than their predecessors, lighter, readier to laugh at themselves, and they see things in less dramatic, less apocalyptic terms than that earlier generation. Or rather, if they see things in apocalyptic terms they also realise the absurdity of such a vision. They are all of them committed to narrative fiction, but they instinctively recognise that we are *in* the world and nothing we do will allow us to step outside it. We grope our way forward as best we can, and our way to find out what we want to say is to speak and see where it takes us. They fully understand how human it is to want to tell stories, to ourselves and to others, and to make forms that have a satisfying shape, but at the same time they recognise that all stories and all forms are only ways of covering up that dark, unformed set of needs and desires which drive us all. Their works of fiction dramatise that contradiction, giving us characters who tell endless stories, but only in order to keep at bay the darkness that lies underneath.

Like Celan, these writers do not feel they are writing 'literature'. Rather, they are struggling with something that cannot be said but that must be said. Their struggles take many forms: the interminable monologues of Samuel Beckett; the spare dialogue of Marguerite Duras; the displaced rants of Thomas Bernhard's characters; the formal games of Georges Perec. There are as many solutions as there are artists, but what unites them all is that they do not tell an already-finished story, only welcome the reader to join them on their journey.

My own artistic hero of the twentieth century is not a writer but a composer: Stravinsky. I love his concision, his wit, and above all his ability to combine plangency with lightness. I love his pragmatism, encapsulated in such remarks as 'For every problem there is a solution', and 'If Beethoven had had Mozart's lyric gifts he would never have developed his rhythmic capacity to the extent he did.' And I love his continuous desire to renew himself, his unwillingness ever to repeat his last success. All this was, I suspect, made possible by his deep faith. He headed his Symphony in C with the words: 'This Symphony, composed to the Glory of God, is dedicated to the Chicago Symphony Orchestra on the occasion of the fiftieth anniversary of its existence.' A similar faith seems to have helped Muriel Spark create an array of short novels that are painfully funny and as profound as anything written in the last half-century. Others, like Bernhard and Perec, seem to have had faith only in their writing.

I too am convinced that writing is a blessing. I know if I can get a story or novel right it will afford me the greatest of joys. Most often 'getting it right' means finding the form to express the feeling, which keeps returning in all sorts of ways, that existence itself is a miracle, one which we too often take for granted. 'A sense of my own strangeness, walking on the earth', is how Virginia Woolf put it as she groped for what it was she wanted her writing to show. That, I think, is about as good a summing up of why we write fiction as I can imagine.

1 Robert B. Pippin, *Modernism as a Philosophical Problem* (Oxford: Blackwell, 1999), p. 155.

Muriel Spark and the Practice of Deception

MURIEL SPARK HAS always had great fun introducing parodies of novels into her own works. 'I have just been re-reading *The Seventh Child*,' an old flame of the once-famous and recently rediscovered lady novelist Charmian Piper tells her, in *Memento Mori*. 'I love particularly that scene at the end with Edna in her mackintosh standing at the cliff's edge on that Hebridean coast being drenched by the spray, and her hair blown about her face. And then turning to find Karl by her side. One thing about your lovers, Charmian, they never required any preliminary discussions. They simply looked at each other and *knew*.' Her son Eric, at fifty-six himself starting to publish fiction, dismisses his mother's books as consisting 'of people saying "touché" to each other.' His father Godfrey, on the other hand, while jealous of his wife's success, is dismissive of his son's latest offering: 'I simply could not go on with it. A motor salesman in Leeds and his wife spending a night in a hotel with that communist librarian [...] where does it all lead you?' In *The Prime of Miss Jean Brodie* the young Sandy Stranger, of whom Miss Brodie is to say: 'Sandy will make a great spy', is busy writing a novel with her friend Jenny:

> This was a story, still in the process of composition, about Miss Brodie's lover, Hugh Carruthers. He had not been killed in the war, that was a mistake in the telegram. He had come back from the war and called to inquire for Miss Brodie at school, where the first person whom he encountered was Miss Mackay, the headmistress. She had informed him that Miss Brodie did not desire to see him, she loved another. With a bitter, harsh laugh, Hugh went and made his abode in a mountain eyrie, where, wrapped

> in a leather jacket, he had been discovered one day by Sandy and Jenny [...]

In a later novel, *Territorial Rights*, the hero's mother watches the news on television while she eats her supper.

> Then she took up her library book, a novel comfortingly like the last novel she had read:
>
> 'Matt and Joyce finished their supper in semi-silence. Somehow she couldn't bring herself to ask the vital question: had he got the job? Was it so vital, was anything so vital anyway? If he had got the job he would have said so without her asking. Matt got up and stacked the dishes. She followed him into the kitchen and ran the hot tap. What had there ever been between them? Had it all been an illusion? The rain poured outside. [. . .]'
>
> Anthea's eyes drooped. And so to bed.

It would be quite wrong, however, to imagine that Muriel Spark is simply laughing at inept writing, or at the extremes of romantic and realist fiction. There is that, of course, but her real quarry is not bad novels but the novel as such, and one clue to why that might be so lies in a later part of the conversation between Charmian and her former lover Guy Leet, from which I have already quoted a comment of Guy's. Though Charmian is in some respects senile, in others she is still sturdily commonsensical, helped in this by her Catholic faith. Guy has been praising the way she plotted her novels, and as she responds she seems to metamorphose into Muriel Spark herself:

> 'And yet,' said Charmian smiling up at the sky through the window, 'when I was half-way through writing a novel I always got into a muddle and didn't know where it was leading me.'
>
> Guy thought: She is going to say – dear Charmian – she is going to say: 'The characters seemed to take on a life of their own.'

'The characters,' said Charmian, 'seemed to take control of my pen after a while. But at first I always got into a tangle. I used to say to myself,

Oh what a tangled web we weave
When first we practise to deceive.

Because,' she said, 'the art of fiction is very like the practice of deception,'

'And in life,' he said, 'is the practice of deception in life an art too?'

'In life,' she said, 'everything is different. Everything is in the Providence of God.'

The villains in Muriel Spark's novels are those who cannot see the difference between fiction and reality. They seek to manipulate the lives of others for their own ends as the novelist manipulates his or her plot. Georgina Hogg in *The Comforters*; Patrick Seaton the spiritualist in *The Bachelors*; Mrs Pettigrew, the ladies' companion in *Memento Mori*; Sandy Stranger in *The Prime of Miss Jean Brodie*; and Miss Rickward in *The Mandelbaum Gate* all fall into that category. But the novels Muriel Spark writes force us to recognise that the plots of men and women often backfire, and to entertain the idea that we are all of us in the Providence of God. More interestingly, it is often through the machinations of the blackmailers and plotters, but in direct contradiction to their aims, that God's benign plot is brought to completion.

Is this the project of a religious, and specifically a Catholic novelist? But in that case why does it make so much sense to a non-Christian like myself?

The answer is that she couches in Catholic Christian terms what is essentially a Modernist enterprise, on which such diverse artists and philosophers as the Protestant Kierkegaard, the militant atheist Nietzsche, Jews without affiliation like Kafka and Paul Celan, and writers in whose lives religion does not seem to have figured at all, such as Proust, Valéry, and Robbe-Grillet, have all been engaged. To understand why this should be the case we need to stand back a little and think about the historical provenance of the novel.

From its origins in the Renaissance the novel has dealt with individuals, at first with individuals, such as Robinson Crusoe, who triumph over the odds by a mixture of luck and skill in controlling their environment, later with tragic individuals, often women, like Anna Karenina and Emma Bovary, who are destroyed by their environment. It is also important to understand that the novel is not a genre, but a form which emerges precisely when the notion of genre starts to become suspect. Genre, in its heyday, provided artists with protection, with a way of working which did not require them to go back to first principles every time, but liberated even as it constrained them. But when genre began to be seen as a barrier to expression rather than as the natural conduit for expression, as it did when Dr Johnson sneered at Milton's exploration of his feelings on the death of his friend Henry King through the genre of Christian pastoral elegy, a new era had dawned, the era Hegel called 'the age of prose'. As Picasso put it (showing that the crisis affected all the arts): 'A painter like Veronese could start at the top left hand of his painting and work his way down; today we know that the first stroke of the brush determines everything.'

The reason why the novel becomes the place where these issues are most clearly explored is that the novel, having shed the formal pointers which guided earlier readers to an awareness of what genre they were confronted with, looks transparent, looks like a piece of pure reporting, while at the same time being as artificial, as much the result of human decisions, as any other artefact. Thus Kierkegaard, desperate to make his readers understand that as we live our lives we are free to make decisions at every moment of the day, but that when a life is recounted it seems somehow inevitable, struggled to explain how 'life is lived forward but told backwards'. I say struggled, because he was all too well aware of the paradox that he himself was only 'telling'. The novel should be entirely in the subjunctive, he explained, because novels are entirely hypothetical; the problem with them is that they are written in the indicative by those who fail to see that they are thereby falsifying reality. Sartre, a hundred years later, put it like this: 'I walk down the street. My life stretches before me. I do not know how it will develop. But when I read a novel, and read about a man walking down the street, who's life stretches openly in front of him, I am comforted by the knowledge (that is why I read the novel) that *something is going to happen to him*, that he will become the subject of a story. Otherwise the novel would have no *raison d'être*.' Valéry put it more coolly and ironically. He imagined a novelistic opening: 'The marquise leaves the house at seven in the evening.' But why not six or eight? Why a marquise? Because the author has arbitrarily decided this, with no constraints on him other than to make the story cohere, to make it lifelike, realistic. But of what interest is it to the maker to make (and to us to read the result of a series of) such arbitrary decisions? To earn a living? To become famous? But then what has happened to the high ideals of art, to the romantic notion of the artist as the seer, the legislator of mankind? Yet novels go on being written and consumed in large quantities. Are Sartre and Kierkegaard right? Is this a form of drug, designed precisely to keep us from seeing the truth, because that would be unbearable. And if that is the case, what is the novelist who is aware of the problem to do about it?

There are, of course, as many answers as there are good modern novelists. What is striking about Muriel Spark is that she sets about the business of subverting the form of the novel with none of the iconoclasm of a Joyce, a Robbe-Grillet or a Thomas Bernhard. Indeed, an inattentive reader might not be aware that she even was subverting the form of the novel, so easy are her novels to read. How does she do it?

Let us go back to *Memento Mori*. At first sight it appears to be a novel about what it means to be old, but a longer acquaintance with it brings us to understand that it is a novel about what it means to be human. All the characters are losing their faculties, some, like Charmian, in blissful ignorance of the fact, others painfully aware of it, while yet others try to pretend that nothing has changed. For Dame Lettie Colston, seventy-nine, lifelong committee woman and organiser of good causes, there is no such thing as old age. When the man (for all are agreed at least on this, that it is a man) rings up and tells her: 'Remember you must die', she immediately informs the police that he has called again and chivvies them on their lack of progress in tracking him down. Nevertheless, she is shaken, and accepts her brother's invitation to spend the night with them. Charmian, her sister-in-law, on the other hand, lives in a twilit world. 'That was a pleasant young man who called the other day,' she says to her husband. '"Which young man?" "From the paper. The one who wrote –" "That was five years and two months ago," said Godfrey.' Godfrey himself is convinced that he alone shows no signs of ageing, but Muriel Spark at once, and brilliantly, shows us the truth. He drives out to fetch his sister from her home in Hampstead and of course on the return journey there is only one topic of conversation:

> 'Nonsense,' said Lettie, 'I have no enemies.'
>
> '*Think*,' said Godfrey. 'Think hard.'
>
> 'The red lights,' said Lettie. 'And don't talk to me as if I were Charmian.'
>
> 'Lettie, if you please, I do not need to be told how to drive. I observed the lights.' He had braked hard, and Dame Lettie was jerked forward.
>
> She gave a meaningful sigh which, when the green lights came on, made him drive all the faster.
>
> 'You know, Godfrey,' she said, 'you are wonderful for your age.'
>
> 'So everyone says.' His driving pace became moderate; her sigh of relief was audible, her patting herself on the back, invisible.

The problems of old age are not just mental. At the funeral tea after the burial of one of their friends a short while later Godfrey finds himself with his friend's housekeeper/companion, Mrs Pettigrew, and the eighty-year-old poet Percy Mannering:

> To Godfrey's relief Mrs Pettigrew refilled his cup. She also poured one for herself, but when Percy passed his shaking cup she ignored it. Percy said: 'Hah! That was strong meat for you ladies, wasn't it?' He reached for the teapot. 'I hope it wasn't me made Lisa's sister cry,' he said solemnly. 'I'd be sorry to have made her cry.' The teapot was too heavy for his quivering fingers and fell from them on to its side, while a leafy brown sea spread from the open lid over the tablecloth and on to Godfrey's trousers.

The resemblance of this to a children's tea-party is not coincidental. We take time to learn to manipulate the objects around us and eventually they once again become intractable. 'Being over seventy is like being engaged in a war,' remarks Jean Taylor, once Charmian's maid and now living in an old people's home. 'All our friends are going or gone and we survive amongst the dead and the dying as on a battlefield.'

> A year ago, when Miss Taylor had been admitted to the ward, she had suffered misery when addressed as Granny Taylor, and she thought she would rather die in a ditch than be kept alive under such conditions. But she was a woman practised in restraint; she never displayed her resentment. The lacerating familiarity of the nurses' treatment merged in with her arthritis, and she bore them both as long as she could without complaint. Then she was forced to cry out with pain during a long haunted night when the dim ward lamp made the beds into grey-white lumps like terrible bundles of laundry which muttered and snored occasionally.

A nurse administers an injection and the physical pain subsides, 'leaving the pain of desolate humiliation, so that she wished rather to endure the physical nagging pain.'

> After the first year she resolved to make her suffering a voluntary affair. If this is God's will then it is mine. She gained from this state of mind a decided and visible dignity, at the same time as she lost her stoical resistance to pain. She complained more, called often for the bed-pan, and did not hesitate, on one occasion when the nurse was dilatory, to wet the bed as the other grannies did so frequently.

But she has regained that wisdom which, we gradually realise, had always been a central feature of her character. When her scientifically-minded one-time lover, Alec Warner, who is making a study of old age, says to her on one of his visits: 'I always like to know whether a death is a good one or a bad one. Do keep a look-out,' she snaps: 'A good death does not reside in the dignity of bearing but in the disposition of the soul.'

Jean Taylor understands what practically none of the others do, that we are never in full control of our own lives and that it would be as well to recognise this sooner rather than later. It is she who deciphers the enigma of the phone-calls, though the others are not willing to listen. 'What should I do about the phone calls?' Dame Lettie asks her on one of her visits.

> 'Can you not ignore it, Dame Lettie?'
>
> 'No, I can not. I have tried, but it troubles me deeply. It is a troublesome remark.'
>
> 'Perhaps you might obey it,' said Miss Taylor.
>
> 'What's that you say?'
>
> 'You might perhaps try to remember you must die.'
>
> She is wandering again, thought Lettie. 'Taylor,' she said, 'I do not wish to be advised how to think.'

Surprisingly, the only other person to respond in this way to the telephone calls is Mortimer, the police inspector. When the friends gather at his house to hear his views on who the criminal hoaxer might be he almost preaches them a sermon:

> If I had my life over again I should form the habit of nightly composing myself to thoughts of death. I would practice, as it were, the remembrance of death. There is no other practice which so intensifies life. Death, when it approaches, ought not to take one by surprise. It should be part of the full expectancy of life. Without an ever-present sense of death life is insipid. You might as well live on the whites of eggs.

Yet when one of the company responds with: 'I consider that what Mr Mortimer was saying just now about resigning ourselves to death is most uplifting and consoling. The religious point of view is too easily forgotten these days, and I thank you, Mr Mortimer,' he replies: 'Why, thank you, Janet. Perhaps "resigning ourselves to death" doesn't quite convey what I mean. But of course I don't attempt to express a religious point of view.'

This is important. Religion, specifically the teachings of the Roman Catholic Church, is vital to Muriel Spark not because it is 'religion' but because it makes more sense than other belief systems. Mortimer and Jean Taylor are not religious but wise. They understand that if you don't remember death, Death will remind you, as Jean Taylor puts it. Lettie Colston is unwilling to listen and is surprised by death in the form of a burglar who has heard that a rich old lady is living alone in a cottage in Hampstead. Alec Warner's files, which will form the basis of his magnum opus on old age, disappear in an instant when his house is engulfed by fire. We came naked into the world and naked we will leave it. We may try to ignore our frailty, our dependence, but sooner or later it will be driven home to us, and if we go on denying it the marks of repression will show on our faces and bodies. Mrs Pettigrew, beautifully groomed and still sexually attractive to elderly gentlemen like Godfrey because she 'looks after herself', passes for sixty-five but is in fact well over seventy. Like Dame Lettie she imagines she is in charge, though for someone of her station that requires a more active pursuit of worldly goals than Lettie. She is determined to get her hands on the money of her old employer and if possible to become Godfrey's mistress. In typical Sparkian fashion there is a story of wills and unexpected discoveries which reveals that even a Pettigrew cannot manipulate the world to her will. Yet by a further twist she does in the end inherit:

> Mrs Pettigrew had her reward. Lisa's will was proved in her favour and she inherited all her fortune. After her first stroke Mrs Pettigrew went to live in a hotel in South Kensington. She is still to be seen at eleven in the mornings at Harrod's Bank where she regularly meets some of the other elderly residents to discuss the shortcomings of the hotel management, and to plan various campaigns against the staff. She can still be seen in the evening jostling for a place by the door of the hotel lounge before the dinner gong sounds.

As in Dante, so here: a person suffers the pangs of hell or purgatory not in some mythical afterlife but here and now, in the very quality of life she has chosen for herself. Her evil is not just an instrument she turns against the world but both the core of her being and an instrument that is turned against herself. Thus Sandy Stranger, the betrayer of Miss Jean Brodie, remains what she always was, though a nun now, and famous, and with a new name, Sister Helena of the Transfiguration: 'What was your biggest influence, then, Sister Helena?' the journalists ask. 'Was it political, personal? Was it Calvinism?'

> 'Oh no,' said Sandy. 'But there was a Miss Jean Brodie in her prime.' She clutched the bars of the grille as if she wanted to escape from the dim parlour beyond, for she was not composed like the other nuns who sat, when they received their rare visitors, well back in the darkness with folded hands. But Sandy always leaned forward and peered, clutching the bars with both hands, and the other sisters remarked that Sister Helena had too much

> to bear from the world since she had published her psychological book which was so unexpectedly famed.

The compassion of the sisters is not just foolish innocence. Jean Taylor no doubt speaks for them when she says: 'We all appear to ourselves frustrated in our old age, Alec, because we cling to everything so much. But in reality we are still fulfilling our lives.' But most readers will feel that both Mrs Pettigrew and Sandy have got what they deserve.

They, like the other manipulators, spies, and blackmailers who throng the pages of Muriel Spark, are living examples of pure selfishness, which in effect means being unable to imagine anyone other than oneself. The ultimate form this selfishness takes is the desire to control your own death. Muriel Spark only once treats the subject head-on, but it forms the theme of the book she often said was her favourite, *The Driver's Seat.* Lise, the protagonist, cannot bear her boring life in London any more and flies to Rome (the city is not named), determined to find a man to kill her there. 'Tie my hands first,' she says, crossing her wrists, when she has at last found him. 'Tie them with the scarf.'

> He ties her hands, and she tells him in a sharp, quick voice to take off his necktie and bind her ankles.
>
> 'No,' he says, kneeling over her, 'not your ankles.'
>
> 'I don't want any sex,' she shouts. 'You can have it afterwards. Tie my feet and kill, that's all. They will come and sweep it up in the morning.'

But even Lise cannot retain total control over her own death:

> All the same, he plunges into her, with the knife poised high.
>
> 'Kill me,' she says, and repeats it in four languages.
>
> As the knife descends to her throat she screams, evidently perceiving how final is finality.

It is interesting that two English novelists, William Golding and Muriel Spark (all right, Spark is Scottish, but 'British novelists' sounds wrong) should, at about the same time (the nineteen sixties) write books every bit as radical as those of the *nouveau romanciers* on the other side of the Channel, and for the same reasons: their sense that the traditional form of the novel was itself complicit in a false and radically impoverished form of life – yet do so in order to stress (in a very English way) moral and religious concerns which one cannot imagine a Nathalie Sarraute or an Alain Robbe-Grillet ever expressing. Both William Golding's *Pincher Martin* and Muriel Spark's *The Hothouse by the East River* are novels which take place in the instant before death, and the plots they develop are gradually understood to be nothing other than the plots devised by the fevered imagination of those about to die in order to stave off the dreaded moment of death. But if you try to blot out the thought of death it will remind you soon enough, and both Pincher Martin and the protagonists of *The Hothouse* have eventually to give in – at which point the novel ends. Thus at one and the same time we are made to understand the effort of will and control that drives the making of novels, and the place of such will and control in the larger vision of our lives as human, fallible, mortal beings. For to both Golding and Spark the refusal to acknowledge death is only a manifestation of what psychologically and ethically can be seen as selfishness, and philosophically as solipsism or the inability to grasp the fact that other people exist.

Jean Taylor, receiving a visit from Alec Warner in the Maud Long Ward, recalls a conversation with him on a country walk almost fifty years before. 'Do you think, Jean,' he had asked, 'that other people exist?' Their walk has led them to the edge of a graveyard.

> She stopped and leaned over the low stone wall looking at the gravestones.
>
> 'This graveyard is a kind of evidence,' she said, 'that other people exist.'

> 'How do you mean?'
> She was not sure. Having said it, she was not sure why. The more she wondered what she had meant the less she knew.

They enter and walk among the graves, stopping to read the names on the stones.

> 'They are, I quite see, they are,' he said, 'an indication of the existence of others, for there are the names and times carved in stone. Not a proof, but at least a large testimony.'
> 'Of course,' she said, 'the gravestones might be hallucinations. But I think not.' [...]
> 'But the graves are at least reassuring,' she said, 'for why bother to bury people if they don't exist.'
> 'Yes, oh precisely,' he said.

In the place of plot, of intrigue, which is the realm of the novelist and the blackmailer, the cemetery confronts us with tombstones – names and dates. The novelist who recognises the temptations of the novel and counters them by placing within his or her novels a traitor and blackmailer, or else someone absolutely determined to hold on to their self forever if necessary, has, perhaps, other possible strategies. Can one make a novel like a graveyard?

Memento Mori concludes with Alec, now in a nursing home, his filing system destroyed in the fire, searching through his mind 'as through a card-index, for the case histories of his friends, both dead and dying.' But what follows is a paragraph which feels less like the transcript of case-histories than like a litany:

> Lettie Colston, he recited to himself, comminuted fractures of the skull; Godfrey Colston, hypostatic pneumonia; Charmian Colston, ureaemia; Jean Taylor, myocardial degeneration; Tempest Sidebottome, carcinoma of the cervix; Ronald Sidebottome, carcinoma of the bronchus; Guy Leet, arteriosclerosis; Henry Mortimer, coronary thrombosis...

This is taken up by the narrator in the final paragraph of the book, speaking of and for all the 'grannies' of the Maud Long Ward who have no one to remember them:

> Miss Valvona went to her rest. Many of the grannies followed her. Jean Taylor lingered for a time, employing her pain to magnify the Lord, and meditating sometimes confidingly upon Death, the first of the Four Last Things to be ever remembered.

This is not the normal way of the novel, and someone turning to the end without having read the rest of the book might dismiss it as mere Catholic piety. That would be a serious mistake. What it is doing is reasserting what Homer, Shakespeare and Spark's beloved border ballads knew instinctively, indeed what every person before the onset of the Enlightenment knew in his or her bones, that life and death are one and that to deny the one is to deny the other. By the same token, to affirm the fact of death is not to rob life of its meaning but on the contrary to remind us of its richness and complexity. 'Thou mettest with things dying,' says the old shepherd to his son in *The Winter's Tale*, 'I with things new-born'. (Interestingly, *The Winter's Tale* is the only work I can think of outside the novels of Muriel Spark where the machinations of a character in order to gain advantage for himself result in the working out of the plot to the benefit of the protagonists, who remain blissfully ignorant of what has led to this.) In Book III of the *Iliad*, Helen, looking from the walls of Troy at the Greek army assembled below, searches in vain for the sight of her two brothers, Castor and Pollux. 'But the two marshallers of the host can I not see,' she says,

> Castor, tamer of horses, and the goodly boxer Polydeuces, even mine own brethren, whom the same mother bare. Either they followed not with the host from lovely Lacedaemon, or though they followed hither in their seafaring ships, they have now no heart to enter into the battle of warriors for fear of the words of

shame and the many revilings that are mine.

'So she said,' says the narrator. 'But,' he adds, explaining to us the real reason why she cannot see them, 'they ere now were fast holden of the life-giving earth there in Lacedaemon, in their dear native land.' They are dead. But the poet does not simply say that, he says that the earth, which gives life, now holds them in its embrace, not anywhere but in the one place everyone wants to be buried in, their dear native land. The effect of this is curiously soothing, both immensely sad and yet deeply satisfying. The same effect is achieved by slightly different means in the ballad of *Sir Patrick Spens*:

'Mak hast, mak haste my mirry men all,
        Our guid schip sails the morne';
'O say na sae, my master deir,
        For I feir a deadlie storme.

'Late late yestreen I saw the new moone,
        Wi the auld moone in hir arme,
And I feir, I feir, my deir master,
        That we will come to harme.'

O our Scot nobles wer right laith
        To weet their cork-heild schoone:
But lang owere a' the play were playd
        Thair hats they swam aboone.

O lang lang may their ladies sit,
        With thair fans into their hand,
Or eir they se Sir Patrick Spens
        Cum sailing to the land.

Two stanzas of dialogue and then a stanza which recounts the feared outcome, but does it by quite wonderful indirection. The first two lines convey the fastidious Scottish nobles high-stepping to keep their shoes dry as the sea starts to cover the decks, and then two doom-laden lines commenting from some position outside the realm of men (as do the two lines in the *Iliad* telling us about the fate of Helen's brothers), describe the whole expedition and the storm as a play or game and then present us with the stark image of the noblemen's hats afloat on the water, the only sign left of the fate of the ship and its occupants. Finally, in the next stanza, as in the Song of Deborah, we cut to the wives and mothers, sitting and waiting for the men to return, 'their fans in their hands', but waiting, of course, in vain.

Prolepsis, the narrative moving forward beyond the immediate moment to the eventual outcome, is a notable feature of the border ballads, and a powerful contributor to the sense of doom and inevitability they convey. It is not normally a feature of the novel, but Muriel Spark has from the start of her career used it to good effect. It contributes to the mood of both *The Prime of Miss Jean Brodie* and *The Girls of Slender Means*, but it of course has a special role to play in *The Driver's Seat*, where, as far as Lise is concerned, she is in a sense dead already. It's most startling use is in *Not to Disturb*, where the servants sit and wait for the master and mistress and the lover they share to shoot each other, but have already written their accounts of the occurrence and warned the papers of what will, by the morning, have happened. It may be that Muriel Spark discovered the possibilities of prolepsis by reading the border ballads, but the essential point is that prolepsis in both is the sign of a vision which extends beyond the perspective of individual, mortal men, which has tended to be the vision of the novel. There are other striking features of her work which are the result of her need to take the novel away from its normal ground and into realms occupied by earlier literature. Take the communal aspect of some of her titles (*The Ballad of Peckham Rye*, *The Bachelors*, *The Girls of Slender Means*), and the curious choric quality of so many of her novels. Think of what Brian Moore would have done with *The Prime of*

Miss Jean Brodie – a study of plucky spinsterhood and muted despair – and recall what Muriel Spark does with it: Miss Jean Brodie is in a sense only the sum of the memories 'the Brodie set' have of her, and she emerges from this, in the novel, as mysterious, imperative, life-affirming, even if slightly dotty, in contrast to the mean and desperate Sandy Stranger. Think of the end towards which *The Girls of Slender Means* drives: Nicholas Farringdon's vision of pure evil on the night of the fire propelling him to a lonely martyrdom far from London, a destiny which makes perfect sense as it comes to us out of the chorus of the voices of the girls and the fragments of English poetry recited by Joanna and her pupils, but which could not be conveyed in the traditional form of the novel. These are books which dance and sing, and they do so because they understand evil in a way a secular novelist like Angus Wilson, for all his concern with the *idea* of evil, never does. Having looked evil in the eye, having meditated on death, the first of the Four Last Things, Muriel Spark can celebrate the wondrous nature of the life we have been given: 'And so, having entered the fullness of my years, from there by the Grace of God I go on my way rejoicing,' as the heroine of *Loitering With Intent* ends her account of an episode of her youth.

My aunt, an avid though undiscriminating reader, with a passion for the sprawling novels of John Cowper Powys, called Muriel Spark a girl of slender means. She could not have been more wrong. But equally wrong was the Penguin blurb writer who commented: 'For comic observation and spicy dialogue it is impossible to outclass Muriel Spark.' That may be a way of selling books, but it sells this author very short indeed. For Muriel Spark is not the cosy English lady novelist the Penguin blurb implies; in fact she has the broad and humane vision of a Sophocles or a Shakespeare, and it is our great good fortune that she had the means and the determination to convey that vision in novels of incomparable lightness and brilliance.

Saying Kaddish[1]

LEON WIESELTIER, the Literary Editor of the *New Republic*, was born in Brooklyn in 1952. When his father died, on March 1996, he decided to follow orthodox Jewish tradition, and, for the next year, every day, three times a day, he went to synagogue (he prefers the non-Greek word *shul*) to say the mourner's Kaddish: 'Magnified and sanctified may His great name be in the world that He created.' In his anguish and bewilderment he also turned to the history of the mourner's Kaddish in an effort to understand where and when it had begun, how it had developed, and what it meant, delving into obscure volumes of rabbinic commentary and *responsa* picked up in *shul* or obtained for him by his New York bookseller.

Wieseltier is not so orthodox as to take the rituals for granted, nor so alienated from tradition that he cannot turn to it; not so learned in Talmud and commentary that he can speak from the inside, yet knowing how to set about his search. He recognises that his father's death has changed everything, including his attitude to tradition: 'All my life I went to shul with my father, that is, I went to shul as a son. It was because I found it almost impossible to stop going to shul as a son that I stopped going to shul.' Now, in *shul*, he is shocked to find himself being addressed as 'Mr Wieseltier': 'I am not Mr Wieseltier. He was Mr Wieseltier.' His book *Kaddish* is thus neither a tract nor a guide to mourning (he loathes such modern compilations), but the record of one man's year, a year, as he says, when nothing for him was trivial. It is much more than a personal memoir; it is an examination of the nature of ritual and of tradition.

What is the mourner's Kaddish? Wieseltier tracks it down to a story about Rabbi Akiva found in the *Mahzor Vitry*, a liturgical, legal, and exegetical record of the practices and opinions of the Jewish community in north-eastern France in the eleventh century.

It tells how Akiva, strolling in a graveyard, meets a naked black man carrying a pile of wood on his head. Akiva stops him and asks him what he is doing. The man explains that he is dead, but is sent out every day to chop wood. In life, he was a tax collector who favoured the rich and harmed the poor. Is there no way your suffering can be relieved? asks the rabbi. I have been told, says the man, that if I had a son and this son were to stand before the congregation and recite, 'Bless the Lord who is blessed', and the congregation were to answer amen, and the son were to say also, 'May the Great Name be blessed', I would be released from my punishment. But I never had a son. I left my wife pregnant and don't know if the child was a boy. And even if it were a boy, who would teach him Torah, since I have no friend in the world? Akiva decides to find out whether or not the man does have a son, tracks him down and, against all the odds – the boy has been brought up a pagan, is uncircumcised, refuses to learn – brings him to the point where he can recite, before the congregation, the prayer his father wanted. Shortly after this, the man appears to Akiva in a dream and tells him joyfully that he has been saved from Gehenna. 'Your Name, O Lord, endures for ever', exclaims Akiva, 'and the memory of You through all the generations.'

At first sight, the ritual seems to be akin to the Christian one of praying for the souls of the dead to speed them through Purgatory (perhaps the most important ritual of the later Christian Middle Ages, and the reason for the founding of a great many colleges, chantries and choirs). That is how Bossuet, in the seventeenth century, understood the Kaddish when he recounted the legend. Yet even as he retells it, he modifies it. For there is nothing about Purgatory in the Jewish tale, and Bossuet confuses the Kaddish with the *kedusha*, which entered the Christian liturgy of the West as the Sanctus: 'Holy, holy, holy is the Lord of Hosts'.

But if the mourner's Kaddish is not a prayer for the dead, then what is it? More specifically, should it be thought of as a prayer in aid of the father or of the son? In the course of his year of reciting it three times a day, whatever the circumstances, wherever he finds himself, Wieseltier worries away at this problem both personally and historically. He is outraged by the overt moralising he finds in Rashi, the great medieval Jewish commentator, who tells a man who has just lost his child that this is an example of God's great mercy, since the child has in effect died for the father's sins. Would this truly comfort the man? wonders Wieseltier. And he confesses: 'Rashi's combination of mercy and justice is not anything I can understand.'

But the beauty of Jewish tradition, perhaps of any living tradition, is that it is a dialogue in which many voices participate. Rashi reads certain verses in Ecclesiastes one way; Abraham ibn Ezra, writing in Spain in the twelfth century, and Yosef ibn Yahya, writing in Italy in the sixteenth, read them differently. And if Rashi is too prone to moralise, then modern Judaism, especially in America, is far too much in love with psychology. After his father's death, Wieseltier is given countless books about 'the Jewish way of mourning'. He is told they are very popular, have helped many to make sense of their sorrow, 'but I disliked the books, because they were psychology tricked out as religion'. For even if Judaism does not 'account for the psychological meaning of grief', as one of the manuals puts it, 'I am still bound by love and by duty to follow its forms'.

Visiting a dance studio, he has a sudden insight into the way ritual works and into why it is ritual and not psychology that is important to him at this time. 'What these men and women are doing is not rote; it is practice [...] The purpose of practice is to repeat the elements of movement over and over until they are absorbed into the body, until they are made to precede reflection, so that they may be combined and recombined, as the result of reflection, into the dance.' It is the same with study and prayer:

> I see that tradition must be an absorption, a second nature, for creation to occur. That is what traditionalists do not understand. They keep tradition in the forefront of consciousness, so that it

> becomes not their second nature but their first nature, so that one can think of almost nothing else. But thinking of tradition is not the same as doing something with tradition.

This is a profound insight. It is one which T. S. Eliot touched on in the early decades of the twentieth century, in 'Tradition and the Individual Talent' and other essays, but it is in the nature of profound insights that they are lost and found and lost again; we only respond to what we are ready for. Wieseltier cannot hold on to the insight of the dance studio for very long. Soon he is once again cursing the iron law that keeps him going to *shul* three times a day, cursing the fact that the words of the prayer seem to make no sense, that his pain is not eased nor his understanding quickened. Even at the end, as he becomes aware of the fact that his year is almost over, he can only say: 'I kept my promise.'

But what of the question which troubled him so much at the start: is it for my father I do it or for myself? If it is for my father, then how can I accept this kind of magic, and if it is for myself, how can I accept this kind of comfort? In the course of his year, he catches many glimpses of a possible answer, but the full answer only comes when he least expects it. Ploughing through an obscure volume by a sixteenth-century rabbi discussing David's prayer for his son Absalom, he finds what he has been looking for: 'In Ovadiah's view, the kaddish is not a prayer for something. It is a proof of something. The son does not request that his father be granted a good fate. The son demonstrates why his father deserves to be granted a good fate. The son is not the advocate, the son is the evidence.' Now everything falls into place. The son, standing up and reciting the Kaddish, demonstrates the worth of the father who taught his son to stand up and recite. It is as simple as that: an example of the workings of tradition; 'the children of parents are the parents of children. The students of teachers are the teachers of students. It will not end.'

Tradition is frail, since it is in the keeping of men, who can forget it or refuse to pass it on. But that fragility is part of tradition. Ritual is there to help us. And the point about ritual is that it can never be wholly understood, only performed. Nothing, for example, had prepared Wieseltier for the pain of ending. His body had grown used, over the year, to his thrice daily performance, and now he finds himself standing up in *shul* and uttering when it is no longer his task to utter. He sits down in embarrassment and confusion. But he comes to see the wisdom of ritual, for that a ritual has an end is an essential part of it. A whole year is to be given up to mourning, but no more than a year. 'There must be no wallowing. The temptation to nestle with nothingness must be resisted.'

How is it possible to be critical of a book which speaks so wisely and unsanctimoniously about the most important things: about mourning and loss; about death and life; about the nature of ritual and tradition? Occasionally, I felt that some of Wieseltier's attempts at aphorism fell flat, reminded me too much of other writers, did not have the penetrative power he sought. Occasionally, too, I felt that his excessive attachment to reason debarred him from understanding the very process he was describing. But that is part of what *Kaddish* is about. It does not set out to teach but to discover, and the way it is written forces us, as readers, to participate in the discovery. Submitting oneself to its process, one discovers that, like the best novels and poems, it illuminates the world.

1 A review of Leon Wieseltier, *Kaddish* (New York: Picador, 1999).

Kafka and the Holy Rabbi of Belz

On 3 July 1916 Franz Kafka celebrated his thirty-third birthday. That, however, is only a manner of speaking, for there is nothing in his diaries or his letters to suggest that Kafka was even aware of the fact that this was his birthday. Indeed, he had quite other things on his mind, for this was the day on which he and Felice Bauer had arranged to meet to spend a week together in Marienbad.

Felice and Kafka had met in the summer of 1912, at the house of their mutual friend, Max Brod, on a visit she had paid to Prague from Berlin, where she worked in the office of a company that manufactured dictating machines. That meeting had triggered an amazing reaction in Kafka, who had for most of the year been feeling a growing sense of crisis both in his writing and in his personal life. In September he wrote in one night the story he felt had finally revealed to him what he was capable of, 'The Judgement', and followed it with 'Metamorphosis' and 'The Stoker', which became the first chapter of *Amerika*. Though their meeting had been brief, Kafka bombarded Felice with letters and soon she became his main correspondent, the recipient of all his dreams, anxieties and desires. From all accounts she was an independent, 'modern' woman, stolid and well-meaning, and the epistolary assault seems to have bewildered and confused her. Nevertheless, Kafka was clearly a charming and passionate man and his wooing at a distance seems to have worked, for by 1914 they were engaged. Yet all was not well. Kafka describes in his diaries the horror of the engagement party in Berlin, and soon after the marriage was called off. It seems, though, that Kafka could do neither with her nor without her, and gradually their correspondence resumed. Tentatively, they began to meet again for brief spells of time.

It is clear that Felice was caught in a private struggle Kafka was having with himself, the unwitting victim of a dialectic which could never be resolved. For she represented for him a way to escape from his family, especially his overwhelming father, at the same time as she represented the means by which he could show his father that he had it in him to become himself a husband and father. But therein lay the problem. For while part of him longed for this, another part loathed and despised all his father stood for. Being a husband and father was thus associated for Kafka with dominance and the total control of others, something that was profoundly alien to him. He also knew very well that what he needed was solitude and invisibility if he was to give expression to all the voices that buzzed inside his head. At the same time the idea of growing old a colourless bachelor who had ventured nothing and so gained nothing filled Kafka with horror. The chance meeting with Felice brought all these things to a head. She was solid, dependable, and, besides, she was interested in things Jewish – as it turned out, something Kafka was finding himself more and more drawn to and which his father, the self-made grocer from a provincial shtetl, had hoped to turn his back on forever. Above all, she was a single woman of marriageable age.

'3 July,' he writes in his diary. 'First day in Marienbad with F. Door to door, keys on either side.'

The diary for these days is actually mainly filled with the beginnings and fragments of stories, with brief comments on the Bible, which he was reading at the time, and with remarks such as: 'What are you? I am miserable. I have two little boards screwed against my temples,' which recur like a leitmotif throughout the *Diaries*. But occasionally it becomes more direct: 'Poor F. 6 July. Unhappy night. Impossible to live with F. Intolerable to live with anyone.' Yet on 10 July he and Felice wrote a joint letter to Felice's mother. Kafka's contribution begins: 'Dear Mother, my right to this mode of address lies not in the past, but in the present. Felice and I have met (such things do happen) here in Marienbad and discovered that years ago we tackled things in the wrong way [...] Good things, however, are not accomplished at the first attempt, nor at the second, but perhaps at the ten-thousandth, and this is where we now are.' He concludes: 'Many things have changed since then, few for the better, this I do know; but one of the few is the relationship between Felice and me and its assurance for the future [...] Kissing your hand most respectfully, I send kindest regards to Erna and Toni. Yours, Franz.'

Felice adds: 'Dear Mother, I hope you will interpret Franz's words the way they are intended. Now you have the opportunity to give him your love all over again.'

By 14 July Felice had gone back to Berlin and Kafka was left alone in Marienbad. In the old way, he inundates her with missives, giving her news of what is going on in the hotel and in the town, and talking about their future: 'Dearest, poor dearest (how the old couple next door keep chattering), alone on the familiar walks, and yet on the whole it would be all right, except that I do nothing but rest. For I am confident as far as you are concerned, as confident as we can possibly be, at this moment, after our fashion.' To Brod he writes:

> The morning of the pencilled card [...] marked the end [...] of a series of frightful days, spawned in still more frightful nights. It really seemed that the rat had been driven to its very last hole. But since things could not have become worse, they took a turn for the better. The cords with which I was trussed I straightened out somewhat while she who had constantly been holding out her hands to help but reaching only into an utter void, helped again and we arrived at a human relationship of a kind I had so far never known and which came very near in its meaningfulness to the relationship we had achieved at the best periods of our correspondence.

But Kafka's ruthless honesty with himself will not let him stop there: 'Much has been torn open that I wanted to shield forever (I am not speaking of anything in particular, but of the whole); and through this rent will come, I know, enough unhappiness for more than a lifetime.' Yet, he goes on, such unhappiness is perhaps a necessary part of something greater:

> I did not really know her up to now. Aside from other doubts, last time I was hampered by an actual fear of the reality of this girl behind the letters. When she came towards me in the big room to receive the engagement kiss, a shudder ran through me. The engagement trip with my parents was sheer agony for me, every step of the way. I have never feared anything so much as being alone with F. before the wedding. Now all that has changed, and is good. Our agreement is brief: to get married soon after the end of the war; to rent an apartment of two or three rooms in some Berlin suburb; each to assume economic responsibilities for himself. F. will go on working as she has done all along, while I — well, for myself I cannot yet say.

However, in the week or so that Kafka stayed on alone in Marienbad something occurred which led him to write to Brod one of the most extraordinary letters ever written by this remarkable letter-writer, and it had nothing, at least on the face of it, to do with Felice. On 18 July, in one of his postcards to Felice, he writes:

> Imagine, we were not even aware of the most distinguished visitor to Marienbad, a man in whom so many place their trust: the Rabbi from Belz, no doubt at present the chief representative of Hasidism. He has been here 3 weeks. Last night for the first time I joined him and some 10 of his entourage on their evening walk. A great deal could be said about it, but I have just written about it at length to Max, who had informed me of the Rabbi's presence here.

Brod had indeed alerted Kafka to the rabbi's visit, and of the presence in his retinue of a Prague friend of theirs, Georg Mordechai

Langer, who had become involved with the Hasidic movement. Kafka's long yet unfinished letter to Brod reports on his meeting up with Langer and his encounter with the rabbi.

He begins as he begins so many letters and diary entries, by complaining about his headache – despite this, though, he says, he ran 'over there' right after dinner. 'I shall only describe the externals,' he goes on, in a sentence which all those who seek to understand Kafka should take to heart, 'since I cannot speak of more than I could see. But all one actually sees is the most minute details; and this is indeed significant in my opinion.' At first he can't find Langer, who is to be his means of entry into the presence of the rabbi, and he wanders about in a labyrinth of rooms and houses very much as he describes such things in *The Trial* and *The Castle*:

> The place has several buildings and annexes, all clustered together on a knoll, that belong to one owner and can only be entered by partly underground stairways and passages. The names of the houses are designed to confuse: Golden Castle, Golden Bowl, Golden Ball, while some houses have two names, one in the front and another in the back.

Gradually, though, he says, a certain order becomes apparent and we realise that what we have here is a small community arranged by social class enclosed between two large and elegant hotels, the Hotel National and the Hotel Florida. But no one seems to have heard of Langer. Someone mentions a few young people living up in the attics, then someone else suggests he look for his friend at the Hotel Florida. And indeed as he approaches the hotel he meets Langer coming out.

'I don't intend to report on what he told me,' he says to Brod, 'but only on what I myself saw.' However, he starts with some background. Every evening at seven-thirty or eight, it seems, the rabbi goes out in his carriage, which proceeds slowly towards the forest while his entourage follow on foot. In the woods he stops and takes a walk with his entourage along the forest paths till nightfall, returning home in time for prayers, at about ten. Thus the evening after meeting Langer at the Florida (Kafka is not very clear about the chronology) he meets up with him again at about seven-thirty at the Hotel National, where the rabbi is staying. The rain is teeming down. 'Langer maintained that it would surely stop, but it did not, only streamed down the harder. Langer said that it had been rainy only once during the rabbi's drive and that the rain had stopped when the rabbi came to the woods. But this time the rain did not stop.' If we are inclined to take this as a hint of scepticism on Kafka's part we would be wrong. He is simply trying to tell everything as it was, just as he did when he encountered other famous people, such as Rudolf Steiner, a meeting that has much in common with this one, and which he describes in the early pages of his diaries.

There follows another episode which could have come straight out of one of Kafka's novels. He and Langer sit under a tree and see a Jew with an empty soda-water bottle run out of the house. Langer explains that he's fetching water for the rabbi (we are in a spa after all). They join the man, who has been detailed to fetch water from the Rudolph Spring, which has been prescribed for the rabbi. Unfortunately he doesn't know where the spring is, and they all rush about in the rain trying to find it. Someone shows them the way but tells them the spring will be closed since it closes at seven. It can't be, says the bottle bearer, and they rush off to find it, but it is indeed closed. Langer suggests the man fetch water from the Ambrosius Spring, since that one is always open. The man agrees and they hurry there, only to find that it is in the process of shutting, and they are shooed away. They hurry back.

> On the way we meet up with two other Jews... They walk along like a pair of lovers, looking affectionately at one another and smiling, one with his hand thrust into his low-slung pocket, the other looking more citified. Firmly locked arm in arm. We tell them the story of the closed springs; the two simply cannot be-

> lieve it, and so the three of them trot off back to the Ambrosius Spring. We go on to the Hotel National, while the water bearer catches up with us and runs ahead, calling out to us breathlessly that the spring really is closed down.

This sense of movement and confusion, first the attempt to find Langer in the labyrinth of the rabbi's headquarters and then the futile search for water in the rain, merely sets the scene for the entrance of the rabbi. To escape the rain Langer and Kafka make for the vestibule of the hotel, but then Langer suddenly jumps back and to one side: 'The rabbi is coming. No one must ever stand in front of him, there must always be a free passage before him, which is not easy to provide, since he often suddenly turns round and in the throng it is not easy to take evasive action speedily.' Indoors it is apparently even worse, and so great are the crowds that throng round him that the rabbi is recently supposed to have cried out: 'You are Hasidim? No. You are murderers.'

But now Kafka finally catches a glimpse of the man he has come to see:

> He looks like the Sultan in a Doré illustration of the Münchausen stories which I often looked at in my childhood. But not like someone masquerading as the Sultan, really the Sultan. And not only Sultan but also father, grammar-school teacher, gymnasium professor, etc. The sight of his back, the sight of his hand as it rests on his waist, the sight of his broad back as he turns – it all inspires confidence. I can detect this peaceful, happy confidence in the eyes of everyone in the group.

Every word counts here. The rabbi reminds Kafka of the Sultan in a book he read as a child, but also of all the other authority figures of his childhood and youth. What he senses is the general aura of the man, but this is conveyed by a thousand little details, details not of dress or appearance but of gestures and ways of moving, and Kafka catches these on the wing, as it were: the rabbi's hand resting on his waist, his back as he turns (compare Eliot's: 'Hakagawa bowing among the Titians' and 'Madame de Tornquist, one hand on the door', and the shortcuts Picasso was taking at the time in his search for a new intensity). In contrast to the wild and pointless movement of his disciples in search of water, these gestures of the holy rabbi are calm and easy, inspiring confidence not only in those who follow him but even in the outsider Kafka.

It is only now that Kafka homes in on the rabbi's appearance, and what is fascinating about this next passage is that though it seems to come out of a nineteenth-century novelistic tradition – the caricature of Dickens, the painstaking descriptions of Flaubert – in fact it flies in the face of such descriptions. For with them there is always a direct link between inner and outer, for the outer details the novelist picks out are meant to give us a picture of the *kind* of person the author wishes us to imagine. With Kafka on the other hand the painstaking accumulation of detail leaves us utterly in the dark as to the inner life of the person being described and anything we might call their 'character'. What we feel, rather, is that Kafka is desperately looking, and finding the language to express what he sees, precisely because he remains in the dark as to how all the details add up:

> He is of medium height, and rather broad of beam, though not sluggish in his movements. Long white beard, unusually long sidelocks [...] One eye is blind and blank. His mouth is twisted awry, which gives him a look at once ironic and friendly. He wears a silk caftan which is open in front; a broad belt about his waist; a tall fur hat, which is the most striking thing about him; white stockings.

It seems that for the first time the rabbi is not going out in his carriage but is going to walk. About ten of his disciples are following close behind or walking on either side of him. One of them carries his silver cane, which he has exchanged for an umbrella, and the chair on which he might want to sit down; another carries a cloth with which to wipe the chair dry; another a glass; and yet another a bottle of water which has finally been acquired from a store. There are four men Kafka calls *gabim* but which Brod in his notes corrects to *gabbaim*, lay communal officials. They play a special role in the rabbi's entourage, are his intimates, secretaries and the like. 'The highest of the four, according to Langer, is an exceptional rogue; his huge belly, his smugness, his shifty eyes seem to bear that out. However,' adds Kafka in one of the most interesting sentences in this extraordinary letter, 'one must not hold that against him, for all the gabim go bad; people cannot bear the continual presence of the rabbi without suffering damage. It is the contradiction between the deeper meaning and the unrelenting commonplaceness that an ordinary head cannot sustain.'

So the procession sets out. The rabbi has a bad leg, he stops to cough, then stops again, fascinated by the most ordinary details of his sightseeing trip. He asks innumerable questions and his whole demeanour is marked by admiration and curiosity.

> All in all, what comes from him are the inconsequential comments of itinerant royalty, perhaps somewhat more childish and more joyous. At any rate they reduce all thinking on the part of his escort to the same level. Langer tries to find or thinks he finds a deeper meaning in all this; I think that the deeper meaning is that there is none, and in my opinion this is quite enough. It is absolutely a case of divine right, without the absurdity that an inadequate basis would give it.

To grasp what Kafka is saying here is to start on the road to responding to his fiction. To try and explain authority either psychologically or sociologically or in any other way is a nonsense, he insists. What we have to start from is that authority is authority *precisely because* it cannot be explained. This does not mean that Kafka is a wide-eyed upholder of all authority or someone likely to fall under the spell of charismatic demagogues. Far from it. But he is aware of the fact that authority is a mysterious force which must be reckoned with and cannot simply be dismissed or explained away. This is the reason for his fraught and complicated relations with his father, and for his fascination with the Hasidic movement. Fraught because he can neither be for nor against. What he grasps so profoundly is that even in our secular times we cannot get away from figures of authority, whether in the family or outside it. Sometimes, as with the Rabbi of Belz, that authority appears to be benign; at others, as with Hermann Kafka, it is tyrannical. In both cases it cannot be gainsaid. Those in authority move slowly and with confidence – the rest of us spend our lives rushing about, lost in the labyrinth of our own confusion. Our one hope is not to be misled into thinking that authority can be explained in historical or psychological or any other terms, for that would lead to our thinking that we can understand it and so to miss the central point, that it is precisely that which transcends understanding.

The rabbi and his entourage move on, and Kafka follows and watches and reports. The rabbi stops at the New Bathhouse. 'The building makes a great impression on him. Golden letters over the door read NEW BATHHOUSE. He has the inscription read to him, asks why the building is called this, whether it is the only bathhouse, how old it is, and so forth. He repeatedly says, with that characteristic East European Jewish wonderment: "A handsome building."'

There is one more paragraph and then the letter breaks off. Brod does not tell us if Kafka sent him the letter as it was or left it unfinished and unposted, or if a leaf has been lost.

He returned to Prague a day or two later. His relationship with Felice sputtered on for a year and then, with Kafka diagnosed with TB and going to his favourite sister Ottla in Zürau to convalesce, she drops out of his life for ever. Before his early death from TB in 1924, however, he will have two rather more fulfilling love affairs, the first with Milena Jesenská and the second with Dora Diamant, with whom he finally found it possible to escape his family and live in some sort of contentment in his final painful year. And, apart from a comment about the rabbi in a postcard to Weltsch sent on 19 July, Kafka, it seems, never mentions him again.

The Lost [I]

THE OPENING OF Daniel Mendelsohn's *The Lost*, an ambitious book, encapsulates both its strengths and its weaknesses. Beneath a small blurred photo of a serious looking little boy we read: 'Some time ago, when I was six or seven or eight years old, it would occasionally happen that I'd walk into a room and certain people would begin to cry.' The sentence is carefully crafted for maximum effect, and it *is* arresting, yet its mock precision ('six or seven or eight years old') and that initial 'some time ago' when we would expect 'a long time ago' (Mendelsohn is in his fifth decade), make it seem mannered, narcissistic even, a feeling reinforced by the silent juxtaposition of image and text. This is dangerous in any memoir, but especially in the kind that deals, as this one does, with the search for the victims of the Nazi genocide.

For the people on whom the young Daniel Mendelsohn had this effect were mainly old East European Jews, members of his grandparents' generation, now in retirement in Miami Beach, and the reason he had this effect on them was (it seems) that he bore a striking resemblance to his maternal great-uncle Shmiel, the brother of his mother's father, and the only one of his family to have been still living in his native town of Bolechów, now in the Ukraine, when the Second World War started. Shmiel, his wife and four daughters all perished in the Holocaust, and it is the need to know precisely what happened to them that preoccupies the growing boy (himself one of five children) and forms the subject of this book. 'It had been to rescue my relatives from generalities, symbols, abbreviations, to restore them to their particularity and distinctiveness that I had come on this strange and arduous trip,' he writes of his first visit to Bolechów. That is why he feels so uneasy with his siblings' insistence that they visit Auschwitz first. 'To me Auschwitz represented the opposite of what I was interested in, and – as I started to realise on the day I actually did go to Auschwitz – of why I had made this trip. Auschwitz, by now, has become the gigantic, one-word symbol, the gross generalisation, the shorthand, for what happened to Europe's Jews – although what happened at Auschwitz did not, in fact, happen to millions of Jews from places like Bolechów.'

To find out what happened to Shmiel and Ester and to their four daughters, Lorka, Frydka, Ruchele, and Bronia, he travels to interview survivors from the town now living in Australia, Israel and Scandinavia, as well as in Bolechów itself (twice). In the course of this he comes to a growing understanding not just of how they died but of how they lived:

> She talked about how she used to ski in the hills outside of Bolechów, how they'd played volleyball in school, how she had played Ping-Pong. (Matt and I exchanged a swift look: *Ping-Pong*!?) She remembered the school uniforms: berets for the girls, caps for the boys. Every school had a different color, she said. She talked about the homework she and her friends had to get through before the Hanoar meetings. What do you expect? she said suddenly. People lived as *usual*... Life as *usual*!

Then the war arrived. First came the Soviets, terrorising the Ukrainians; then came the Germans, with their pestilential dream of a world without Jews. All that time Shmiel was writing more and more desperate letters to his relatives in America, begging them to find a way of helping him and his family get out. Perhaps they tried, but if so they failed. And why, Mendelsohn wonders, did his grandfather, that dapper gentleman, that great ladies' man and raconteur, the one who first told him about the old place, end his life by committing suicide? He does not speculate, merely notes that the Holocaust is not something that happened in the past; it's something that's happening now. And now, in the present of the narrative, he contacts his informants and asks his questions, while his brother takes pictures:

> Now, for the first time, I got a clear picture of the first Aktion. I needed to know about it in as much detail as possible [...] How, I wanted to know, did they round up the people for this Aktion? Bob said, The Germans were going round with Ukrainian policemen, because at first they had a list.

In this first Aktion, in all probability, the third daughter, Ruchele, died, having been picked up as she walked the streets of her home town with her girlfriends. She was sixteen. A year later there was a second Aktion. This time the Germans were better organised. Men, women, and children were caught in their houses, attics, hiding-places. About 660 children were taken. After the usual incarceration in the Catholic community centre, with the usual beatings and tortures, those still alive were herded to the cattle trucks and taken to the extermination camps. Here Shmiel, his wife and the youngest daughter most probably died.

In his search for the detail that will rescue these events from the banalities of generalisation ('Killed by the Nazis'), Mendelsohn does not spare himself or us. He copies out an account of what happened in the Dom Katolicki in the first Aktion:

> The rabbis were especially targeted. Rabbi Horowitz's body was literally chopped and shredded. Rabbi Landau was ordered by one of the Gestapo men to stand naked on a chair and declaim a speech in praise of Germany. When he said that Germany is great, the Gestapo man beat him with a rubber stick, shouting: 'You're lying!' After that he shouted: 'Where is your God?' [...] Szancia Reisler, the wife of Friedmann the lawyer, had to dance naked on naked bodies. At midday, the Rabbis were led out from the hall and there is no trace of them. It is said that they were thrown into the sewer.

Later he spends four pages describing in detail exactly what he thinks Shmiel, Ester and Bronia would have experienced as they were dragged out of the cattle trucks, made to strip naked, and entered what they thought was the shower-room.

But there is a problem here. The idea that we need to know what happened in the past in order to be free of it is an old and powerful one, given a new impetus by Freud. But, as J. M. Coetzee has noted, there are some places into which we venture at our peril, places of the imagination where we may easily be corrupted by what we find. Even the need to know, far from being an unquestioned good, may, as Nietzsche thought, be just as much the product of pathology as the refusal to face the past. For, like jealousy, it has no end and can become a drug without which we cannot live. We find ourselves wanting to know more and more and more and nothing will ever wholly satisfy this thirst. Mendelsohn is too American, too much a child of his age and place, to see this. 'As a profoundly Jewish person,' he writes of his one-time classics teacher and companion on some of his trips, Froma Zeitlin, 'and, in a way, as a person who had devoted her professional life to the nature of tragedy, how could she not, in the end, become obsessed by the Holocaust?' (My answer, not an American answer: Not all Jews NOT obsessed by the Holocaust are in denial.)

Though his travels make Mendelsohn acknowledge that 'the world is so much bigger than you can possibly imagine, if you grow up in a provincial place: a New York suburb, a Galician shtetl,' one does not feel that he really understands this. He writes, for instance, about 'my later desire to study the culture and language not of the Jews, the people to whom I belonged, but of the Greeks and Romans, the Mediterraneans of whom Nino himself was so obviously one [...]' For him Jews are the inhabitants of East European shtetls; it never enters his mind that Jews have lived in Mediterranean lands for more than three millennia.

To differentiate his book from other accounts of the search for Holocaust victims, he interlaces the story of his quest with meditations on the different portions of Genesis read in synagogue on different days, the *parashot*. Thus the start is linked to the opening chapters of Genesis; the exploration of the tensions between his grandfather and the brother who returned to Boleshow and died there, and of the relations over the centuries between Poles, Ukrainians, and Jews in Eastern Europe is linked to the episode of Cain and Abel; the deluge that overwhelmed European Jewry to the *parashah* of Noah; his travels in search of information to the *parashah* of Abraham and God's injunction to him to leave his home and family and set out on his travels. This at first seems like a brilliant insight, but what is it really saying? That history repeats itself? That it's all in the Bible? Besides, his actual discussions of the *parashot* do little to inspire trust in him as a Bible reader. He parades his knowledge with an air of authority but what he says is too often banal and rarely incisive.

Nor is he much more reliable on the classics, his academic speciality. There is a wonderful early moment when a remark by his mother suddenly makes him realise that the man in a photograph with his great-uncle, which he had often looked at without ever thinking of the other person, is none other than the frightening and repulsive old man he used to see as a child in those Miami apartments, Herman the barber. The shock caused (to him and to us) by this collision of two worlds which had previously seemed hermetically sealed off from one another, is worthy of Proust. A similar shift of perspective occurs when, in Australia, he hands some family photos to the survivors he is interviewing. Suddenly he realises what he is doing: here he is,

> travelling around the world talking to these survivors, who had survived with literally nothing but themselves, and showing them the rich store of photographs that my family had owned for years, all those photographs I had stared at and, later, dreamed about when I was growing up, images of faces that, for me, had no emotional meaning at all in and of themselves, but which to the people to whom I was now showing them had the power to recall,

suddenly, the world and the life from which they'd been torn so long ago. How stupid, how insensitive I had been.

This is terrific. But the insight is diluted, if not negated, because it is followed by a long excursus on Aeneas arriving in Carthage and seeing, depicted on the walls, the story of the sack of Troy, from which he himself had only narrowly escaped. 'For the Carthaginians, the war is just a decorative motif,' writes Mendelsohn, 'something to adorn the walls of their new temple; for Aeneas, of course, it means much more.' But that is spectacularly wrong: the whole story of Dido and her infatuation with Aeneas cannot be understood without realising that she has long heard of and admired him, and that it is she who has had his deeds painted here – hardly 'a decorative motif'. Not a very important point in the general economy of Mendelsohn's book, but indicative of the way in which his style and how he has chosen to tell his story, far from enriching it, as he seems to imagine, actually detracts from it because it dilutes his points, and, in the search for large and powerful resonances, makes even what is genuine in his book start to sound hollow.

The same holds of his use of photographs, which is clearly indebted to Sebald, but without Sebald's sure touch both as to what to show and how to position it on the page. Too often it feels like a rhetorical ploy.

This is a pity because the themes he is dealing with are important and, once he gets caught up in his quest, what he has to say is very much worth hearing. One strand, which grows in significance as he interrogates the survivors and visits the town in which the events took place and talks to the present-day inhabitants, is that of moral responsibility. By refusing to talk in generalities, by searching for specific details, he slowly unpacks the role of chance and choice in human affairs. There are no evil peoples, he insists. Phrases like 'the Ukrainians were the worst of the lot' are unhelpful. When the Russians came in the Ukrainians cowered and the Jews felt safe; when they retreated and the Germans replaced them, the Ukrainians were at last able to give vent to the anger and resentment they had felt for generations at what they saw as their privileged neighbours. But there were good Ukrainians and Poles, who sheltered Jews, knowing full well that their lives were at risk, just as there were bad ones who denounced them out of spite or, worse, tortured them in a spirit of sadism, encouraged by the Germans. There were also Jews who did the Germans' dirty work for them, the so-called Jewish policemen, because if they did not they and their families would suffer, and there were Jews who refused. Who can say how you or I would have acted in the circumstances?

Another strand, which gathers significance as the book nears its climax, concerns the nature of stories. When he began he was full of confidence that 'a story, however ugly, would give their death some meaning – [...] make their deaths be *about* something.' But he soon comes to see that no one who has lived to tell would actually have been there when others were killed, so that everything comes to us at second or third-hand. And then gradually he comes to see that perhaps all we can ever have are conflicting stories and defective memory. In the end, though, he understands that it was not, after all, stories he was in search of, but something else, something much more difficult to grasp, but fundamental to our relationships with others.

Frydka, the second daughter, is the one who from the first seemed the most independent, more beautiful and wilful than her sisters. Did she join the partisans, as one rumour has it? Or was she hidden in the town by her Polish lover? Was she pregnant by him at the time? Was her father with her? (Then he hadn't died in the gas chambers?) And who denounced them? Rumour had it that they were concealed in a *kessle*, as Mendelsohn writes it, anxious to give us a flavour of Yiddish accents whenever he can. But as he enquires about a possible castle in the vicinity no one seems to have heard of one. Then, by a series of extraordinary chances he suddenly finds himself in a house where, he is told, a Jewish girl and her father were hidden by her Polish lover with two Polish teachers. He is shown a cellar, reached by a trapdoor, and, though he suffers from claustrophobia, he descends into the darkness. The cellar, which is no more than an underground box, is now used to store jams. Suddenly he understands: he had the information all along but his romantic imagination had misled him once again: *kessle*, he now remembers, is the Yiddish word for box; his informants were using a Yiddish word, not an English one with a Yiddish accent. He emerges. How were they killed? he wants to know. Shot in the back garden, he is told, while the Poles who hid them were taken to the nearest big town and hanged, *pour encourager les autres.* He asks to be taken out into the garden. He is shown the tree next to which they were shot. And as he stands on the spot where they met their end, he has a final revelation:

> For a long time I had thirsted after *specifics*, after *details*, had pushed the people I'd gone all over the world to talk to to remember more, to think harder, to give me the concrete thing that would make the story come alive. But that, I now saw, was the problem. I had wanted the details and the specifics for the *story*, and had not – as how could I not [*sic*], I who never knew them, who had never had anything *but* stories – really understood until now what it meant to be a *detail*, a specific [...] As I stood in this most specific place of all, more specific even than the hiding place, that place in which Shmiel and Frydka experienced things, physical and emotional things I will never begin to understand, precisely because their experience was *specific* to them and not me, as I stood in this most specific of places I knew that I was standing in the place where they had died, where the life that I would never know had gone out of the bodies I had never seen, and precisely because I had never known or seen them I was reminded the more forcefully that they had been specific people with specific deaths, and those lives and deaths belonged to them, not me, no matter how gripping the story that may be told about them.

So, in the moment he finally 'finds' them, he understands that he has to let them go. At such a moment, as religions from time immemorial have always known, thought and imagination need to be replaced by a gesture, an act. And as Jews have always done in the presence of their dead, he bends down, picks up a stone, and places it in the cleft of the branches.

As I read this book I could not help but think of two great novels, one about the search for one's lost ones – Nabokov's *The Secret Life of Sebastian Knight* – the other about the return to a Ukrainian town after the war, Appelfeld's *The Age of Wonders*. At the end, though, it was Wallace Stevens who came to mind, as Mendelsohn finally grasps (and helps us grasp) that there comes a point when all stories must be left behind in the acknowledgement of the mystery of other lives and deaths. That the book can make one think of such illustrious predecessors, in spite of the sometimes annoying preening and self-consciousness of the early pages, is a testimony, in the end, to Mendelsohn's hard-won artistic and ethical integrity.

1 A review of Daniel Mendelsohn, *The Lost: A Search for Six of Six Million* (New York: HarperCollins, 2006).

Cousins

FOR GOOD OR ILL we are the products of our past. On a visit to Israel ten years ago I spent a week with a distinguished novelist touching seventy who was also a Holocaust survivor. 'They penned us into ghettos in Europe and then exterminated us,' he told me, 'and now they are planning to do the same in the Middle East.' I asked him who 'they' were. 'The forty million Arabs,' he said. The second week of my stay I spent with Israeli-born friends in Tel Aviv, a couple in their forties. 'The disastrous policies our governments have pursued for so many years,' they said to me, 'have set back the possibility of our children and grandchildren ever growing up in peace. Maybe our great-grandchildren will, but we won't be there to see it.' Two histories, two views of the present and the future.

I too, of course, am a product of my past, and how I see myself as a Jew and how I relate to the state of Israel is of course strongly coloured by that past. My mother was born in Egypt. Her mother's grandfather was a Jewish doctor who had come to Egypt from Ferrara in the 1830s to seek his fortune. Her father was another Jewish doctor, from Odessa this time, who had come to Egypt on the first leg of a tour of the world he planned to make after serving as a medical orderly in the Russo-Japanese war. He fell in love with the country and with my grandmother, settled in Egypt, had two daughters, converted and became a Muslim, and died of an unspecified disease (probably syphilis) when my mother and her sister were five and six years old. The distraught widow eventually fell in love with an Australian journalist in Egypt on his way to cover the war on the Western front. When he died at Messines in Belgium the following year my poor grandmother, barely thirty and twice bereaved, sought comfort from an Anglican missionary and eventually decided to convert. One day, my mother told me, she called her and her older sister into the drawing room and said to them: 'Sister Margaret would like to tell you a story. Please listen carefully.' At the end of her story, which was very moving, Sister Margaret said: 'Now, girls, which would you rather be, the cruel people who killed our Lord or the good people who loved him?' Even then, at the age of seven or eight, my mother told me, she had the uneasy feeling that something was wrong with this story, but that feeling was drowned by the general mood of the occasion, and the two little girls were duly baptised. Three years later their mother herself died in the great cholera epidemic of 1920 and the little girls went to live with their grandparents.

Yet while my aunt went on to marry a Catholic and to convert to Catholicism (and her elder daughter to marry a Muslim and convert to Islam while her younger daughter married a Greek Orthodox but remains a committed Roman Catholic), my mother married a Jew and repudiated her Anglican conversion. For though she had never been in a synagogue or had any Jewish instruction, she had obscurely felt, all the time she was growing up with her freethinking grandparents, that she was Jewish. There was no content to this thought, just an obscure conviction. When she married, she and my father moved to France, in 1935, to pursue their studies, and the ten years she spent in France, the last three if not exactly in hiding at least in the daily fear of death for both her and her child, gave her ample opportunity to discover just what Jewishness meant to her.

There is one episode in particular which, to me, encapsulates my mother. She and my father had separated and he had gone off to Paris, leaving her with a child of two and pregnant with a second child. She was living by then in a pension in Nice, which had rapidly filled up with Jewish refugees from all parts of France, since this corner of the country was under the jurisdiction of the Italians, who protected 'their' Jews. When Italy fell to the Allies, however, in September 1943, the Germans at once sealed off the region and on 8 September began what historians describe as the biggest 'raffle' or round-up of Jews in the West. By sheer chance my mother, who had decided that it was safer to be out in the open, was pushing my pram along the sea front when she felt a hand on her arm and looked up to see her one-time neighbour from her years in the small hillside town of Vence, Ida Bourdet, the wife of Claude Bourdet, the Resistance leader. Horrified to find her there, alone with her child, Ida told her if she did nothing she would soon be rounded up and deported. She and her young son must come back with her and she would get them forged papers and put them on a train the next day for the *massif central* with some friends, also making a getaway. And this is what happened. But, my mother told me later, she had left me in one carriage with the friends and gone to sit by herself in another carriage. For though she now had forged papers, she said to me, she was not sure, when it came to it, if the Germans got into the train and challenged her, whether she would be able to deny her Jewishness. Even though that would mean her death and, even more, the abandoning of her child to strangers. When my mother told me this she was not boasting. She was almost apologetic. She was certainly puzzled. But she knew that there are moments that define one, and that if that moment came she might find it impossible to deny a Jewishness she knew little about and certainly never 'practised'. Fortunately for both of us the test never came. The train slowly moved away from Nice, to Lyon and finally to La Bourboule, where we spent the rest of the war. Her second child was born there, but died ten days later.

She told me these stories in Egypt, where we lived from 1945 to the summer of 1956. Because she had had no Jewish upbringing I didn't either, yet because we had almost perished because we were Jewish, that marked me too, and set me apart from the friends I made at school and at the Sporting Club which was the hub of the social life of the middle classes. My circle of friends was just as likely to contain Muslims, Copts, Armenians, Americans or Germans as Jews, and even with the Jewish boys I played with, as with the various (I now realise, Jewish) friends of my mother's, questions of race or ritual never obtruded. This was the world of assimilated well-to-do Europeanised Sephardic Jewry, and it is because I grew up in its ambiance that in later life the world Proust paints of Marcel's childhood seems much closer to mine than anything to be found in the pages of Isaac Bashevis Singer or Saul Bellow.

As a student at Oxford, then, when I went through my adolescent religious crisis, it was couched in Christian terms, since I was at the time reading Dostoevsky, Milton, and Donne. And though a friend put me on to Gershom Scholem's *Major Trends in Jewish Mysticism*, I found the book a bore and it made me realise that I was not, as I had supposed, in the least bit interested in mysticism. It was only much later that I found myself growing interested in Jewish matters. This had partly to do with a discovery: I had thought that I differed from my English friends and contemporaries because of my European interests, and indeed sought out friends who shared those interests and found a job teaching literature in the School of European Studies at the University of Sussex. The models I looked to in my writing were European authors, Proust as well as Virginia Woolf, Mann as well as Eliot, Robbe-Grillet as well as William Golding, Claude Simon as well as Saul Bellow. But now I began to feel that there was a part of me that was not being catered for by this way of perceiving myself. Oddly, it was a new-found interest in the Bible that led me to it. For I found in the Bible what I realised I had experienced in contact with my mother and with members of her family, and which I now described to myself as a 'middle-eastern' quality: a kind of flexibility, a complex sense of irony, a wise realism. Abraham, Isaac, Rebecca, Jacob, Rachel, David, Bathsheba – they were the great-aunts and uncles I had never known but who came to life in the stories my mother and my aunt told me and each other. At the same time I found, as a writer, that the pared-down quality of the biblical narratives, the emphasis on action rather than description, the willingness to let actions remain mysterious and unexplained, was something I cherished and which stimulated my own work, though these narratives had been written down so long ago.

I learnt enough biblical Hebrew to read these narratives in the original, and started teaching a course with an Anglican colleague on 'The Bible and English Literature'. And naturally I began to read modern Hebrew literature, delighted to find in the poems of Bialik, Leah Goldberg, Amir Gilboa, and Yehuda Amichai, as well as in the novels of Yakov Shabtai and Aharon Appelfeld, the kind of sustenance I had always found in Yeats and Eliot and Stevens and Borges. But, I soon discovered, there was another Hebrew literature, an Israeli literature, whose best-known representatives seemed to be Amos Oz and A. B. Yehoshua, and which felt as alien to me as the novels of Angus Wilson or Claude Mauriac – realistic tales of people I could not summon up an interest in, within a culture I felt was very far from my own. Amichai and Appelfeld, it became clear to me, were European writers who were Jews and wrote in Hebrew, as Kafka was a European writer who was a Jew and wrote in German; Oz and Yehoshua were Israeli writers who happened to be Jewish and wrote in Hebrew.

As with assimilated Jews in Europe, but perhaps slightly differently, given that we lived in close proximity to it, Israel had never really been an issue for us as I was growing up in Egypt. It was almost as alien as Japan or Brazil. Of course I was aware of it, and became more aware of it as my interest in the Jewish elements in my make-up grew. But it seemed to have nothing to do with me. As a child in Egypt in 1948 I heard about a war in Palestine, but I personally never experienced any anti-Semitism in all my time there, only the growing sense, in an increasingly nationalist environment, of my status as a foreigner. I became more aware of it in 1956 when, after we had moved to England, all the Jews were expelled from Egypt, along with the French and the English. This was perfectly understandable, given the unprovoked attack on Egypt by Israel and the two Western powers and the long years of quasi-colonial rule the Egyptians had been forced to endure. Nevertheless, in retrospect, it seems like one of the first examples of that confusion between Jews and Israel which has become such a feature of the past twenty-five years. Jews, as I have tried to suggest, had been living in Egypt for centuries, and most of them considered themselves both Jewish and Egyptian, as Greeks living there considered themselves both Greek and Egyptian. To be informed that they were enemy aliens and expelled was a shock from which many of them never recovered. But my mother and I had never felt that much at home in Egypt. We had left voluntarily several months before the Suez war, and we found the life we had chosen for ourselves, in England, congenial. I went up to Oxford to read English and then on to a teaching job at the University of Sussex, and took no interest in either my Jewishness or in Israel. I had no wish to visit the country.

Israel, I understood, was where the Jews had made a homeland, dispossessing hundreds of thousands of Palestinians in the process. I had no wish to visit the country, which seemed, like South Africa, to be a place where whites bossed over natives, something I felt I had had my fill of in Egypt in the last days of King Farouk. Yet when in 1967 the papers and the airwaves (I did not yet own a television set) were suddenly full of the threats of the Arab countries to throw Israel into the sea, I found to my surprise that the survival of that country did matter to me. The thought of Jews once again about to perish *en masse* with the world standing by and doing nothing was unbearable. I had thought of myself as uninterested in anything but my writing and my teaching, and suddenly I had the feeling that I should perhaps go and enlist or at least make an effort to find out what I could do to help. The war was of course over so quickly that all such thoughts disappeared almost as soon as they arrived, but it was this, perhaps, which lit the fuse that would, several years later, make me wake up to the realisation that Jewish matters were important to me, and were bound up, somehow, with my feelings about the region in which my family had lived for so long. Nevertheless, I still had no wish to visit Israel and totally agreed with my mother when she said: 'They've got to give back the land they've occupied as quickly as possible or they'll be storing up trouble for themselves.'

I realised after 1967 that the particular relation I had with this country I had never visited was very much like the relation one has with distant relatives. If one learns of something admirable they have done one is proud of them, if they do what one finds shameful one is embarrassed. What one cannot be is completely indifferent. Because, in a strange sense, both their glory and their shame reflect upon oneself. I suppose the citizens of most countries feel that way about the ways in which their country acts. The protests that have greeted the decisions of Bush and Blair to go to war in Iraq attest to that: not in our name, the protesters want to say, even though the leaders of the USA and Britain have been democratically elected. Liberal South Africans felt the same way about their country in the days of apartheid, and I imagine liberal Russians (there are a few of them) feel the same way about the war in Chechnya and the elimination of investigative journalists. The oddity of Israel is that Jews who are citizens of other countries, and who therefore have absolutely no say in the ballot-box, feel that they have not only a right but a duty to speak out about the way that country is going about its business. When criticised by such people, Israelis say: 'What do you know about it? If you had to live here...' And: 'Why should we be purer and more ethical than other countries? We're a sovereign state and this is the real world. Wake up, buddy.' Perhaps that's true. As a writer and an academic I feel both ignorant and innocent. By and large, as long as I have the space and time to work undisturbed I am happy to let those who enjoy doing such things take charge of politics. Nevertheless, cousins are not like strangers. I can hate what Russia is doing in Chechnya and wish the United Nations and the rest of the world took some sort of a stand, but I don't feel I have much say in the matter. Being a fellow human being is one step further away than being a fellow-Jew. Hell, these are not just human beings, they are *cousins*!

In 1982 I was invited to lecture in Israel and decided to accept. If I didn't like what I saw there I could always put on my British Council lecturer's hat, I thought, and if I did, well and good, I could come out as – what? A Jew? One of 'them'? I didn't know. Of course what I found was a country more sharply divided even than the Britain of Margaret Thatcher I had just left, and I found that on the whole the people I met and mingled with were more strongly against the policies of the Likud government than I was. I made some wonderful friends, people I felt I understood and who understood me perhaps as few people did in Europe. I began to return regularly to see these people and to take part in various literary and educational projects. Then came the first *intifada* and I felt I did not want to visit a country where it seemed to be official policy to break the arms of children. My liberal friends begged me to come: 'If people like you don't show solidarity with us, who will?' they said. I tried to explain that it was not a question of solidarity. I was not making an ideological or a political point. I simply had no wish to be in a country where this sort of thing was happening. Of course those were innocent days compared to what has followed, the derailing of the Oslo talks, the murder of Rabin and the whole avalanche of disastrous decisions on all sides that have led us to what is surely the darkest time ever in the history of the region.

The seeds of that darkness of course lie far back in time – in the Zionist dream, in the horrors of the Holocaust, in the establishment of the state of Israel on land that no one had the right to give to anyone. But different decisions along the way would surely have led to a different present. And even today one must believe that there is still hope, if only the right decisions are taken and leaders of courage and vision come to the fore. History is full of mistakes and human beings eventually accommodate themselves to them. International law is there to help smooth the path of accommodation. To flout it is surely a recipe for disaster.

When cousins do things you don't like the sound of, you wince. You may be wrong, and you certainly can't expect to be listened to if you offer advice, even though you mean well and have your cousins' best interests at heart. But what is intolerable is your father telling you never to criticise because a family must always present a united front. That is the ultimate betrayal of the family's humanity. Jews should know this better than most.

Against the 'Idea of Europe'

TODAY WE ARE ALL only too well aware of the dangers of talking about any country or continent in terms of purity or cleanliness. The hideous history of those words resonates through the dark twentieth century, for in their name were carried out some of the worst crimes human beings have ever committed. And it is instructive to note that even after the end of World War II, when one would have thought the lessons had been learned, it turned out that they hadn't. The Balkan wars of the 1990s showed us that the idea of purity could survive in the minds of men even when what had been done in its name had been well documented and its lessons apparently learned. But though politicians and intellectuals could mouth the slogan 'Never again!', it turned out that the dream of ethnic purity had not died and could be revived at any time by unscrupulous or idealistic demagogues. It could be revived because it elicited clear resonance in the masses they led.

I want to argue that the notion of the 'idea' of Europe, though espoused by some of the finest and most humane thinkers of our time, is itself merely an intellectual version of ethnic cleansing. It suggests that there is such a thing as an essence of Europe, with which the writer is in touch; that it is better than the essences of other continents and cultures; and that it must be walled in and preserved at all costs while other, inferior notions, are rooted out. While not denying the noble idealism of many of those who espoused such claims, I want to suggest that they are part of the problem of Europe, not any solution to them.

I am no historian, but it seems to me that these notions of a unique European destiny and calling, while they may have been in the air since Plato, or since the establishment of Christianity as the universal religion of Europe, really came of age as the result of a particular educational formation, which has its roots in sixteenth-century Humanism, but which comes to its full flowering in the German-speaking lands (the 'heart' of Europe) in the nineteenth century. George Steiner could be regarded as its last eminent representative, and his Nexus lecture, 'The Idea of Europe', embodies, sometimes consciously, at others unconsciously, many of its assumptions.[1] Those of us who were not formed by this education, who come not from central Europe but from its periphery, who do not regard ourselves as humanists or scholars but as artists and teachers, feel deeply uneasy with these assumptions and I will try in what follows to explain why.

Steiner proposes five elements which for him define Europe:

> the coffee house, the landscape on a traversable and human scale, [...] streets and squares named after the statesmen, artists, writers of the past [...], our twofold descent from Athens and Jerusalem, and, lastly, the apprehension of a closing chapter, of that famous Hegelian sunset, which shadowed the idea and substance of Europe even in their noon hours.

With the first three I have no quarrel. They show Steiner at his best. It is a fascinating insight into our past to think of the coffee house and the street sign as unique to Europe (though one might want to ask about the role of the coffee house in Middle Eastern culture), as is the one that the continent of Europe is a *walkable* continent, unlike the Americas, Asia or Africa, where deserts, rainforests and impassable mountains hem populations in to the river valleys and the seaboard, and can only be traversed by train or plane. These three first elements make us understand the geology and geography of Europe as the ground upon which its spirit of human intercourse and dialogue could grow. It is when we come to the fourth element that I balk. Here Steiner gestures towards the twofold inheritance of Athens and Jerusalem to make his point that in what he calls 'three pursuits or addictions or games of a wholly transcendent dignity', to whit music, mathematics and philosophy, Europe has been pre-eminent.

Steiner immediately seems to feel uneasy with his formulation. 'We know of no ethnic community, however rudimentary, which does not practise some mode of music,' he writes; however, 'what is worth pondering' (a Steinerian formulation which should alert us to the fact that proof is thin on the ground) 'is the question of whether any of these manifold musical constructs or executive forms entail the miracles of the meanings of meaning which are conveyed to us by Bach, Mozart, Beethoven or Schubert.' I cannot be the only one to hear in this formulation the simple assertion of cultural prejudice. We all know, the words seem to say, that the best music, the music in which music comes into its own, so to speak, is that of Bach, Mozart and the rest. But do we? I yield to no one in my love of and admiration for the music of Bach and Mozart, but I find equally rich and interesting the music of Machaut and Perotin, of Okeghem and Monteverdi, of Josquin and Tallis, of Stravinsky and Webern, of Stockhausen and Berio, as well as the music of Bali, central Asia, and the African pygmies recently brought to our attention by the great Hungarian composer Georgy Ligeti. What gives Steiner the right to elevate his chosen quartet above these? Because of a certain cultural formation, which we may for the sake of brevity call German. Steiner, like Gombrich, responds to a particular tradition of fairly recent European art with passion and understanding, but at the expense of much else. Those with a different cultural formation will simply not agree. But – and this is crucial – they will not feel the need to privilege their favourite art over the others, but simply accept that the world has provided us with a wondrously rich diversity of cultural traditions, for which we must be grateful.

Steiner's other two 'pursuits [...] of a wholly transcendental dignity' are mathematics and philosophy. I know far less than he does about these topics, but I would suggest that though it is well known that China and Africa, while developing rich visual and oral cultures, did not develop philosophy or mathematics, India certainly did. I find it amazing that a man of Steiner's extensive learning should not be aware of the rich tradition of both mathematics and philosophy in India, and of Arab mathematics, which was so important to Europe. Again, he tries to cover himself by saying that 'there are philosophic moments and systems extraterritorial to Europe'. 'But', he goes on, in the now familiar vein, only in Europe does 'the sovereign stream of supposition and argument' fully flow.

It is this sense that Europe is best and that only those brought up in the best traditions of Europe can understand this and should tell the rest of the world what to think, which comes across as so insufferable. Steiner calls in support two famous lectures on his topic, Max Weber's 1919 lecture on learning and science (*Wissenschaft*) as vocation, and Edmund Husserl's on 'Philosophy and the Crisis of European Man'. Both are splendid examples of the best and worst of the German cultural formation. 'Whoever lacks the ability to put blinders on himself,' Steiner quotes Weber as saying, 'and to convince himself that the fate of his soul depends on whether his particular interpretation of a certain passage of manuscript is correct, will always be alien to science and scholarship.' This, to someone not brought up in the German tradition, is both sublime and faintly distasteful. The fate of his soul? Why this religious, this Christian language? As for Husserl, Steiner paraphrases him saying that only in ancient Greece does there evolve 'the pursuit of theory, of disinterested speculative thought in the light of infinite possibilities. Only, moreover, in classical Greece and its European legacy, is the theoretical applied to the practical in the guise of a universal critique of life and of its goals. There is a sharp distinction to be drawn between this phenomenology and the "mythicopractical" fabric of Far Eastern or Indian models [...]. Europe,' he concludes, 'forgets itself when it forgets that it was born from the idea of reason and the spirit of philosophy.' But was it? What does it mean that Europe is 'born'? Is it not simply a way of saying 'The Idea of Europe I espouse was born...?' But to put it like that would of course be to render it a mere idea, whereas both Steiner and Husserl want to elide 'What I think' with 'What is'. These German professors are splendid representatives of their respective disciplines, but can they really be allowed to speak for 'Europe'?

The problem with the 'idea' of Europe is that it is not only very far from the complex and messy reality of Europe or any other entity, but that its proponents, excited by their own visions, quickly become prescriptive: anything that does not fit into their idea has to be got rid of. Thus, 'If young Englishmen choose to rank David Beckham high above Shakespeare and Darwin in their list of national treasures [...] the fault is very simply ours,' George Steiner states in his peroration I don't want to comment on the false gravitas of the last phrase, the meaningless assumption of a meaningless guilt, but only on the opening remark that it is profoundly wrong for 'young Englishmen' to rate Beckham more highly than Shakespeare. It offends the German professor in Steiner. Would it have offended Shakespeare? I doubt it. Just as Humanism, with its idealism, humourlessness and tendency to pomposity was sweeping through the intellectual circles of Europe, Shakespeare was on hand to put it in its place. For what do the young princes of *Love's Labour's Lost* live by except a Humanist idea? And the play rebukes them: one cannot live by ideas alone. Just as Theseus and his court are implicitly rebuked in *A Midsummer Night's Dream* by Bottom and the 'rude mechanicals'. Theseus thinks he knows the answers, but Shakespeare, like Bottom, knows that Bottom's dream 'hath no bottom'. What is important for Shakespeare is not an *idea* of Ovid as a monument of European culture, but getting Ovid *to work* for him; not an *idea* of England in the history plays, but the conflicts of ideas and desires, both base and noble, which lead to that less than perfect entity, the English State.

Shakespeare reminds us that the glory of Europe has always been that it was the opposite of pure, that it was, in fact, porous, permeable, open to other cultures and influences. Steiner half understands this when, in a footnote, he quotes Herodotus: 'Every year we send our ships at the risk of life and very expensively to Africa to ask: "Who are you? What are your laws? What is your language?" They never sent one ship to us.' But it is not just that Europe asks questions, is curious about other cultures, while they are satisfied to remain within their own spheres; it is that Europe has always been open to other cultural influences. Think of the crucial importance to Europe of the Bible, that quintessentially Middle Eastern document. Think of what the discovery of the Americas did for the Europe of the Renaissance, how Montaigne and Shakespeare used those discoveries to show Europeans that there were other ways of life, very different from their own, which raised questions about their own political and metaphysical ideas. Think of what artists of the late nineteenth century learned from Japanese prints, what those of the twentieth learned from African sculptures, what modern composers learned from the music of Bali and India. Europe more than any other continent, European culture more than any other culture, has been open to the outside world, has been ready to learn from those seemingly alien cultures how to renew itself, how to escape the constraints of its own most deeply cherished beliefs. Indeed, we can see from our perspective that the painters of the late nineteenth century turned to Japan precisely to escape the constraints of the Renaissance Humanist tradition in art, just as the composers of the twentieth turned to late medieval and Far Eastern music to escape the constraints of that tradition in music.

Of course there is another side to Europe, a side exemplified by the Crusades, by the suppression of the Albigensian 'heretics', by the burning of witches and the pogroms against Jews, by the wars between Catholics and Protestants in the early modern period, by the arrogance and racialism behind its various colonising ventures, and, of course, by the Nazis, with their crazy dream of a pure, Aryan race which would only flourish by the suppression of Slavs and Jews, Gypsies, homosexuals, the sick and the mad. But our revulsion at these aspects of Europe should not blind us to the positives I outlined a moment ago.

In the summer of 2004 I spent a week in Northumberland. In the northeast tip of that enormous and beautiful county lies the island or peninsula of Lindisfarne (it is, like Mont S. Michel, an island when the tide comes in, twice a day, and a peninsula, joined to the mainland by a causeway, when the tide retreats). I suspect that even those who know England well would have some difficulty in placing Lindisfarne on the map. But here, at the beginning of the eighth century, was created one of the greatest English works of art, the *Lindisfarne Gospels*. The monastic community of Lindisfarne was one of a number of such communities in the Europe of the so-called Dark Ages. Looking at the map one is struck by how few of them there were, isolated in the midst of unfriendly landscapes, surrounded by sea, marsh, forest and mountain, and by sparse settlements of peasants living in conditions similar to those that had prevailed in Europe since the Iron Age. Yet when one learns a little about those times one is struck by the fact that these monastic communities maintained close ties with each other and were in fact far more open to a wide range of influences than many later cities and countries. The monks of Lindisfarne had links with Egypt, Syria, Byzantium, Rome, Trier, Cologne, Iona in Scotland, and the Irish houses. They were profoundly influenced by the Egyptian Desert Fathers, and consciously tried to emulate their way of life in the very different wilderness of the Northumbrian coast. The art of the Lindisfarne gospels owes much to that of Syria, Byzantium, Rome, and Ireland. The so-called 'carpet pages', which are one of the glories of the Lindisfarne Gospels, ultimately derive, like Islamic carpets, from the prayer mats which featured in the liturgical-devotional practices of Rome. These religious men may have been physically distant, but they felt themselves to be spiritually one with other communities across the British Isles, Europe, and the Middle East. Michelle Brown, Curator of Illuminated Manuscripts at the British Library, has even argued, persuasively in my view, that the *Lindisfarne Gospels* are a conscious attempt at the reconciliation and fusion within a single artefact of many different styles and traditions.[2]

Is not the Lindisfarne community a better model for the twenty-first century than the later models of nation states? Today, when the mayors of Lille and Bruges, of Genoa and Barcelona, tell us that they feel they and the cities they represent have more in common with each other than with Paris or Brussels, Rome and Madrid, we should make sure that the history we teach our future Europeans is a history that brings to the fore communities like those of Lindisfarne in the eighth century or like those of Alexandria in Hellenistic times. It should not be a history of nation states and of modern Europe, with their dangerous myths of land and race, of oppression and the desire for revenge, but a history of cities and monastic communities, proud of their achievements in matters of art and culture, achievements embedded in their very stones. Such a history will reveal to today's Europeans that there was a time when there was no concept of Europe as a fortress, but rather as a rich variety of communities and urban settlements, ready to exchange ideas and practices as well as goods with their distant fellow-communities and cities, unfettered by any 'idea' of Europe.

1 George Steiner, *The Idea of Europe* (London: Duckworth, 2015).

2 Michelle Brown, *The Lindisfarne Gospels & the Early Medieval World* (London: The British Library, 2010).

Interruption and the Last Part

In memory of John Mepham

1. WHAT IS INTERRUPTED by an interruption? Continuity. The classic novel presents us with narratives that are continuous and with narratives of continuity. Let Smollett's *Roderick Random* stand for the genre:

> I was born in the northern part of this united kingdom, in the house of my grandfather; a gentleman of considerable fortune and influence who had, on many occasions, signalled himself on behalf of his country; and was remarkable for his abilities in the law, which he exercised with great success, in the station of a judge, particularly against beggars, for whom he had a singular aversion.

Roderick Random appeared in 1748. Eleven years later a very different kind of novel was launched on the English public:

> I wish either my father or my mother, or indeed both of them, as they were in duty both equally bound to it, had minded what they were about when they begot me; had they duly consider'd how much depended upon what they were then doing: – that not only the production of a rational Being was concern'd in it, but that possibly the happy formation and temperature of his body, perhaps his genius and the very cast of his mind; – and, for aught they knew to the contrary, even the fortunes of his whole house might take their turn from the humours and dispositions which were then uppermost: – Had they duly weighted and considered all this, and proceeded accordingly, – I am verily persuaded I

> should have made a quite different figure in the world, from that, in which the reader is likely to see me. – Believe me, good folks, this is not so inconsiderable a thing as many of you may think it; – you have all, I dare say, heard of the animal spirits, as how they are transfused from father to son, etc. etc. and a great deal to that purpose: – Well, you may take my word, that nine parts in ten of a man's sense or his nonsense, his successes and miscarriages in this world, depend upon their motions and activity, and the different tracks and trains you put them into; so that when they are once set a-going, whether right or wrong, 'tis not a halfpenny matter, – away they go cluttering like hey-go-mad; and by treading the same steps over and over again, they presently make a road of it, as plain and as smooth as a garden-walk, which, when they are once used to, the devil himself shall not be able to drive them off it.
>
> *Pray, my dear,* quoth my mother, *have you not forgot to wind up the clock? – Good G—!* cried my father, making an exclamation, but taking care to moderate his voice at the same time, – *Did ever woman, since the creation of the world, interrupt a man with such a silly question?* Pray, what was your father saying? – Nothing.

In *Tristram Shandy*, Sterne cuts straight to the heart of the matter, and his questioning of the principles of the novel is all the more telling for being encapsulated in a conceit which is itself grotesque and ridiculous: that lack of concentration in the act of coitus will lead to the creation of a child who is less than human, not quite 'all there', thus not only endangering the continuity of the species, but, perhaps more importantly, that of the 'house'.

A book is not a tree, which, once the seed is planted and it is given sufficient light and water, will grow of its own accord – though the classic novel would persuade us that it is. Writing means in the first instance interrupting the continuum: I decide to write a book and then I decide how I want to write it, and the writing of it will take time and effort and ingenuity, which I will not be able to devote to other pursuits. Writing will depend on the decisions of the writer, who may, if he wishes, obey the rules of genre, rhetoric, and grammar, but is under no obligation to do so. He may in fact prefer to stress the arbitrary nature of writing, its dependence on chance, on whim, and so produce a work which is, literally, whimsical. So, just as Roderick Random, the hero of the novel of that name, is both the product and the guarantor of continuity, Tristram Shandy is the product and mischievous perpetrator of interruption. The bulk of readers feel happier with the Smollett tradition, but a few have found that Sterne speaks more truly to their condition.

2. *Tristram Shandy* begins with an interruption and ends with a cock and bull story – or rather, volume nine ends like that; Sterne would no doubt have written further volumes had death not interrupted him, for a book that makes interruption rather than continuity its theme cannot have an ending.

A century after Sterne, Kierkegaard was to provide the rationale for Sterne's apparently eccentric performance, arguing that for a writer to end a book was evidence that he was not a writer at all, that he had misunderstood his vocation. 'It is not improbable that the lives of many men go on in such a way that they have indeed premises for living but reach no conclusion,' he wrote in the introduction to his book *On Authority* (1847). 'For it is one thing that a life is over and a different thing that a life is finished by reaching its conclusion.' To reach a conclusion, he implies, life must have a meaning; without that meaning it is merely 'over' when a man dies. Now the ordinary man, the one whose life has no conclusion, may, for one reason or another, decide to become an author. But, says Kierkegaard, though

> he may have extraordinary talents and remarkable learning [...] an author he is not, in spite of the fact that he produces books [...] He will be capable of writing the first [...] and also the second part, but he cannot write the third part – the last part he cannot write. If he goes ahead naively (led astray by the reflection

> that every book must have a last part) and so writes the last part, he will make it thoroughly clear by writing the last part that he makes a written renunciation of all claim to be an author [...] If he had been thoroughly aware of the inappropriateness of the third part – well, one may say, *si tacuisset, philosophus mansisset* [had he kept quiet he would have remained a philosopher].

In other words, we live in an age where talent is no longer enough; any artist worthy of the name must come to terms with the question of meaning and so of authority, both in his life and in his work: What authority does he have for what he does? What is it that confers authority on his work? For without authority of some kind a work remains no more than the private expression of a private whim. To reach the end and not have at least shown awareness of these issues is to reveal your unfitness for the task you have set yourself. But that doesn't mean that meaning or authority exist and it is just a question of finding them. Indeed, Kierkegaard goes on: 'To find the conclusion it is necessary first of all to observe that it is lacking, and then in turn to feel quite vividly the lack of it.' Or, to go back to Sterne, if the conclusion is lacking then interruption becomes the figure of truth.

3. In his *Theses on the Philosophy of History*, that wonderful meditation on time and how we make sense of it, which was the last thing he wrote, Walter Benjamin explains the power of dialectical thinking as opposed to historicism: 'Thinking involves not only the flow of thoughts, but their arrest as well. When thinking suddenly stops in a configuration pregnant with tensions, it gives that configuration a shock.' That ability to arrest thoughts is what Benjamin cherished above all in the theatre of Brecht. Epic theatre, says Benjamin, breaks up the stream of continuity and allows us to see that events could be other than they are. 'Epic theatre is gestural [...] The more frequently we interrupt someone engaged in action, the more gestures we obtain. Hence the interrupting of action is one of

the principle concerns of epic theatre.' And, elsewhere: 'Epic theatre makes life spurt up high from the bed of time and, for an instant, hover iridescent in empty space. Then it puts it back to bed.' Often it does so through laughter, for laughter, as Sterne knew, is a form of blessed interruption.

4. Yet Brecht, in his theoretical writings on the epic theatre, makes it seem too easy. The truth is that we long for continuity and dread interruption. That is why the classic novel has a deep hold over us. But what exactly is the nature of that hold? Sartre, the avid reader of Kierkegaard, suggested it was because it gave tacit meaning to life. I would go further and venture to suggest that it is because it is secretly reassuring us that we will not die. Peter Brooks, one of the most thoughtful modern critics, suggested, making rich use of Freud, that it was because it helped us integrate in dynamic fashion the scattered portions of our past lives. The three views are not incompatible.

With *To the Lighthouse*, it is well-known, Virginia Woolf was able finally to come to terms with the early death of her mother and lay her ghost to rest.[1] She did it by forging a fictional form for interruption which would make us experience death as an essential element in our lives. In Part Three, 'The Lighthouse', Lily Briscoe stands looking out to sea, painting and letting her mind wander over the past and especially over the presiding angel of the house, Mrs Ramsay, now dead, as she watches the boat carrying Mr Ramsay and his two children being rowed across the bay by Macalister's boy. Suddenly (we are at the end of section 5) she finds there are hot tears in her eyes:

> Was she crying then for Mrs Ramsay, without being aware of any unhappiness? […] What was it then? What did it mean? Could things thrust their hands up and grip one; could the blade cut; the fist grasp? Was there no safety? No learning by heart of the ways of the world? […] 'Mrs Ramsay!' she said aloud. 'Mrs Ramsay!' The tears ran down her face.

6

[Macalister's boy took one of the fish and cut a square out of its side to bait his hook with. The mutilated body (it was still alive) was thrown back into the sea.]

7

'Mrs Ramsay!' Lily cried, 'Mrs Ramsay!' But nothing happened. The pain increased. That anguish could reduce one to such a pitch of imbecility, she thought! [...] Heaven be praised, no one had heard her cry that ignominious cry, stop pain, stop! [...] No one had seen her step off her strip of board into the waters of annihilation. She remained a skimpy old maid, holding a paint-brush on the lawn.

And now slowly the pain of the want, and the bitter anger (to be called back, just as she thought she would never feel sorrow for Mrs Ramsay again [...]) lessened; and of her anguish left, as antidote, a relief that was balm in itself, and also, but more mysteriously, a sense of someone there, of Mrs Ramsay, relieved for a moment of the weight that the world had put on her, staying lightly by her side [...]

Why does Virginia Woolf feel compelled to introduce Macalister's boy at this point? Why interrupt our communion with Lily in her moment of anguish? For that interruption is no simple Brechtian alienation – it is a wrench, a tearing at the fabric of our being, quite as powerful in its way as Lily's sudden and unexpected experience of the death of Mrs Ramsay.

'To find the conclusion it is necessary first of all to observe that it is lacking and then in turn to feel quite vividly the lack of it,' said Kierkegaard. In Part Two of the novel Virginia Woolf had already begun to make us feel the lack when she killed off Mrs Ramsay in a bracketed aside. There she had used ordinary round brackets. Now she interrupts our communion with Lily's anguish with a whole new section, set in remorseless square brackets, and the effect is to make us experience, against our will, the fact that the world consists of more than our sorrows and joys, that many things go on simultaneously, that there is Lily Briscoe engaged with her painting, that there is the journey (at last) to the lighthouse by the children, that there is the daily life of the sea for Macalister's boy, that there is a dreadful death for the fish, mutilated and thrown without a thought back into the sea. That does not mean that Lily's loss is any the less real; but then neither is the pain of the fish. Both form part of the fabric of a larger life, fragments of a whole that can never be grasped except negatively, when for an instant we see one of the fragments from a perspective other than our normal one. And, as Kierkegaard understood, it is only with the almost unbearable realisation of this (realisation is hardly the word, this is something we have to experience viscerally or not at all) that some sort of healing can occur: the anguish lessens and leaves a sense of relief 'that was balm in itself'; but also, 'more mysteriously, a sense of someone out there, of Mrs Ramsay, relieved for a moment of the weight that the world had put on her, staying lightly by her side'.

5. Post-Modernism, so-called, has made a fetish of interruption – but by that token is in danger of robbing it of its meaning and power. Sterne, Kierkegaard, Benjamin, and Virginia Woolf are wiser: they recognise that we are pulled along by the desire for continuity; that perhaps, indeed, continuity is so potent because it is a denial of mortality, a refusal on the part of our bodies to acknowledge that death is a part of life. Yet such a denial is dangerous and unhealthy, both in the body politic (the Thousand Year Reich, the Communist Utopia) and in the private sphere. The task of the modern artist (if he or she is a real author, in Kierkegaard's terms) is to make something that will catch both the power of continuity and at the same time, through interruption, to break its hold over us.

6. Yet even to talk about interruption is to turn it into something else and so rob it of its force.

Interruption and the Last Part

1 My comments on *To the Lighthouse* owe much to John Mepham's wonderful essay, 'Figures of Desire: Narration and Fiction in *To the Lighthouse*', in Gabriel Josipovici (ed.), *The Modern English Novel*, Open books, 1976.

How to Make a Square Move

I'VE ALWAYS BEEN FASCINATED by the kind of structure I call A...B...C...Z...A, that is by the idea of a story that moves ineluctably forward into its own beginning. My early novel, *The Echo Chamber*, was an attempt to write such a story. I've also been fascinated by what I call the X structure, where A moves into B as B moves into A. My most successful version of that is a story I wrote in the early 80s called 'Brothers'.

Why do such forms excite, almost obsess me? This is very complicated – but I think it has to do first of all with a love of the impossible, with the feeling that art which merely mirrors life is not very interesting, but that art becomes interesting (to the artist at any rate) when it succeeds in creating an impossible object. Stories of the kind I have outlined above, if successful, have a quality of the *unheimlich* or uncanny, which appeals to me – that, at any rate, is the kind of story I like to read, and which I seem to feel drawn to write.

But behind this lies another, related reason, one which is linked to Valéry's famous remark that he would never want to write the kind of novel that began with 'La Marquise sortit à cinq heures...' In other words he wants fiction which escapes the merely anecdotal and becomes *the enacting of an event* – or, from another point of view, he wants fiction which is an object rather than an *anecdote*, an *object* you can hold up and examine from every point of view. This is what I too am drawn to, and why I love Borges and Sterne but am left indifferent by Iris Murdoch and George Eliot.

That is what excited me about Robbe-Grillet when I first read him, this sense of the novel as the enacting of an event, as well as the feeling of strangeness or uncanniness that his early novels evoked. And of course his very first novel, *Les Gommes*, was a modern version of *Oedipus Rex*, the archetypal work that moves forward into its own beginning. Oedipus, the detective who has set himself to solve the riddle of who is responsible for the blight afflicting the city, uncovers clue after clue until he arrives at the truth: it is himself. In Robbe-Grillet the detective too turns out to be the murderer, though the murder he is investigating turns out not to have taken place at the beginning of the narrative, as all had supposed, but to be brought about precisely *by* the investigation.

I lack Robbe-Grillet's clear, engineer's mind, so my novel *The Echo Chamber* took a rather different turn. As I was trying to get into it, the sense that I wanted a narrative that would move forward into itself nearly drove me crazy, till I enlisted the help of a philosopher friend, John Mepham, who, when I had explained my problem to him, produced a diagram of a Marxist analysis of the production chain of shoes originating in Taiwan, and I suddenly saw how to do it.

With my story 'Brothers' it was easier: two brothers, one hiding away in the country, the other driving down from London to persuade him to return. At the start we are with the country brother, as he imagines his brother approaching – or are we with the town brother as he imagines his brother waiting for him – or with the country brother imagining he is the town brother? As the story progresses the possibilities multiply.

What about variations on the X shape? Could one do it not with two characters but with four? At first sight the idea of fourness seems very static. I have been working on a novel that deals in an oblique way with the fascinating and eccentric Italian composer, Giacinto Scelsi, 1906–1988. Scelsi claimed to have a profound knowledge of Buddhism and to have spent time in India, but people now think he never did. Anyway, in one of his notes on Buddhist geometry he argues that Buddhism moves from the triangle to the pentangle, by-passing the square, because while all the other forms, from the triangle to the dodecahedron and beyond, are dynamic, approximating ever more to that ultimate dynamic form, the circle, the square is irredeemably static. His disciple Luciano Martinis writes:

> Seeing that I was puzzled, he explained that he considered the symmetry of the square made of it the figure of the static par excellence, a kind of stutter in the evolution towards perfection. It is the refuge, the receptacle of mediocrity, he explained, the place where most of mankind feels secure. In effect it is the symbolic form of the *tamasic* state, the force of inertia that Shri Aurobindo talks about, and to be avoided at all costs.

And, indeed when Scelsi came to write a string quartet, he treated the strings not as four separate voices in quadrologue, but as one instrument of sixteen strings. But that is, literally, another story.

How then to go from two to four and keep the dynamism? What about this: Not A into B, but AB and CD becoming AC and BD? Then you have a dynamic structure consisting of four players rather than two. You have, let us say, two couples, who cross over and exchange partners.

I tried this out in a novel I wrote in the early 90s called *In a Hotel Garden* – but there it got entangled with stuff about the Holocaust and about memory. So, more recently, I thought I'd have another go and try and do it in a purer form. The result was a novel called *Making Mistakes*, which came out in 2009. *Making Mistakes* had its immediate origins in a night at the opera. Not the Marx Brothers film but a visit to Glyndebourne with a musician friend to see the recent production of Mozart's *Cosi fan tutte*. As the opera came to an end my friend turned to me and said: 'That's not the end of the story, is it?'

Why did she say this? *Cosi fan tutte* is Mozart's tightest and most perfect opera. It tells the story of two couples, Ferrando and Dorabella, and Giuglielmo and Fiordiligi, the women sisters, the men officers and friends, who are betrothed to each other; and of the bet made with the two men by an older man, a sort of eighteenth-century *philosophe*, don Alfonso, that he can, in twenty-four hours, make each of the two women fall in love with the other's fiancé. The philosopher wins the wager, of course, but this is comedy, not tragedy, and he does so with the help of the spirited serving-maid, Despina, and a great deal of farcical dressing up; more importantly, the couples, brought face to face with what has happened, return each to his and her respective lover, acknowledging in a final ensemble that this is just how women are: *cosi fan tutte*.

The opera has had a chequered history. Disapproved of by the nineteenth century for its cynicism, it has been much revived in recent years, but the feeling has been that the final reconciliation is tacked on and forced. Mozart's music, it has been suggested, tells us that the new-found love of Dorabella for Giuglielmo, and especially of the love of the much more serious and troubled Fiordiligi for Ferrando, is far deeper and more genuine than that between the original set of lovers, and that the ending is thus a forcing back into what society wants of what the heart rebels against. Fiordiligi, in the great arias of the second act, as she struggles against and then finally succumbs to the pressure put on her by Ferrando, has, it is suggested, discovered a new passion, more real and more lasting than her original 'love' for Giuglielmo, and Mozart cannot have seriously meant us to believe that at the end all return to their original positions as though nothing had happened. This, we could say, is the Romantic reading. And, since we still live in the aftermath of Romanticism, it seems far more in tune with our attitudes today, and it is the one strongly hinted at by the Glyndebourne production I saw and which led to my friend's remark that this was not the end of the story – in other words, that, far from happily returning to their original pairings, these two, at any rate, would find a way to live out their hearts' secret desires, which had been revealed to them less by the machinations of don Alfonso than by the very music Mozart gave them to sing. *Cosi*, in this reading, prefigures *Tristan*.

But, such is Mozart's musical and dramatic genius, that there are actually three, not two possibilities inherent in the opera. There is the obvious or surface version, in which, though women will always stray, wisdom, reason and intellect can help to overcome this. Then there is the Romantic version, in which something has been released in Act II which cannot be simply put back in its box, and all four protagonists will never be the same again. But what if Mozart, in the opera, is opening up a space for the *recognition* of Passion – for the reasons of the heart as opposed to the reasons of Reason, in Pascal's formulation – but that this is recognised as only a possibility, and perhaps one that, though it has to be acknowledged, has also, in the grown-up person, to be (albeit reluctantly) renounced? This would fit in with the theme of Mozart's two other collaborations with da Ponte, with the *Marriage of Figaro* and its great last act, in which the lustful count comes to understand that his middle-aged wife has charms which the young Susannah can never match, and with *Don Giovanni*, where we see what happens when you give free rein to your quite natural desires. Mozart, on this reading, is neither a Puritan nor a Wagnerian *avant la lettre*. Rather, like the Shakespeare of *Twelfth Night*, he explores the various conflicts of desire and duty in order to come to a richer view of human possibility, one that transcends both repression and the giving in to every desire.

This, naturally, is the Mozart I favour, the Mozart I believe I discern in the dramas and the music. It is a Mozart who has much in common with other artists and thinkers who had one foot in the eighteenth century and one in the nineteenth – Goethe, whose *Elective Affinities* is the other great exploration of the crossing over of two couples, but also Byron, Pushkin, and Kierkegaard. It does not matter that Mozart died before the nineteenth century started and Kierkegaard was only born in 1812 – they share a sensibility which is neither that of Pope and Handel nor that of Keats and Beethoven, but which recognises, as it were, the imperatives of both.

Which is why, while I was excited by my friend's remark that the story was by no means finished at the end of the opera, I felt that somehow it didn't quite get at the heart of the matter. And I began to think of ways of writing a sequel which perhaps would. Which, in other words, would do something other than show either the suffering the characters would endure when put back in their boxes or the joy they would experience when finally able to throw off the shackles of convention and each turn to his or her true love.

As I was pondering all this it came to me that I should start my novel with the two couples *having already switched*. In my terms, A is now with D and C with B. I had already decided to call my characters Anthony (always called Tony, so as not to make the ABCD element too obvious, as it were), Beatrice, Charley and Dorothy. Their initial paring of Tony with Bea (AB) and Charley with Dot (CD) is now ancient history – but recalled in the first chapter, by my *philosophe*, called, as in Mozart, Alphonso, but here a Spanish professor of linguistics at London University. The occasion is a dinner party given by Tony and Dot, which is interrupted by a phone call from Dot's sister Bea, to say she is (once again) leaving her husband Charley, and could she come and shelter with them for a few days. The rest of the novel would be devoted to a kind of dance which would see Tony eventually partnering Bea (AB) and Charley Dot (CD) – returning them, as it were, to their original Mozartian/da Pontian pairings.

But not in order to moralise about the ways of women (or of men). My motto, I realised, as I worked on the book, had to be, not *cosi fan tutte*, but 'there is no such thing as a mistake' – so that the title, *Making Mistakes*, would come to be seen as ironic. Or rather, not so much ironic as symptomatic of the kinds of clichés which are a part of the moral fabric of our modern lives, and which the book would, I hoped, deconstruct, or reveal to be a glossing over of a much deeper and perhaps more uncomfortable truth. For, as you can imagine, all four protagonists are much given, especially in the later stages of the book, to talking about the mistakes they have made – the mistakes they thought they had made in their youth, the mistakes they did indeed make in trying to rectify those first mistakes, and so on. What Alphonso – and life – has to teach them is that we demean ourselves by talking about our past in terms of mistakes. Rather, these are the choices we all make all the time in our lives, and they are what have made us what we are today. To talk about them as mistakes is to dismiss our past selves and by contrast to put too much value on our present (supposedly wise) selves. The truth is, Alphonso says, there is no such thing as a mistake, for that suggests its opposite, a correct choice – and who is to say what is correct and what is not? We can none of us stand outside our lives and say with certainty what was and was not a mistake. What we can say is that our lives consist of choices and living with the consequences of those choices, to which are added others and yet others, until we die.

Not for the first time in my life I have had what I felt was a profound insight, forced upon me by my work, only to discover later that it had already been anticipated by Proust. And this is what happened here. I wrote *Making Mistakes* in 2006–08, and it was published in 2009. Recently I've been re-reading *À l'ombre des jeunes filles en fleurs*, what Scott-Moncrieff called *Within a Budding Grove*, and I came across this passage. Elstir, the painter Marcel has got to know at Balbec, and whose work is to prove so important for his development as a man and an artist, has just revealed to Marcel that he was none other than the ridiculous figure known as M. Biche, who had been a member of Mme Verdurin's circle in the old days. Marcel can't believe it, and Elstir proceeds to deliver what is in effect a little secular sermon. 'There is no man,' he says,

> however wise, who has not at some period of his youth said things, or lived a life, the memory of which is so unpleasant to him that he would gladly expunge it. And yet he ought not entirely to regret it, because he cannot be certain that he has indeed become a wise man – insofar as it is possible for any of us to be wise – unless he has passed through all the fatuous or unwholesome incarnations by which that ultimate stage must be preceded. I know that there are young people, the sons and grandsons of distinguished men, whose masters have instilled into

> them nobility of mind and moral refinement from their schooldays. They may perhaps have nothing to retract from their past lives, they could publish a signed account of everything they have ever said or done, but they are poor creatures, feeble descendants of doctrinaires, and their wisdom is negative and sterile [*ce sont de pauvres esprits, descendants sans force de doctrinaires, et de qui la sagesse est négative et stérile*]. We do not receive wisdom, we must discover it for ourselves, after a journey through the wilderness which no one else can make for us, which no one can spare us, for our wisdom is the point of view from which we come at last to regard the world. The lives that you admire, the attitudes that seem noble to you, have not been shaped by a paterfamilias or a schoolmaster, they have sprung from very different beginnings, having been influenced by everything evil or commonplace that prevailed round about them. They represent a struggle and a victory. I can see that the picture of what we are at an earlier stage may not be recognisable and cannot certainly be pleasing to contemplate in later life. But we must not repudiate it, for it is a proof that we have really lived, that it is in accordance with the laws of life and of the mind that we have, from the common elements of life, [...] extracted something that transcends them.' [*In Search of Lost Time*, Chatto & Windus six-volume reprint (1992), pp. 512–13; 1954 Pléiade, I, 864]

This is a sermon about life, but it is also a tract about art. What I learned from Proust when I first read him at seventeen – and it was a liberating blast that transformed my life forever – was the rule that you do not need, when you start a novel, to have a great plot or a profound thought or moral to expound – what you need is to trust enough in your ability, in time, and in the material, to plunge in, with nothing more than a rhythm and a desire – the precise contours of both certainly hidden from you, but a sense of them there, driving you forward. There is no 'father' to guide you, no Virgil to show you the way – there are only other pilgrims who can provide you with comfort – pilgrims like Proust himself, or, in his case, Elstir.

What this passage now brings home to me is how in Proust, and, indeed, in all great art since the Romantics, life and art are deeply intertwined – not as modern biographers want to suggest, because the details of an artist's life can be clues to their art, but because the same imperatives apply for both: 'We do not receive wisdom, we must discover it for ourselves, after a journey through the wilderness which no one else can make for us, which no one can spare us. The lives you admire, the attitudes that seem noble to you, have not been shaped by a paterfamilias or a schoolmaster, they have sprung from very different beginnings [...] They represent a struggle and a victory.' Ethics and aesthetics cannot be separated; the Proustian law applies to both.

It is an exciting but a difficult law to put into practice. Not to have a model and a sure guide, to have to rely on instinct and on trust in time and the material, is hard indeed. The up side, though, where art is concerned, is that, if you can carry it through, you will end up not with a story but with an object, I would even say a *moving* object – moving in both senses of the word – something that cannot be pinned down because it is always in motion and something that moves the reader – because it is *alive*. And so my hope is that *Making Mistakes* will be closer, in the reading, to listening to the performance of a quartet than to the reading of a novel by Balzac or even Tolstoy.

When I Begin I Have Already Begun

In memory of Stephen Medcalf

I REMEMBER READING a series of interviews with Stockhausen. This was in the eighties, when the composer was at the height of his fame. I was particularly struck by his account of a visit to Japan, which made a deep impression on him. The Japanese, he noted, did not have the same sense of time as we have in the West. For them time was either something that passed extremely swiftly or extremely slowly, and the large middle range we inhabit did not seem to exist. An example of this was Sumo wrestling. The two enormous combatants, artificially fattened for years, would size each other up in total stillness for what seemed an eternity, and then suddenly, almost before the spectator could see it, one had thrown the other out of the ring. Stockhausen, whose own music had from the start followed a route far removed from the major traditions of the West, was enchanted. He was also much taken by the Japanese attitudes to space. He grew fascinated by the Japanese use of sliding doors and windows, which had the effect, he said in the interview, of blurring the boundary between inside and outside, an effect heightened in many of the temples by the winding and labyrinthine paths which led to them, so that as one approached one felt oneself to be sometimes almost on top of them and then, seconds later, as far away as ever.

For reasons I did not understand, these remarks of Stockhausen's excited me, and they led, eventually, to my writing a little story called 'Second Person Looking Out'. I decided to write about a rather formal party in a house with sliding doors and windows, in which the protagonist is at times approaching the house, at times within it, and at times departing from it. At first I thought I would write the story in nine parts – in the past, present and future, and in the first, second and third persons. In the end I realised that it only needed three parts, in the first, second and third person, each part involving a protagonist who was approaching, within, and departing from the house, and therefore moving between past present and future. Here is an extract from the start of the second section, in the third person:

> He has walked through the seventeen rooms. He has talked to many of the guests as well as to his host. At times he has stopped alone in front of a window and stared out at the landscape.
>
> It has been explained to him that the house is approached by numerous paths, some of which, he has been told, will be closed, when he leaves, with a bamboo stick laid across the path, but, by following those stones which have a piece of string tied round them and fastened in a triple knot he will be able to find his way out again.
>
> 'How much further is it?' he asks his guide.
>
> 'Not much further,' the man says, hurrying ahead.
>
> They round a hillock, and there is the house ahead of them.
>
> 'There are seventeen rooms in the house,' the guide explains. 'Each room has three windows, which can be moved to any position on the walls or covered over if necessary.'
>
> His host has moved away from him and wandered into the next room. The young lady to whom he has just been introduced asks him: 'Is this a temple or something?'
>
> 'No. Just a private house.'
>
> 'It reminds me of a temple,' she says.
>
> They are standing in the fourteenth room. The three windows all face the tall trees at the back of the house. The light from the downstairs rooms illuminates the lawn, but that only serves to make it darker under the trees. His host, in answer to a question, explains: 'The windows are always moved once a guest has looked through them.'

'That must be disconcerting for the guest,' he says.

'It is the custom,' his host says, standing beside him in the dark.

He advances slowly, feeling each step ahead of him for fear of treading on a bamboo stick laid across his path.

Why had reading the interview with Stockhausen excited me and led me to the writing of this story? Probably because I too, without quite realising it, had been as unhappy with the narrative traditions I had inherited as Stockhausen had been with the musical ones; because I too was looking for ways of escaping from the beginning-middle-and-end form which seemed to be the only way to write narrative, as it seemed to be the only way to compose music. Those novels and stories which began, like *David Copperfield*, with 'I was born on…' or, 'I was born at…' or, 'Had you been in such and such a place at such and such a time you would have seen…' did not, I obscurely felt, correspond to how I felt in my own life. There I could find no beginnings and no ends but rather obscure correspondences, repetitions and foldings, which nevertheless demanded to be explored in a narrative mode – but where was that mode to be found?

As I discovered, narratives did exist which corresponded to my secret intuitions, but though they were hardly marginalised – they were among the most famous works of literature in the Western canon – they seemed to lead their lives in a parallel universe, not impinging on the territory of the novel, which had become, in the West, the dominant narrative tradition. When I came across them my heart leapt and I obscurely knew that these were the narratives for me:

Nel mezzo del cammin di nostra vita
  mi ritrovai per una selva oscura
  chè la diritta via era smarrita.
Ah quanto a dir qual era è cosa dura
  esta selva selvaggia e aspra e forte

che nel pensier rinova la paura! [...]
Io non so ben ridir com'io v'entrai
tant'era pieno di sonno a quel punto
che la verace via abbandonai.
Ma poi ch'i'fu al piè d'un colle giunto,
là dove terminava quella valle
che m'avea di paura il cor compunto,
guardai in alto, e vidi le sue spalle
vestite già de'raggi del pianeta
che mena dritto altrui per ogni calle.
Allor fu la paura un poco queta
che nel lago del cor m'era durata
la notte ch'i' passai con tanta pièta.

[In the middle of the journey of our life / I came to myself within a dark wood / where the straight way was lost. / Ah, how hard a thing it is to tell / of that wood, savage and harsh and dense, / the thought of which renews my fear! [...] I cannot rightly tell how I entered there, / I was so full of sleep at that moment / when I left the true way; / but when I reached the foot of a hill / at the end of that valley / which had pierced my heart with fear / I looked up and saw its shoulders / already clothed with the beams of the planet / that leads men straight on every road. / Then the fear was quieted a little / which had continued in the lake of my heart during / the night I had spent so piteously.]

So begins Dante's *Commedia*. Though the poem is regarded as one of the four or five classics of European civilisation, when I first read it I sensed at once that it was quite different from Virgil's *Aeneid* or Milton's *Paradise Lost,* in that it did not require a great effort of the historical imagination, or great erudition, to enter into it, as those two works did, but spoke to me directly and immediately. Of course it is rich in learning, richer perhaps than those other poems, and the commentaries on every canto are so numerous that no one but a dedicated scholar could read them all; but that does not alter the fact that it is possible to read the poem as, somehow, telling one's own story and telling it in a way which, for me at any rate, made immediate sense.

Someone has been lost in a dark wood and now emerges into an open valley to see, touching the mountains that tower above, the first beams of the rising sun. But this narrator, unlike the first person narrators of nineteenth-century novels, is quite ready to confess that he does not know how he got into the wood, how his way was lost. Everything in those opening lines (and the opening is not over) speaks of renewal, of emergence from darkness and confusion, but we do not know if wood and valley and rising sun are metaphor or reality. And it does not matter, for all reading is in a sense the reading of metaphor, making mine what the writer has put out there, what the protagonist is experiencing. We open the book, we start to read. What happened before the book starts is lost precisely because there were no words for it; or, to put it another way, the beginning of words is the beginning of a coming to consciousness. Time and space have lost their rigidity, and when we begin to read we are straight away inside something whose threshold we have not consciously crossed because, in a sense, when the poem begins it has already, long ago, begun. Partly this is a function of Dante's way with language: 'In the middle of *our* life, *I* found myself'. That the narrator's life and mine share a basic structure is attested by the 'our': the middle of our life, thirty-five by the biblical reckoning; that one element in this structure concerns finding again what was lost is brought out by the next phrase, '*mi ritrovai*', '*je me suis retrouvé*' as the French would put it (English, lacking the reflexive, has to opt for the clumsy 'I found myself' or the too specifically psychological 'I came to'). I was lost in a dark wood but now I begin to find my way again; I was lost to myself, but now, as I start to read, I begin to find myself again.

And in the third line of this extraordinary first tercet (a three-line stanza invented by Dante for his poem, which is not quite a *stanza*, a (closed) *room*, since it links with the next in a chain, ababcbcdc, each line consisting of eleven syllables), *diritta* and *smarritta* – straight and lost or confounded – echo ironically one with the other, forcing us, as we read, to recognise how easily that which is straight can be lost but, by the same token, how easily that which is lost can be recovered, made straight (how, at the level of speech production, even internal speech production, the complicated tongue and lip movement which produces the hissing of '*sma*' can relax into the easy '*di*').

Did Proust know Dante? It would be surprising if he did not, but there are no references in the letters or in *À la recherche* (which has such extended passages on Giotto, on Saint Mark's in Venice, and on medieval French cathedrals) to show that Proust had actually read Dante. Perhaps he hadn't and it was simply that he and Dante were working the same seams that led him to find, after much patient labour, testified by the number of drafts we have for the opening pages, a first sentence that also blurs all thresholds and also hinges on a reflexive: '*Longtemps je me suis couché de bonne heure*'. As numerous commentators have pointed out, it is impossible to translate this sentence, for what exactly is the force of that *longtemps* which will find its echo in the last word of the massive work, many thousands of pages later, *temps*? And how to translate '*je me suis couché*'? 'I went to bed' or 'I used to go to bed' or 'I laid me down' are all impossibly wordy or archaic. The sentence leads into an extended meditation on how fluid the border is between sleep and waking: having finally managed to get to sleep the narrator is woken by sounds of the city coming to life at dawn only to realise that it is in fact the night watchman in the hotel doing his rounds putting out the lights at midnight; he then meditates on how, in sleep, we hold within us, like Adam, all the innumerable possibilities of the human race and how, on waking, we have to revert to the one possibility which is the life we actually have, a life which is partially given and partially chosen. In the course of this meditation Proust/Marcel passes in lightning review all the rooms in which he has slept and which we will come to know in the pages that follow, rather as a Mozart overture compresses all the major themes of the opera to follow in music which seems so carefree, so intent only on its own inner logic, that these overtures are often performed by themselves. The effect of this is that when we do meet those rooms later we sense that we have already been there. Once again it seems that in order for the story to begin it must, in a sense, have already begun.

Eliot, of course, did know Dante, and references to Dante in his great later poems, like *Ash Wednesday* and *Four Quartets* are explicit and unironic, in contrast to *The Waste Land*, where the distance between Dante's Europe and the Europe of the years immediately after World War I is highlighted. In the later poetry what is important is similarity, not difference. As in Dante and Proust, the first lines of *Burnt Norton*, the first of the *Four Quartets*, convey the impression that the poem has started long before its actual start. As in those other two works it manages to do this because the poet has found a series of very specific and local ways of conveying a radical vision. After a few lines which do not so much convey information about time and eternity as establish a mood (which I tend to think of as the mood in which, at four in the morning, unable to sleep, we talk to ourselves and imagine that what we are saying has enormous profundity – and perhaps it has, but by morning that profundity has evaporated), the poem takes a new turn, one which is, as with Dante and Proust, both surprising and somehow long-predicted. In fact, this much shorter work retains from first to last the sense that it is both a narrative and a commentary on how this narrative has come into being, maintains itself, and arrives at its end:

> Time present and time past
> Are both perhaps present in time future
> And time future contained in time past.
> If all time is eternally present
> All time is unredeemable.

What might have been is an abstraction
Remaining a perpetual possibility
Only in a world of speculation.
What might have been and what has been
Point to one end, which is always present.
Footfalls echo in the memory
Down the passage which we did not take
Towards the door we never opened
Into the rose-garden. My words echo
Thus, in your mind.
                                        But to what purpose
Disturbing the dust on a bowl of rose-leaves
I do not know.
                                Other echoes
Inhabit the garden, shall we follow?
Quick, said the bird, find them, find them,
Round the corner. Through the first gate.
Into our first world shall we follow
The deception of the thrush? Into our first world.
There they were, dignified, invisible,
Moving without pressure, over the dead leaves [...]

The world of memory and of the imagination, like the world of the unconscious as Freud described it, does not know the meaning of the word 'no'. So 'footfalls echo in the memory / Down the passage which we did not take', and that passage leads us into a rose-garden. The definite article before 'passage' and 'rose-garden' helps persuade us that there was one and only one passage, one and only one rose-garden; but note also the tact whereby what starts as only a sound, the echo of feet, turns into a passage and then into a door and then into what is to be found beyond the door. And so, as we read the poem, the magic is worked and we *are* in that rose-garden, where the rest of this opening section takes place.

The echoes are not only of Dante but also of *Alice in Wonderland*

and Frances Hodgson Burnet's *The Secret Garden*, which suggests that the Victorians and Edwardians, particularly in their children's books, tapped unconscious material which the official culture tended to repress, so that what the first wave of Modernist authors, such as Eliot and Joyce and Conrad and Forster, can be seen to be doing is only making this material explicit. Like the narrator of *À la recherche*, 'more destitute', as he wakes up, 'of human qualities than the cave-dweller', but for whom then 'the memory, not yet of the place in which I was but of the various other places where I had lived, and might now very possibly be, would come, like a rope from heaven to draw me from the abyss of not-being, from which I would never have escaped by myself'; like Dante the pilgrim emerging from the dark wood into the valley still bathed in shadow, the peaks of whose surrounding mountains the rays of the rising sun are already striking, the narrator of *Four Quartets* is somehow given the opportunity, by the words that have gone before, to hear the footfalls and to follow them in memory or imagination (remember that what is Marcel's *memory* is Proust's and the reader's *imagining*) down a passage never taken and then open a door never opened so as to emerge into a garden that is somehow familiar. The poem has only just begun but it has already, we feel, been going on for a long time, has been going on, in fact, all our lives.

We all know how, in our own lives, decisions are rarely taken strictly on their merits, but because of who and what we are, and who and what we are is something mysterious to us, though clearly made up of genetic, social and other factors, which include all the decisions we have and have not made in the years we have lived. We know too how dreams and involuntary, chance memories – memories triggered by smells or tastes or perhaps something felt or half seen – suddenly put us in touch with areas of ourselves we did not know were there or had lost touch with, and how important these seem to us to be. The classic novel, good as it is in dealing with some things, seems not to know how to deal with these, or perhaps can only deal with them in very indirect ways. What my reading of Proust, Dante, and Eliot gave me, and what reading those interviews with Stockhausen helped me articulate, was that there are other ways of writing narrative, as of conceiving of space and time, which, to me at any rate, seemed more true to lived experience and more rewarding.

It might be thought that traditional cultures – those with a strong sense of the importance of thresholds, of rites of passage – would have been inimical to such modes of narration, but the opposite is true. As the case of Dante might have suggested, these modes are actually closer to the ways of thinking of traditional societies than is the classic novel, and a little thought suggests why this might be so. Traditional societies have a strong sense of the porousness of individuals, of how we each of us merge into others and into the community at large. It is the novel which sets up the individual as a closed vessel against society and makes a fetish of individual freedom and success. Those rites of passage which clearly mark at least birth, puberty, marriage, and death in traditional societies also clearly mark the places where the individual joins the group: in baptism or circumcision in Christianity and Judaism, at the start; in the first communion and the *bar mitzvah* when the individual is deemed old enough to acknowledge for him or herself a membership of that community; in marriage where the joining of two families is seen as sanctioned by God in both Christianity and Judaism; and in death, when the individual is recognised by the community he or she has left behind as now entering that larger communion of the dead.

These thresholds, being communal, bring the individual in touch with the larger group. This means that they are moments when the individual is helped to escape the narrow unfolding of his or her unique life, made to see that '*io*' and '*nostra vita*' are forever conjoined, and that the recovery of the 'I', '*mi ritrovai*', is one with the recognition that it is not only my life but our life too. It is as though the threshold between the various aspects of one life are the moments when we can recognise this, and it suggests that in my three examples what the authors have attempted is in a sense to naturalise the sacramental: this is how our lives are, not as Balzac and Stendhal depict it. Dickens is a fascinating case, for it is clear – from his early embracing of the rigours of serial publication to his later public readings, from his powerful sense of childhood terrors as infecting the later life to his attempts, almost single-handedly, to give a meaning to Christmas for his age – that he hungered for a more inclusive form of narration, for a closer contact between himself and his audience; that the effect was often merely sentimental suggests partly that the age was inimical to such efforts and partly that he perhaps did not have the imagination to make the radical breaks with the form that were required.

Let me give just three examples of the porousness of thresholds in the great monotheistic cultures, so as to bring home the perhaps surprising closeness between radical modernism and ancient tradition.

Monotheism, it is sometimes claimed, brought with it a new sense of the historical: in the place of the cyclical world-view of the irrigation-based and sedentary cultures of the Ancient Near East – Egypt and Mesopotamia – the Israelites, a nomadic people, brought with them the idea of a God who created the world once and for all and acted in it at decisive moments, notably in the freeing of the Chosen People from enslavement in Egypt. But this is not, as Protestant theologians sometimes take it to be, the moment of a clear transition from repetition to linearity, from cultures whose rituals are based on the annual cycle to ones which recognise the decisive intervention of God in history in a unique moment. At least that is not how the Jews themselves, the descendants of the biblical Israelites, chose to see it. That once-and-for-all moment in which God acted in history is recalled and symbolically repeated every year at Passover, when the participants in the Passover meal are enjoined to see what happened then as happening now, and those who experienced those events in the past not as 'them' but as 'us'. A similar paradox pertains, of course, to the Easter ceremonies of the Catholic and Orthodox Churches, and indeed, to the daily celebrations of the Mass in those two Churches. When one grasps this, one can see that one of the things Dante is trying to do is make of his poem a parallel both to the Easter liturgy and to the Mass. And the parallels one finds between Dante and Proust and Eliot would then suggest that these modern writers have only found ways of extending the life of these ancient rituals, both Christian and Jewish, and in a sense naturalising the sacraments.

My second example has to do not with the Israelites but with later Jewish commentary on the Bible. The first sentence of Genesis is familiar to nearly everyone: 'In the beginning God created the Heaven and the Earth' – in the Hebrew: '*bereshit bara elohim et ha-shamayim va-et ha-aretz*'. There are as many difficulties with this opening sentence as there are with Proust's, but for our purposes what is important is that first word, *bereshit*. The word derives from *rosh*, head. The letter B with which, in this form (in-the-beginning) it starts, is written, in Hebrew, 'ב'. It is called *beth*, which means a house, and it is the second letter of the Hebrew as of the English alphabet. The rabbis argued that it is not by chance that the Bible begins not with the first but with the second letter, and that this second letter has the shape it has. As it is open on the left and closed on the right (remember that Hebrew is written from right to left), what follows, i.e. the whole Bible, is open to examination, but what precedes is closed off. That is, we must not ask what came before, we must simply start. One does not search for origins, for these can never be found (to imagine one can find them is to usurp the place of God), one simply starts somewhere and gradually finds oneself and one's subject. This is precisely what the implicit argument is in Dante, Proust and Eliot.

My third example comes from Islam and it demonstrates a lack of concern with thresholds as decisive transitions, this time not in the realm of time or text but of space and architecture. Visitors to the great ninth-century mosque of Ibn Tulun in Cairo can make their way to the roof of the building. From there they will look down on a vast courtyard with an elaborate well in the centre, from which four grooves lead to the four corners of the building which surrounds the yard (not shown on the diagram). These symbolise the four rivers of Paradise. All round the courtyard are arcades, which, seen from ground level, are found to be two deep on three sides and five deep on one, but this is not visible from the roof, where the four sides appear uniform, as in the cloister of a medieval cathedral. But the crucial difference is that the cloister is only an adjunct to the cathedral, an ambulatory area distinct from the sacred area which is entered through the imposing doors in the Western façade, which often themselves lead only to an antechamber which then leads into the main body of the Church (two superb and very different examples are New College chapel in Oxford and the Romanesque church of Vézelay in France). In the mosque of Ibn Tulun, by contrast, *there are no doors, because there are no walls*. The *mihrab* and *minbar*, the prayer niche and pulpit, which are aligned towards Mecca, and which are what define the communal focus of the building, are to be found in the side of the courtyard where the arcades are five columns deep, and the floor there is covered with carpets. But that is all. Like the other three sides enclosing the central courtyard, it is only separated from the courtyard by the pillars which constitute the arcades. This is a huge shock to the Westerner. What, he asks, is inside, what out?

Like Stockhausen's Japanese temples, this sacred edifice has no clear inside and outside, only degrees of innerness and outerness.

What is the explanation for this? At one level there is a simple historical reason why early mosques were often like Ibn Tulun. They were built on the model of the Prophet's house in Mecca. In regions where the distinction is not between cold (outside) and warmth (around a fire, inside), but between sun and shade, there is much less reason to build walls and doors. What you need is protection from the sun, not from the cold. But this, like the nomadic origins of the Israelites, has a profound effect on the religious practices and perceptions of the inhabitants of the region: inner and outer are not shut off from one another, nor the individual from the community: not only are thresholds porous, they are almost non-existent.

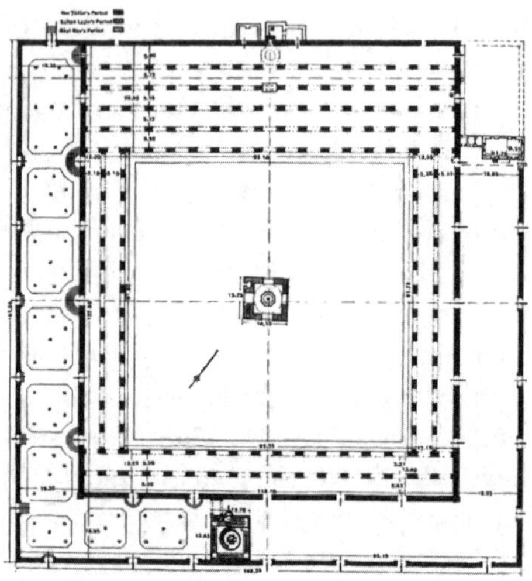

Floor Plan of the Mosque of Ibn Tulun, Cairo.

These three examples suggest that the great monotheistic religions of the world, at any rate, while recognising the importance of thresholds and rites of passage, also see the individual as far more open, far more a part of a larger community, than does the post-Enlightenment West. Only the High Priest could enter the Holy of Holies in the Israelite Temple, the place where the Ark of the Covenant was kept, but the Ark itself was a portable house, so to speak, and the God of the Israelites had expressly forbidden David to build him a temple, since he dwelt everywhere and nowhere, and no merely human building could ever house him. It was perhaps in response to some such imperative that Stockhausen, no less than Dante, Proust and Eliot, was drawn to the creation of works which do not so much have beginnings, middles, and ends as move forwards in a circular fashion towards an end which, when it is eventually reached, is discovered to be the true beginning.

We shall not cease from exploration
And the end of all our exploring
Will be to arrive where we started
And know the place for the first time.
Through the unknown, remembered gate
When the last of earth left to discover
Is that which was the beginning;
At the source of the longest river
The voice of the hidden waterfall
And the children in the apple-tree
Not known, because not looked for
But heard, half-heard, in the stillness
Between two waves of the sea.

(T. S. Eliot, *Little Gidding*)

The Ouse's Muddy Bank

IF YOU TAKE the path over the Downs it is four miles from the old market town of Lewes, in Sussex, to the village of Rodmell. If you choose to walk along the bank of the Ouse the distance is more like six, for the river swings east towards Glynde in a great loop, and for the last mile or so you have to leave the high bank and venture down across the water-meadows in a perpetual zigzag as you skirt ditches, streams, and mini-canals.

Here, where the path from Rodmell reaches the river, on 28 March 1941, Virginia Woolf drowned herself. This is how her nephew and biographer Quentin Bell describes the incident:

> On the morning of Friday 28 March, a bright, clear, cold day, Virginia went as usual to her studio room in the garden. There she wrote two letters, one for Leonard, one for Vanessa – the two people she loved best. In both letters she explained that she was hearing voices, believed that she could never recover; she could not go on and spoil Leonard's life for him. Then she went back into the house and wrote again to Leonard:
>
> > Dearest,
> > I feel certain I am going mad again. I feel we can't go through another of those terrible times. And I shan't recover this time. I begin to hear voices, and I can't concentrate. So I am doing what seems the best thing to do. You have given me the greatest possible happiness. You have been in every way all that anyone could be. I don't think two people could have been happier till this terrible disease came. I can't fight any longer. I know that I am spoiling your life, that without me you could work. And you will I know. You see I can't even write this

> properly. I can't read. What I want to say is I owe all the happiness of my life to you. You have been entirely patient with me and incredibly good. I want to say that – everybody knows it. If anybody could have saved me it would have been you. Everything has gone from me but the certainty of your goodness. I can't go on spoiling your life any longer.
>
> I don't think two people could have been happier than we have been.
>
> V.

She put this on the sitting-room mantelpiece and, at about 11.30, slipped out, taking her walking-stick with her and making her way across the water-meadows to the river. Leonard believed that she might already have made one attempt to drown herself; if so she had learnt by her failure and was determined to make sure of it now. Leaving her stick on the bank she forced a large stone into the pocket of her coat. Then she went to her death, 'the one experience,' as she had said to Vita, 'I shall never describe.'

There were many reasons why she might have acted as she did. First of all, as she herself says in her letter to Leonard, she had a history of madness (and each time she felt it coming upon her, of course, she felt she would never emerge from it). Leonard had in fact been so worried by her demeanour in the past weeks that he had persuaded her to go and see a physician friend with a practice in nearby Brighton. Then there was the war. The summer of 1940 had witnessed the horrors of the Battle of Britain and in September of that year bombs were still falling on London and on Sussex. One had even fallen close to Monk's House. The Woolfs were not the only people who felt that Hitler might invade at any time, and they had made clear-eyed plans to kill themselves should that occur. And, finally, Virginia Woolf had finished *Between the Acts* on 23 November, and she and Leonard knew well that the period when she (like all writers) was most vulnerable was when a book, worked on long and hard, had finally come to an end.

Nevertheless, the abruptness and finality of suicide is always shocking. The potential suicide, someone once explained to me, is like a person who lives in a room with a precious vase. Every day he circles the vase, admires it, and wonders what it would be like if by some accident he were to brush against it and bring it crashing to the ground. No one should be surprised if that is precisely what does happen one day, though it might very well never happen. Elizabeth Bowen's wise words, quoted by Bell, should always be borne in mind. Bowen visited Rodmell on 13 and 14 February and recorded her memories of that visit. She describes Virginia kneeling on the floor as the two women attempted to mend a torn curtain:

> And she sat back on her heels and put her head back in a patch of sun, early spring sun. Then she laughed in this consuming, choking, delightful, hooting way. And that is what has remained with me. So that I get a curious shock when I see people regarding her entirely as a martyred, or a definitely tragic sort of person, claimed by the darkness.

Of course, as I leave the river and cut across the water-meadows to Rodmell, I am aware of the fact that this is the place where Virginia Woolf committed suicide. But that knowledge does nothing for me, and I walk on down the muddy track. I know that stopping and attempting to meditate on her suicide would not help. The water would keep on flowing and my mind would remain a blank.

Is this because I am particularly callous or unfeeling? I don't think so. I never knew Virginia Woolf, so the fact of her death can mean nothing to me, except for a general sense of sorrow at its manner, but no more really than reading about the death of Mozart or of Kafka at an absurdly early age. And because I cannot feel her death, the fact that she died here, at this junction of river and path, does not invest the spot with any more significance than the field above

Lewes where, I have read, the great Battle of Lewes took place in 1264, which altered for ever the balance of power in England between the monarch and the nobility.

As you enter the village of Rodmell and walk up the single street to the pub, you pass Monk's House, the house in which Virginia and Leonard lived for many years and where Leonard died in 1969. In 1963, when I first came to live in Sussex, I was taken to tea there by a friend, to meet Leonard. The first words he said to us were: 'There was a Mexican photographer here just now, wanting to photograph my wife's house.' I detected a note of bitterness in his voice and in his designation of the house he had lived in for forty-four years as 'my wife's '. Then he offered us tea and talked about Samuel Butler.

I have even less desire to linger by Monk's House than by the river Ouse. I abhor writers' houses and all they stand for. Henry James surely said the last word on the subject in his wonderful story about Shakespeare's house in Stratford, 'The Birthplace'. For many decades admirers of Wordsworth or Jane Austen or Shakespeare have traipsed to these houses in a vain attempt to commune with the spirit of their beloved author, by seeing the views they had seen, touching, perhaps, the very furniture they had once touched or sat on. Nowadays this is in the process of being superseded by the Literary Festival, in which there is no longer any need to imagine one's beloved author; if one attaches oneself to a living writer one can actually see and hear him or her in the flesh and even get them to sign a copy of their book for one.

All this – the visits to authors' houses, the attendance at festivals to listen to the author of one's choice and perhaps even to talk to him or her – is of course nothing other than a secular version of pilgrimage. In Christianity, as in Hinduism, the pilgrim travelled, often for months and over thousands of miles, in order to enter the sacred presence of the long-dead holy man. Once there, pilgrims had to be (often forcibly) prevented from trying to take away a piece of the holy man, even if only a thread from his garment.

Pilgrim manuals tried to explain that what was important was entering the *praesentia* of the saint, and being in the right frame of mind, rather than seizing any material possessions – but the human spirit being what it is, the desire to hold, to possess, could never be entirely eradicated.

Pilgrimages, as we know, fell into disrepute in the West in the Protestant era, though Catholics will still undertake them to Lourdes and Santiago de Compostela, while Christians of all denominations feel driven to visit Jerusalem and the Holy Land. Nevertheless, for a largely secular West, the notion of pilgrimage is now meaningless. Yet a sociologist might well ask what else is tourism if not secularised pilgrimage. The modern-day pilgrim will visit a church or tomb in the same spirit as he or she visits a library, a museum, or the house (if they are in Amsterdam) of Rembrandt or Anne Frank. It is all one.

No one understood the continuity between pilgrimage and tourism better than the English novelist Laurence Sterne, who was writing his masterpiece, *Tristram Shandy*, in the 1750s and 60s – surely, if one is required, the moment of transition from a religious to a secular culture. Volume Seven of *Tristram Shandy* is taken up with the account of Tristram's journey through France in a vain attempt to escape death. Or should it be Death? For from the start of the book Sterne teases us by moving between a medieval, allegorical mode, in which death is a person who comes to call, and a modern, secular mode, in which death is the failure of the body, which may be kept at bay by doctors for a certain period. For the patient suffering from bad lungs, as Tristram/Sterne was, the best advice is to go South to warmer climes. Sterne also teases the reader by bringing out the absurdities, once Tristram sets off on his journey, of both secular travel narratives (what are they purporting to describe, the sites along the route or the author's interesting experiences?) and secular tourist guides.

In good Protestant fashion Tristram has nothing but contempt for relics, but he is hardly more positive about what has replaced them.

In Lyon, for example, he first of all wants to see the great clock, then the Jesuit library with its famous collection of Chinese books, and only when 'these curiosities are seen', ''twill be no hurt if WE go the Church of St Ireneus, and see the pillar to which Christ was tied – and after that, the house where Pontius Pilate lived'. On learning that these are actually in the next town he replies that he is glad of it, 'for so much the sooner shall I be at the Tomb of the two lovers' (VII.xxx). But, if the tomb of two lovers of bygone times is of more interest to the modern traveller than visiting the house of Pontius Pilate, just what kind of interest does it elicit? What, to rephrase the question, is the status of these objects, these clocks and libraries and tombs of lovers, which we now visit as our ancestors once travelled to visit relics? Once again Sterne is content to raise questions, not answer them. Having expatiated at length on the story of the two lovers and lamented their sad fate, when he finally comes to the place where the tomb should be – 'there was no tomb to drop [my tear] upon' (VII.xl).

Sentiment and empathy have replaced *praesentia*. We visit the tomb of the two lovers to shed a tear or Anne Hathaway's cottage in Stratford to wonder at the mystery of Shakespeare. Once there, we try to imagine ourselves into the lives of the dead. But sentiment is a weak, subjective thing. The notion of *praesentia* has a public, social dimension (the pilgrim rarely travels alone and has to follow a strict code of practice, followed by all the other pilgrims, when once within the holy precincts), but sentiment is only to be found in the recesses of our subjectivity; by the late eighteenth century it is everywhere, filling the gap left by the departure of the gods. And Sterne's relation to it is as ambiguous as his relation to allegory and the writing of fiction: he plays with it, laughs at it, but also half accepts it.

I think about this and about that muddy river bank which was once the scene of Virginia Woolf's suicide. Sussex rivers, cut into chalk, not limestone, have none of the mysterious beauty of the quick-running rivers of the Yorkshire Dales or Dartmoor. They are sluggish streams, no doubt with a certain melancholy beauty of their own, but barren and windswept and quite lacking in grandeur. The Ouse is tidal well past Lewes; two miles below Rodmell it enters the sea at Newhaven, one of the most unattractive towns in England. The gulls follow the tide in and twice a day the town of Lewes teems with them. When the tide retreats the banks are left exposed and muddy, and in winter Wellington boots are essential for any walk along the river. Once, on such a walk with a friend, on a particularly windy spring day, in the water-meadows close to Rodmell, we heard a loud rushing noise and looked up to see six swans, rising out of a canal and struggling to make headway against the wind. After what seemed an eternity but was probably not much more than a few seconds they gave up the struggle and swung round, flying off with the wind behind them.

Unless you know where to turn it is easy to miss the track through the water-meadows to Rodmell. I enjoy the walk in most weathers and look forward to lunch in the pub. But I know that if I want to enter the imaginative world of Virginia Woolf it is not by pausing there at the place where she died, still less by visiting Monk's House, that I will do so. It is by reading her books. This will not, of course, enable me to 'hold' her, to 'make her my own', but it will enable me, effortlessly, to enter her 'presence'. There, and only there, will she, like any other writer, be found.

Notes of First Publication

'The Legends of the Jews', 'Sacred Trash', 'The Hebrew Poetry of Medieval Spain', 'The Tallith and the Dishcloth', 'Medieval Matters', 'The Stories of the Germans', 'Empty Rooms', '*A Napoleon of Thought*: Paul Valéry and his Notebooks', 'Reading Kafka Today', '*Like a Bad Russian Novel*: T. S. Eliot in his Letters', 'Claudel and the Bible', 'Boris Pasternak', '*The Itch to Write*: Beckett's Early Letters', 'The Lost', and 'Saying Kaddish' were all published in the *Times Literary Supplement*. 'Why Write Fiction?' was first published as a Catalan translation in *Avenc*. 'How to Make a Square Move', 'The Ouse's Muddy Banks', and 'Why Write Fiction?' (in English) were first published in *PN Review*. 'Against the "Idea of Europe"' and 'Györgi Kurtág: *Samuel Beckett What is the Word*' first appeared in *Nexus*, the Journal of the Nexus Institute, Amsterdam. '*Tristram Shandy:* Not Waving But Drowning' was delivered as the annual Sterne Lecture at Shandy Hall in 2011 and subsequently published in *The Shandean*. 'Muriel Spark and the Practice of Deception' was first published in *Hidden Possibilities: Essays in Honour of Muriel Spark*, edited by Robert Hosmer (University of Notre Dame Press, 2014); 'Interruption and the Third Part' was first published in *The Book of Interruptions*, edited by David Hillman and Adam Phillips (Peter Lang, 2007). 'When I Begin I Have Already Begun' was first published in *Thinking On Thresholds: The Poetics of Transitive Spaces*, edited by Subha Mukherji (Anthem Press, 2011); 'Cousins' was first published in *A Time to Speak Out: Independent Jewish Voices on Israel, Zionism and Jewish Identity*, edited by Anne Karpf and Brian Klug (Verso, 2008). The rest of the essays are previously unpublished.

Acknowledgements

As always with non-fiction, and especially with a book of essays, a great many people have helped me, over the years, with advice and encouragement. I want to thank particularly David Herman, George Craig, Rosalind Belben and Stephen Mitchelmore. Tamar Miller, as usual, was both utterly supportive and usefully sceptical. My thanks, of course, to the editors of the *TLS*, *PN Review*, and Rob Rieman of the Nexus Institute who commissioned many of the essays and subsequently published them; to Patrick Wildgust at Shandy Hall, who invited me to give one of the annual Sterne Lectures there and to Peter de Voogt, who subsequently published it in *The Shandean*; to the editors of the Catalan literary journal *Avenc*, who commissioned and subsequently published 'Why Write Fiction?'; to Robert Hosmer and the University of Notre Dame Press, who commissioned and subsequently published the essay on Muriel Spark; to David Hillman and Adam Phillips who commissioned 'Interruption and the Third Part', and to Peter Lang who published it; and to Subha Mukherji and Anthem Press, who commissioned and subsequently published 'When I Begin I have Already Begun'. Michael Schmidt at Carcanet was, as ever, encouraging and open-minded, and Luke Allan an exemplary editor.

About the Author

Gabriel Josipovici was born in Nice in 1940 of Russo-Italian, Romano-Levantine parents. He lived in Egypt till 1956, when he came to Britain. He read English at St Edmund Hall, Oxford and, from 1963 to 1998 taught literature in the School of European Studies at the University of Sussex. He is the author of eighteen novels, three volumes of short stories, nine books of criticism, numerous plays for stage and radio, and a memoir-biography of his mother, the poet and translator Sacha Rabinovitch.

Also by Gabriel Josipovici

Fiction:

The Inventory (1968)
Words (1971)
Mobius the Stripper: Stories and Short Plays (1974)
The Present (1975)
Four Stories (1977)
Migrations (1977)
The Echo Chamber (1979)
The Air We Breathe (1981)
Conversations in Another Room (1984)
Contre Jour: A Triptych after Pierre Bonnard (1986)
In the Fertile Land (1987)
Steps: Selected Fiction and Drama (1990)
The Big Glass (1991)
In a Hotel Garden (1993)
Moo Pak (1994)
Now (1998)
Goldberg: Variations (2002)

Everything Passes (2006)
Two Novels: *After* and *Making Mistakes* (2009)
Heart's Wings (2010)
Infinity: The Story of a Moment (2012)
Hotel Andromeda (2013)

Theatre:
Vergil Dying (1977)
Mobius the Stripper: Stories and Short Plays (1974)

Non-fiction:
The World and the Book (1971, 1979)
The Lessons of Modernism (1977, 1987)
Writing and the Body (1982)
The Mirror of Criticism: Selected Reviews (1983)
The Book of God: A Response to the Bible (1988, 1990)
Text and Voice: Essays 1981–1991 (1992)
A Life (2001)
The Singer on the Shore: Essays 1991–2004 (2006)
What Ever Happened to Modernism? (2010)
The Modern English Novel: The Reader, the Writer and the Book (ed., 1975)
The Siren's Song: Selected Essays of Maurice Blanchot (ed., 1980)
The Spirit of England: Selected Essays of Stephen Medcalf (ed. with Brian Cummings, 2010)